Instrumentation
for
Psychology

Instrumentation
for
Psychology

ALAN CLEARY

Department of Psychology
University of Newcastle upon Tyne

JOHN WILEY & SONS
Chichester · New York · Brisbane · Toronto

Library of Congress Cataloging in Publication Data:

Cleary, Alan.
  Instrumentation for psychology.

  1. Psychological apparatus. I. Title.
BF190.C58   150'.28   77–1250

ISBN 0 471 99483 9

Photosetting by Thomson Press (India) Limited, New Delhi.
Printed by The Pitman Press, Bath.

Acknowledgements

Part of Chapter 5 is based on the contents of the Mullard publications *Semiconductor Devices* and *Introducing Integrated Circuits*. I am grateful to Mullard Ltd. for granting permission to use this material and to reproduce their copyright figures.

Ken Kapota of BRD (Electronics) Ltd. kindly supplied some notes which helped me in the writing of Chapters 5 and 6.

Many equipment manufacturers have given permission to use illustrations of their products. The manufacturer and model number are credited in the captions of the appropriate illustrations.

I wish to express my appreciation to the following individuals, institutions, journals and publishers who have granted permission to use copyright figures:

Figure 7.17. D. W. Robinson and The Institute of Physics. From Robinson and Dadson (1956).

Figures 8.1, 8.2, 8.4. Illuminating Engineering Society of North America. From IES (1959).

Figure 8.7. The Royal Society. From Stiles and Crawford (1933).

Figures 8.8, 8.10. McGraw–Hill Book Co. *The Principles of Optics* by A. C. Hardy and F. H. Perrin, McGraw–Hill (1932).

Figures 8.17, 8.18, 8.20. John Wiley & Sons, Inc. From Riggs (1965).

Figures 8.28, 11.9. John Wiley & Sons Ltd. From Cleary, Mayes and Packham (1976).

Figure 9.5. J. W. Davenport and The Psychonomic Society, Inc. From Davenport, Chamove and Harlow (1970).

Figure 9.6. D. M. Baer and The Society for Research in Child Development, Inc. From Baer (1962); copyright © 1962 by The Society for Research in Child Development, Inc.

Figure 9.7. McGraw–Hill Book Co. From Bitterman (1966).

Figures 10.8, 10.9. J. G. Bauer, Jr. and The Psychonomic Society, Inc. From Bauer, Woods and Held (1969).

Figures 10.10, 10.11. A. C. Downing.

Figure 10.12. W. H. Freeman & Co. From *Experimental Psychobiology: A Laboratory Manual* edited by Benjamin L. Hart, W. H. Freeman & Co. Copyright © 1976.
Figures 10.16, 10.19. P. H. Venables and North-Holland Publishing Co. From Venables and Martin (1967a).
Figure 10.18. P. H. Venables and Academic Press, Inc. From Venables and Christie (1973).
Figure 10.24. John Wiley & Sons, Inc. From Geddes and Baker (1975).
Figure 10.26. Peter Peregrinus Ltd. From Greatorex (1971).
Figure 10.28. Baillière Tindall. From *The Physiological Basis of Medical Practice* by C. H. Best and N. B. Taylor, 7th edition, Baillière, Tindall & Cox (1961).
Figure 10.31. Elsevier/North-Holland Biomedical Press. From Jasper (1958).
Figure 10.32. Digital Equipment Co. Ltd. From Ross, F., Fleming, N. I., and Willey, T. J. (1975). 'Frequency profile of long duration EEG', *Decuscope*, **14**, 3–5.
Figures 10.33, 10.34, 10.35. O. C. J. Lippold and North-Holland Publishing Co. From Lippold (1967).
Figures 10.39, 10.42. B. Shackel and North-Holland Publishing Co. From Shackel (1967).
Figure 10.41. B. Shackel.
Figure 11.1. Beckman–RIIC Ltd.
Figures 11.7, 11.8. Digital Equipment Co. Ltd.
Figure 12.2. Bell Telephone Laboratories, Inc. From Julesz (1971).
Figure 12.3. Hewlett–Packard Ltd. From (1968) *Hewlett–Packard Journal*, **19**, (8).

Contents

Preface

In recent years, the instrumentation used in psychology has become increasingly sophisticated. Many students, however, still enter the subject from a non–science background; these students in particular have a poor understanding of the elementary principles and practice of scientific instrumentation, and, in many cases, the deficiency continues into professional life. This is particularly sad, because much modern electronic equipment is designed so that its use does not require a detailed knowledge of electronics.

For the last ten years, I have taught a course on instrumentation methods at the University of Newcastle upon Tyne, and the structure of the book reflects this experience. I have started with digital logic instead of electronics, because experience with solid-state programming equipment gives students confidence in the use of equipment, and also puts science and non-science students onto a more equal footing. It is, of course, important that students should have suitable practical work to accompany the text. In the laboratory at Newcastle, we have prepared programmed texts which teach logic and introduce the students to practical work with modular programming equipment. (I will supply a copy of this material on request to anyone teaching or planning an instrumentation course.)

Although this book is mainly intended as a student text, it should also be suitable for postgraduates and others who find they need to work in an area of psychology which demands the use of instrumentation, and for which they are ill-prepared. The scope of the book is not encylopaedic, but the coverage should be sufficient to allow the reader to move on to the specialized literature in most areas of the subject. To assist those readers who do not need to work through the whole book, there is extensive cross-referencing in the text, and a technical glossary as an appendix.

So many people have given freely of their time to comment on the various drafts of the book that I am unable to mention them all by name. Special thanks, however, are due to Richard Bird, Joe Dawson, Terry Mayes, Hugh

Smith and the second-year students of 1975–76. I also wish to thank Peter Sanderson for giving a clear and consistent style to the many figures in the book.

ALAN CLEARY
Department of Psychology
University of Newcastle upon Tyne
Newcastle upon Tyne NE1 7RU
England
October 1976

CHAPTER 1

Role of Instrumentation in Psychology

1.1 Instrumentation in experimental science

Instrumentation in science has evolved from a need to set the values of experimental variables and to measure the resulting effects. It is, therefore, a basic part of all experimental sciences, including psychology. It is true that, traditionally, instrumentation has played a small part in some areas of psychology, such as clinical and developmental psychology; in these areas, the traditional tools have been, for example, observation and questionnaires. Even here, however, there is an increasing use of technologically based devices such as video tape recorders and devices for presenting and scoring tests.

In recent years, a large industry has developed around the manufacture of equipment for measurement and control. Its largest customers are manufacturing industry and the military, who demand reliable devices with well defined functions. Modern laboratory instrumentation is largely a matter of appropriately interconnecting such pieces of commercially manufactured equipment. The aim of this book is to give guidance on the principles and practice involved in using such equipment in the psychology laboratory. It is not intended as a manual for the design and construction of laboratory instruments.

In the early days of scientific instrumentation, the main effort was directed towards the development of high-precision measuring instruments, such as the micrometer and thermometer. Many modern measuring instruments are capable, in addition, of producing a permanent recording of their measurements. One of the earliest of such instruments was the smoked-drum kymograph, which was used by physiologists in the last century. Today, a wide variety of recording equipment is used in psychology laboratories, for example multi-channel pen recorders and instrumentation tape recorders.

A second aspect of instrumentation is its use for controlling the physical environment. Such methods have been used for many years in some areas of psychology, for example in visual research, where optical filters are used to vary the colour and intensity of light, but the widespread availability of such

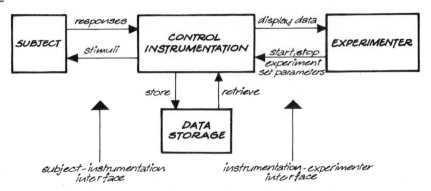

Figure 1.1. *The organization of an instrumented experiment.*

devices as audio tape recorders and automatic slide projectors has now brought instrumented presentation of stimuli into most areas of psychology.

It has become increasingly common to think of the physical instrumentation as forming more than just a small part of the complete man–machine system for the control of an experiment. Totally instrumented experiments have become fairly common in psychology during the last 20 years or so, the first major application being operant conditioning experiments. Early equipment for this purpose was electromechanical in nature, being largely composed of relays, but, in recent years, electronic control systems and laboratory computer systems have also been used in animal laboratories, and, in general, a wide variety of instrumentation techniques is now used for the control of psychological experiments.

When considering psychological experiments, the experimenter, instrumentation and the subject are typically organized according to the scheme illustrated in Figure 1.1. The experimenter communicates with the experiment through his instrumentation, and exercises a supervisory control. The precise control of stimuli, detection and measurement of responses and storage of data may all be performed by the instrumentation. The use of instrumentation for detecting and recording events increases the objectivity of an experimental procedure. In psychological experiments, the reduction in the need for direct contact between the experimenter and the subject is particularly valuable, because the experimenter's expectations can influence the results of the experiment (Rosenthal, 1976). The interfaces between experimenter and instrumentation and between the subject and instrumentation should be designed on ergonomic principles, for ease of use and reliability of operation.

1.2 The function of instrumentation

Six main functions may be provided by instruments in an experiment:

(1) They can present stimuli, for example, words in a tachistoscope, thereby allowing systematic control of the independent variable.

(2) They allow the experimenter to control other potentially independent variables, as when white noise is used to mask possible auditory cues.

(3) They are used to measure responses, the dependent variable. The responses may be simple pushbutton operations, or they may be a response not otherwise observable, such as changes in skin resistance.

(4) They can control the sequence of events in an experiment, as with the memory drum, which allows the presentation of a predetermined sequence of stimuli. Decisions about the presentation of stimuli can even be made during the course of an experiment, as in the correction-trials procedure for discrimination-learning experiments.

(5) They can record data. Discrete responses, for example, may be counted on an electromagnetic register. Continuous variables, such as skin resistance, can be recorded on an ink-writing oscillograph.

(6) Finally, they can analyse data and present the results to the experimenter, as in computer-controlled experiments.

Functions (1), (2) and (3) occur at the subject–instrumentation interface, whereas functions (4), (5) and (6) occur at the instrumentation–experimenter interface.

During the early development of an experimental science, individual workers need specially constructed apparatus for a wide variety of rapidly changing techniques. As the discipline matures, standardized forms of instrumentation emerge, thereby facilitating the replication of experiments by workers in different laboratories. Commercially manufactured, standard equipment has a number of advantages. It is generally more reliable than purpose-built equipment, and provides standardized experimental conditions, thereby simplifying the reporting and replication of experiments. A pool of such equipment in a laboratory can be of great convenience to investigators by allowing them to implement quickly a wide range of experiments. Although commercial equipment may seem expensive, it is often much cheaper than the full cost in time and materials of constructing items individually in a laboratory workshop. The savings are particularly great with modern modular instrumentation, which has been designed to facilitate re-use of the instruments in various experiments.

1.3 Electronic instrumentation

Electronics is now widely established in instrumentation. The advantages of electronic instrumentation are:

(1) A wide variety of physical events or changes in energy can be transformed into an electrical representation.

(2) Electrical signals can be transformed readily into other forms of energy.

(3) Logical operations can be performed easily in electronics, and the techniques are highly developed.

(4) Electrical signals can be transmitted over great distances.

(5) Data can be stored and retrieved very rapidly.
(6) Sophisticated mathematical transformations of data are possible.

Because of the increasing use of electronic equipment in the psychological laboratory, it is important that the psychologist who is likely to be involved in highly instrumented work should have some appreciation of electronics. We shall be returning to this matter in Chapter 5, where an elementary introduction to electronics is given.

1.4 Discrete events and continuous data

It is usual to think of data as being either continuous or discrete. Skin resistance would normally be considered to be a fairly typical continuous variable, whereas the number of errors in a recognition test is clearly discrete. When we take a note of the value of skin resistance, however, we implicitly quantify it into small steps, the size of the steps normally being indicated by the least significant digit. For example, a weight stated in the form 83·4 kilograms (kg) suggests that we are working in increments of 0·1 kg.

It has been argued that continuous functions are the invention of mathematicians (Poincaré, 1905). They are, of course, a convenient and elegant invention, particularly in respect of the powerful analytical techniques which they provide. We should not be overawed, however, by these techniques; they merely provide an approximate method for the representation of quantified measurements. They were used originally because of the labour involved in dealing directly with numerical data. With the advent of high-speed digital computers, the situation is changing, and it is now possible to use numerical techniques with much more convenience.

Information theory suggests that we can convert a continuous signal to a quantized representation without necessarily incurring any loss of information. This follows from two considerations. The first of these is that, in any physical channel of communication, some interfering disturbance or noise is always present; the second is that there is always a limit to the rate of change of signal which can be achieved in any real communication channel, that is the channel is of limited bandwidth.

In order to understand the concept of bandwidth, we need to know something about the sine wave. This curve, which is characteristic of simple harmonic motion, may be generated by rotating a point around the circumference of a circle at a constant angular velocity. A sine wave results when the vertical distance between the point and a horizontal line through the centre of the circle is plotted as a function of time.

The generation of such a sine wave is illustrated in Figure 1.2. One complete revolution of the point produces a single cycle of the sine wave. The figure shows one and a half cycles. The value of h at any instant is known as the amplitude of the curve. Clearly its maximum value is equal to the radius of the circle. If this is taken to be the unit of amplitude, then the maximum value is one positive

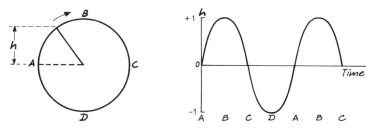

Figure 1.2. *The generation of a sine wave by circular motion.*

unit and the minimum value is one negative unit. The number of complete cycles in any one second is a measure of the frequency of the wave in cycles per second or Hz, the abbreviation for hertz, which is now the internationally agreed unit of frequency. The importance of sine waves for our purpose derives from the work of the French mathematician Fourier (1768–1830), who showed that any continuous curve could be analysed into a number of sine waves of related frequency. Conversely, these sine waves, when added together, would reproduce the original curve (Figure 1.3).

Suppose we wish to record a physiological signal with a continuous waveform similar to that shown in Figure 1.4. It may be quantified by sampling the signal at regular intervals. If we sample the signal more frequently, then we shall be able to specify the shape of the curve with greater accuracy. The question may

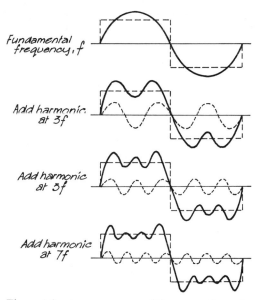

Figure 1.3. *A square wave of frequency f can be analysed into a series of sine waves of frequencies f, 3f, 5f, 7f, 9f etc. As the higher-frequency harmonics are restored to the fundamental, the square wave is reproduced with increasing fidelity.*

6

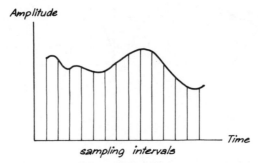

Figure 1.4. *Signal amplitude as a continuous func-*
tion of time.

be asked as to whether a signal can ever be fully specified by sampling. Fourier analysis suggests the answer, for, as long as the frequency range of the component sine waves is finite, then the frequency of sampling necessary to completely define the signal is also finite. In fact, if the highest frequency present is W Hz, then the waveform can be fully specified by sampling at the rate of not less than $2W$ per second (s), so that at least one sample is taken for each change in direction at the highest frequency present. This result is of great importance when recording data, for, if frequencies higher than half the sampling rate are present, it is impossible to reconstruct the original waveform. In such circumstances, many different waveforms might have produced the same sampled data, and therefore the process is often termed aliasing. The solution is to increase the sampling rate or to filter out the high frequencies before sampling.

Figure 1.5 shows a continuous signal of maximum amplitude s being transmitted over a channel which introduces noise of maximum amplitude n. The received signal is the sum of the original signal and the introduced noise; it therefore has a maximum amplitude of $s + n$. At the receiver, we know that the noise may achieve a maximum value n, although we do not know its precise value at any particular instant. We also know that the highest frequency represented in the signal is W Hz. Let us consider how we might proceed to sample the received signal with the minimum loss of information.

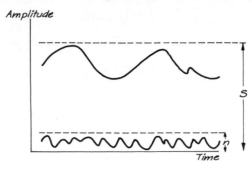

Figure 1.5. *Signal and noise amplitudes as time*
functions.

7

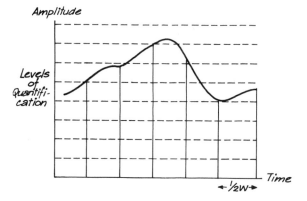

Figure 1.6. *Quantification of a continuous signal.*

First, we should take $2W$ samples/s in order to eliminate loss of information by too infrequent sampling. Second, we need to determine the number of categories into which we should classify the amplitude of the samples. The received signal will have an amplitude in the range zero to $s + n$. The maximum difference between the transmitted and received signals, that is the maximum error, will be n, the maximum amplitude of the noise. We must, therefore, quantify the received amplitudes in increments of n units, since we are unable to distinguish the signal from noise with any greater precision. The number of distinguishable categories is therefore $(s + n)/n$. In Figure 1.6, a continuous signal has been quantified into eight levels, with samples taken at a rate of $2W\,\mathrm{s}^{-1}$ or $1/2W$ s apart on the time axis.

From information theory, we know that the channel capacity T is maximized when the amplitude categories are equiprobable. Therefore

$$T = \log_2\left(\frac{s+n}{n}\right) \text{ samples/s}$$

and, since there are $2W$ samples/s,

$$T = 2W \log_2\left(\frac{s+n}{n}\right) \text{ bit/s}$$

Measurements of signals are often expressed in the form of power rather than amplitude. The power of a signal is proportional to the square of its amplitude, and so we can write

$$T = 2W \log_2 \sqrt{\left(\frac{S+N}{N}\right)} \text{ bit/s}$$

or

$$T = W \log_2\left(\frac{S+N}{N}\right) \text{ bit/s}$$

where S is the signal power and N is the noise power. This expression gives the maximum value of capacity of a noisy channel, a result which was given in

Shannon (1948) as Theorem 17. A useful introductory text on information theory for psychologists has been written by Edwards (1964).

So, if we know the noise level n which accompanies the signal in which we are interested, and we know the highest frequency W which we wish to resolve, we can completely represent our signal in digital form by converting it into quantized samples with increments not greater than n at a sampling rate of at least $2W\,s^{-1}$.

In practice, conversion of this kind is usually achieved by electronic devices such as analogue–digital converters (ADCs). These converters are becoming fairly common as digital computers become less expensive. Digital signals may be converted back into analogue form by another electronic device, the digital–analogue converter (DAC). Digital data is usually represented in electronic devices in binary or 2-state form, because this gives the greatest resistance to corruption of the data by noise. In order to understand how this takes place, it is necessary to give some basic consideration to the working of number systems.

Our system of counting in units of ten has probably developed because man has ten digits on two hands. The use of the number ten as the base of our number system is not of itself of any great importance; any other universally agreed number would do just as well. Historically, two basic concepts were important in simplifying the operations which are needed to manipulate numbers. These were the concept of position and the digit zero. The concept of position consists in assigning to a number a value which depends both on the symbol itself and on the position of the symbol in the whole number. For example, the digit 8 has a different value in each of the three numbers 138, 482 and 805. In the first number, the digit 8 represents its unmodified value of 8; in the second number, it has a value of 80, or 8 times 10; and, in the last number, it has the value of 800, or 8 times 100. Sometimes the position in a number does not have a value between 1 and 9. If this position were simply omitted, there would be no difference in notation between, say, 406 and 46. This is where the digit zero is used to fill the space. In the number 406, there are four hundreds, zero tens and six units. Thus, by using the concept of position and the digit 0, arithmetic in the form with which we are familiar becomes possible.

In order for an instrument to handle digital data in decimal form, it must in some way represent the ten different digits 0 to 9, that is it needs to have ten different states with which the digit values may be associated. For example, if we have an electronic circuit which can produce a voltage varying over the range 0–9 volts (V), we could decide to represent the digits 0 to 9 by 0, 1, 2, 3, 4, 5, 6, 7, 8 and 9 V, respectively. A disturbance of 1 V of noise would then be sufficient to cause an error by shifting the signal to an adjacent voltage level. If we used the same voltage range to represent only two digits, 0 and 1 at levels 0 and 9 V, respectively, we would then need 9 V of noise to produce the corresponding error. Most physical quantities are easy to categorize as being in one of two states. For example, a light may be on or off, current flow may be positive or negative, material may be magnetized or demagnetized, and so on. Because it can be represented by two such physical states, the binary number system is the one which is generally used in digital instruments and computers.

In the decimal or base-10 number system, the value of a digit depends upon its position in the number. For example,

$$1564 = 1 \times 10^3 + 5 \times 10^2 + 6 \times 10^1 + 4 \times 10^0$$

The value of each position in a number is known as its position coefficient or weight.

The decimal weighting table from the example above would be

$$10^3 \qquad 10^2 \qquad 10^1 \qquad 10^0$$

Weighting tables may seem to serve little purpose in the familiar decimal number system, but their usefulness becomes more obvious when we consider the binary or base-2 number system. In this system, we have only the two digits 0 and 1, and so, to represent larger numbers, we use the count-and-carry principle, which will be familiar from the decimal system.

When we count in decimal, we proceed as follows

0   starting in the units, or 10^0, column
1
2
3
4
5
6
7
8
9
10   with a carry to the tens, or 10^1, column

and so on. When we reach 0 in the units column again, we carry another 1 to the tens column for 20. This process is continued until the tens column becomes 0, and a 1 is carried into the hundreds column, as shown below

90
91
92
93
94
95
96
97
98
99
100   with carries to the 10^1 and the hundreds, or 10^2, columns.

In the binary number system, the carry principle is used with only the two

10

digits 0 and 1. Thus, the numbers used in the binary system to count up to a decimal value of ten are as follows

0000	0
0001	1
0010	2
0011	3
0100	4
0101	5
0110	6
0111	7
1000	8
1001	9
1010	10

When using more than one number system, it is a common convention to subscript the numbers with the value of the base, for example

$$110_2 = 6_{10}$$

It is very tedious to write binary numbers containing many bits, and errors are very easily made. Accordingly, they are often formed into groups of 3 bits, starting with the last significant bit. Each group of bits is expressed as a number to base 8, or an octal number. Thus, the binary number 110101001010 would be grouped and written in octal as

110	101	001	010	grouped binary
6	5	1	2	octal

Octal representation is often used with the minicomputers which are used in laboratory computer systems (Chapter 12). Large computer systems of the type found in computer centres usually group the bits into sets of 4 and use hexadecimal or base-16 notation. Octal notation only needs the characters 0 to 7, but hexadecimal needs 16 separate characters, one for each of the numbers of value 0 to 15. The numbers 0 to 9 followed by the letters A to F are used for this purpose. Thus, the same binary number would be represented in hexadecimal as

1101	0100	1010	grouped binary
D	8	A	hexadecimal

A weighting table of the form

$$\ldots 2^4 \quad 2^3 \quad 2^2 \quad 2^1 \quad 2^0$$

is used to convert binary numbers to the more familiar decimal form. For example

$$1101_2 = 1 \times 2^3 + 1 \times 2^2 + 0 \times 2^1 + 1 \times 2^0$$
$$= 1 \times 8 + 1 \times 4 + 0 \times 2 + 1 \times 1$$
$$= 13_{10}$$

The binary weighting table may be extended as far as necessary, just as with decimal numbers. In general, to find the value of a binary number, each digit is multiplied by its weight, and the results are summed.

By convention, the weights are always arranged in the same order, with the highest value of weight on the extreme left and the lowest value on the extreme right. Therefore, the position coefficients begin at 1 and increase from right to left. This convention has two advantages. First, it is not necessary to label each digit in a binary number with its appropriate weighting value, as the digit on the extreme right is always multiplied by 1, the next digit by 2, the next by 4 and so on. Second, it allows the elimination of some of the zeros. Those zeros to the right of the highest valued 1 are needed to maintain the position of the columns in signifying the correct position of the 1s. The zeros to the left of the highest valued 1, however, provide no information about the value of the number, and may be discarded. Thus, the number 0001110011 may be written as 1110011, just as, in decimal, 00115 is usually written as 115.

Many digital laboratory instruments do not use a pure binary code, but use binary-coded decimal (b.c.d.). In this code, each decade has a 4 bit binary representation, so that the number 1359_{10}, for example, would be represented by

$$0001 \quad 0011 \quad 0101 \quad 1001$$

Within each group of 4 bits, the weights used for the bits are 8, 4, 2 and 1, respectively. This code has advantages when it is necessary to display the information to human operators, but it clearly uses more bits than are strictly necessary to represent the data. In each decade, the binary numbers 1010 to 1111 do not exist, and so a 3-decade system would need 12 bits to represent numbers from 0 to 999_{10}, whereas a pure binary system with only 10 bits could represent numbers from 0 to 1023_{10}.

1.5 Validity of an instrumented system

It is important to consider both the validity of an instrumentation technique and the reliability of the instrument. First, the validity of the instrumentation technique, that is does it exclusively and completely perform the function that is specified for the experiment? We should consider the possibility that the instrumentation may give rise to some additional unspecified stimulus, thereby providing unintended cues for the subject. If relay equipment is used, for example, the click of the relays may be audible to the subject. The results of the experiment will be especially difficult to interpret if the relay operation varies with the stimulus conditions, because any effects observed could be attributable to auditory cues from operation of the relays.

When recording responses, we should consider the possibility of false positives and false negatives. Azrin and Powell (1968) wanted to record the number of cigarettes smoked per day, and devised a special cigarette case with a counter coupled to the lid. Because the subjects might have access to other cigarettes (false negatives), or might open the case without removing a cigarette (false

12

positives), the instrumentation method was validated by an independent check using a different system. Azrin and Powell used volunteer observers to report the numbers of cigarettes smoked at work and at home by the subjects.

The control logic may give unexpected experimental conditions if all possible input states have not been considered. A common fault is failure to consider the effects of the subject responding at inappropriate times, for example, anticipating the stimulus in a reaction-time task. It is important to specify the control requirements for all the conditions which could possibly arise.

Finally, the data gathered by instruments may be corrupted directly by electrical interference from other sources, such as stimulus generators; this may result in correlations arising which are entirely artefacts of the instrumentation.

1.6 Reliability of an instrumented system

It is important that the operation of instrumentation should be repeatable so that reliable results are obtained. For example, it is a common failure of tachistoscopes that the light level does not remain constant for a given setting of the controls. Again, early electronic timer/counters using glow transfer tubes were notoriously erratic and very sensitive to minor fluctuations in the power supply.

Contacts and leads can be a very frustrating source of trouble, particularly when using modular programming equipment. Intermittent connections can transiently change the control functions, causing spurious operation of equipment. It is false economy to use poor quality leads or connectors.

Mechanical unreliability can also cause problems. If the drive of a chart recorder slips, then it may be impossible to analyse the record of the responses; certainly the time scale will be distorted.

It is good practice to build some redundancy into an instrumentation system. To give a simple example, as a check to find corrupted data, we could record the total number of responses independently of the correct and incorrect responses. A small amount of redundancy can provide an error-checking system which will alert the experimenter to a failure, but, with more redundancy, it is possible to design systems which can automatically correct certain specified kinds of error (Cherry, 1964).

1.7 Summary

The main features of instrumentation for behavioural sciences are:

(1) It increases the objectivity of the procedure and results. It is important to realize that sophisticated instrumentation will not, of itself, improve a poor design or remove the effects of a biased sample; an experiment is only as strong as its weakest link.
(2) It allows the elimination of some biases by removing the human experimenter from direct participation in the experimental situation.

(3) A completely instrumented experiment can be a completely specified experiment, thereby allowing convenient replication.

(4) It can provide a permanent record of both the course of the experiment and of the data which have been collected. Even the use of an audio tape recorder during an otherwise manual experiment may provide this facility.

(5) It can present stimuli, record responses and make decisions which may not be possible without the assistance of instrumentation.

(6) Techniques can be embodied in products which are then available to other workers, thereby speeding the development of the science.

A useful chapter on the role of instruments in research will be found in the introductory text on methodology by Plutchik (1974).

CHAPTER 2

Digital Logic

2.1 Introduction

Many of the devices which are used to instrument experiments are stable in either one of two states. A toggle switch of the type commonly used to operate ordinary room lights is such a device: its two states are ON and OFF. Similarly, a pushbutton such as is used to operate a doorbell may be either pressed, causing the bell to ring, or not pressed, causing the bell not to ring. Devices such as these come in two forms, those with memory and those without memory. The toggle switch is an example of a 2-state device with memory, because it remains in the last state into which it was set. The pushbutton, however, is a 2-state device without memory, because the circuit is completed, causing the bell to ring, only while an input is present, that is while it is pressed. Immediately the pressure is removed, the pushbutton reverts to its normal state and the bell stops ringing.

Events are often 2-state, or can be reduced to a number of 2-state representations. Consider a car driver; if he sees a red light OR a halt sign OR an obstacle in the road ahead, then he will stop. Symbolically, we could represent his decision to stop in the form of Figure 2.1. Each of the variables considered in arriving at the decision is a 2-state or binary event, that is it is either present or not present. The red light can either be on or off, the halt sign can be present or absent and the obstacle is in the road or not in the road. If one or more of these conditions is present, then the driver will stop. We may represent all possible combinations of input conditions in the form of a table. Figure 2.2 shows such a table for this driving decision. The table also shows the output decision for each combination of input conditions. Tables of this type, which completely

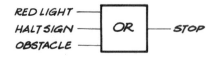

Figure 2.1. *Stop decision.*

CONDITIONS			RESPONSE (STOP)
RED LIGHT	HALT SIGN	OBSTACLE	
No	No	No	No
No	No	Yes	Yes
No	Yes	No	Yes
No	Yes	Yes	Yes
Yes	No	No	Yes
Yes	No	Yes	Yes
Yes	Yes	No	Yes
Yes	Yes	Yes	Yes

Figure 2.2. *Truth table for logical stop decision.*

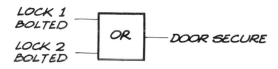

Figure 2.3. *Door with two locks.*

LOCK 1 BOLTED	LOCK 2 BOLTED	DOOR SECURE
No	No	No
No	Yes	Yes
Yes	No	Yes
Yes	Yes	Yes

Figure 2.4. *Truth table for door with two locks.*

specify the output for all combinations of input, are called truth tables. The number of rows (that is different combinations of input states) required for a truth table is 2^N, where N is the number of variables under consideration.

Mechanical systems may also be represented in this symbolic form. A door fitted with two locks would be secure if either lock were bolted. Figure 2.3 shows how this lock system may be represented symbolically. The truth table (Figure 2.4) for this system has four rows because there are only two input variables.

2.2 Logic gates

The two examples above demonstrate logical decisions. The decision in the first example would be to stop or not to stop, and the decision in the second examples would be that the door is secure or not secure. The 2-state outcome of such decisions depends both on the states of the input conditions which are being examined, and upon the nature of the decision rule which is being applied. In the first example, the inputs were the red light, the halt sign and the obstacle. In the second example, the inputs were the state of each of the two locks. In

16

both examples, the decision rule used was OR. Other decision rules are possible, for example room lighting will operate only when the wall switch is on AND when an electric light bulb is in the fitting.

Logical decisions can be made by various devices, but those which are designed specially for this purpose are called logic gates. Although most logic gates are electronic in nature, the formal logical properties being discussed in this chapter are independent of the physical nature of the gate, and, for many applications, where silence and operating speed are not the main criteria, mechanical or hydraulic logic gates may be used. Regardless of the physical form of the gate, the decision can be symbolically represented in a standard form.

2.2.1 OR *gates*

The logical OR decision has been demonstrated in the driving and lock examples. The symbol most commonly used for an OR gate is shown in Figure 2.5. The inputs or conditions examined by the OR gate are on the left of the figure, and the output or the result of the logical decision is on the right of the figure. OR gates may have two or more inputs, although more than four is uncommon. There is only one output, but it may be connected to the inputs of many other logic gates, allowing complex logical functions to be implemented. We shall return to this point in Section 3.6.

As we have seen, if one or more of the inputs are present, the OR condition is satisfied; or, to use a technical term, we may say that the gate is enabled. There are other types of gate, and, in general, we say that any gate is enabled when the state of its inputs is such that the gate gives an output. The driving decision considered earlier can be represented in the standard logic diagram form using a 3-input OR gate, as shown in Figure 2.6. The operation of the gate is defined by the truth table of Figure 2.2.

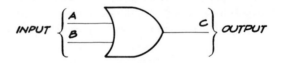

Figure 2.5. *Standard OR symbol.*

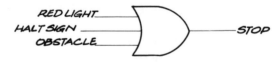

Figure 2.6. OR *driving decision.*

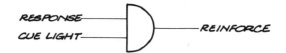

Figure 2.7. AND *decision for CRF.*

RESPONSE	CUE LIGHT	REINFORCE
No	No	No
No	Yes	No
Yes	No	No
Yes	Yes	Yes

Figure 2.8. *Truth table for* AND *decision.*

2.2.2 AND *gates*

As mentioned earlier, another type of logic gate is one which makes an AND decision. In an operant conditioning experiment employing a continuous schedule of reinforcement, we might give reinforcement only when the cue light is on AND when the subject makes a response. Both input conditions must be satisfied before an output is provided and a reinforcer dispensed. Figure 2.7 shows a symbolic representation of the AND decision, and the truth table in Figure 2.8 shows all the possible input conditions and the resulting output. Note that, as there are 2^2 possible combinations of the two input variables, there are four rows to the truth table. In a like manner to an OR gate, an AND gate may have more than two inputs, in which case all the inputs must be satisfied for the gate to be enabled.

2.2.3 *Inverters*

There are occasions when it is necessary to take a logic signal and change it to its opposite state. For example, in the case of the reinforcement schedule just considered, the reinforcer may be the presentation of a food hopper for 2 s. We would then probably want to switch off the cue light during presentation of the reinforcer. This could be arranged by deriving a signal of opposite value to that used to drive the food hopper, and then using this new signal to operate the cue light. A device which performs such an operation is known as an inverter. The logic-diagram symbol for an inverter is shown in Figure 2.9. If an inverter

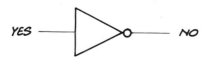

Figure 2.9. *Standard inverter symbol.*

INPUT	OUTPUT
1	0
0	1

Figure 2.10. *Truth table for inverter.*

receives a signal at its input which represents a YES, then it will produce at its output a signal which represents a NO. Conversely, if it had received a signal at its input representing a NO, it would produce at its output a signal representing YES. Figure 2.10 gives this definition in truth-table form with the more convenient symbols 1 and 0 substituted for YES and NO.

If we consider a logic state represented by the variable name A, which may represent either a logic 1 or a logic 0, then the inversion of this is represented by NOT A. Thus, if A is the input of an inverter, then NOT A will appear at its output, and, conversely, if the input to an inverter is NOT A, then its output will be A.

2.3 Binary arithmetic and digital logic

In Section 1.4, we discussed the importance of the binary number system for the coding of data. We have just seen how 2-state logic can be used in control and decision making. In order to demonstrate the unity of ideas in these two areas, we will show how logic gates can be used to carry out the operations of binary arithmetic.

Consider the addition of two binary numbers X and Y, for example

$$X = \ \ 101$$
$$Y = \ \ 110$$
$$Z = X + Y = 1011$$

The rule for addition in the 2^0 column of such a pair of binary numbers can be expressed in the form of a truth table (Figure 2.11).

By considering the input conditions for each of the rows which has a logic

INPUT		OUTPUT	
digit in X	digit in Y	digit in Z	carry to 2^1 column (c)
0	0	0	0
0	1	1	0
1	0	1	0
1	1	0	1

Figure 2.11. *Truth table for binary addition in the 2^0 column.*

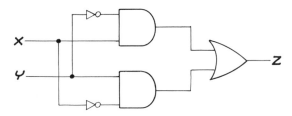

Figure 2.12. *Binary addition without carry.*

INPUT			OUTPUT	
digit in X	digit in Y	carry from 2^{N-1}column(F)	digit in Z	carry to 2^{N+1}column(C)
0	0	0	0	0
0	0	1	1	0
0	1	0	1	0
0	1	1	0	1
1	0	0	1	0
1	0	1	0	1
1	1	0	0	1
1	1	1	1	1

Figure 2.13. *Truth table for binary addition in the 2^N column.*

1 for Z, we can express the rule in the form

$Z = \{(\text{NOT } X) \text{ AND } Y\} \text{ OR } \{X \text{ AND } (\text{NOT } Y)\}$

The resulting logic diagram for the computation of the least significant bit of Z is given in Figure 2.12. The carry bit to the 2^1 column is given by

$C = X \text{ AND } Y$

A system of logic gates for such binary addition is termed a half adder. A full adder is a system of logic gates which will not only add the bits in the 2^N column of the two binary numbers X and Y, but also take into account the value of the carry from the 2^{N-1} column. The general rule for addition with carry in the 2^N column is given in Figure 2.13. The value of Z is now given by

$Z = \{(\text{NOT } X) \text{ AND } (\text{NOT } Y) \text{ AND } F\} \text{ OR } \{(\text{NOT } X) \text{ AND } Y \text{ AND } (\text{NOT } F)\}$
$\quad \text{OR } \{X \text{ AND } (\text{NOT } Y) \text{ AND } (\text{NOT } F)\} \text{ OR } \{X \text{ AND } (\text{NOT } Y) \text{ AND } F\}$

The carry is given by

$C = \{(\text{NOT } X) \text{ AND } Y \text{ AND } F\} \text{ OR } \{X \text{ AND } (\text{NOT } Y) \text{ AND } F\}$
$\quad \text{OR } \{X \text{ AND } Y \text{ AND } (\text{NOT } F)\} \text{ OR } (X \text{ AND } Y \text{ AND } F)$

A logic diagram of a system which performs this complete binary addition

20

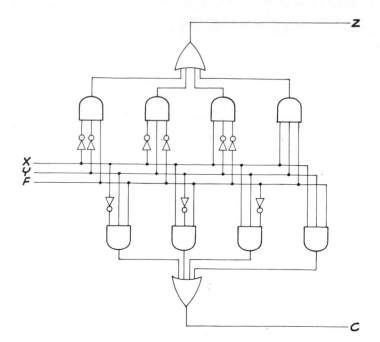

Figure 2.14. *Binary addition with carry.*

for any one column of a pair of binary numbers is given in Figure 2.14. Although this diagram shows a possible way to carry out binary addition, the diagram would be considerably simplified for a practical application, such as in the arithmetic section of a digital computer. Chapter 3 will introduce some of the techniques which are available for the manipulation and simplification of logic systems.

2.4 Summary

In an OR gate, the output is at logic 1, or the gate is said to be enabled, whenever one or more of the inputs are at logic 1. In and AND gate, the output is at logic 1, or the gate is said to be enabled, only when all the inputs provided on the gate are at logic 1. An inverter has an output which always takes the opposite logic value to the input, that is the output is at logic 1 when the input is at logic 0, and vice versa.

This chapter and the following two chapters provide a brief, intuitive introduction to digital logic and to its application in the control of psychological experiments. If a more rigorous treatment is required, there are many specialist books on the subject (for example, Flegg (1971)), but, in order to become proficient in the use of logic in the laboratory, there is really no substitute for practical experience with logic devices. For this purpose, the logic training

21

kits manufactured by a number of companies are very convenient. They are usually accompanied by a manual which gives an introductory course in logic design. One such logic training kit is illustrated in Figure 2.15.

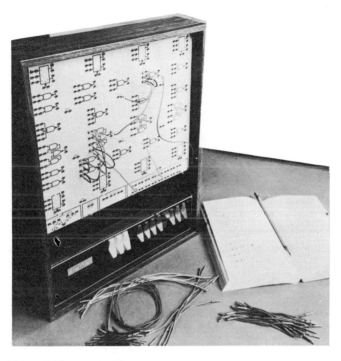

Figure 2.15. *A typical logic trainer and workbook. The student uses the leads to patch up or interconnect different logic diagrams. Logic inputs can be set by the switch registers, and lamp indicators which glow for a logic 1 allow the outputs of logic elements to be examined (DEC Computer Lab).*

CHAPTER 3

Boolean Algebra

3.1 Introduction

Boolean algebra (Boole, 1854) is a branch of mathematics designed to deal with 2-state entities. It allows the logic functions described in Chapter 2 to be expressed in an algebraic form and to be manipulated in a simple mathematical fashion. This is often preferable to the more cumbersome logic diagrams and truth tables. In this chapter, we will discuss the basic Boolean relations and their use in the design and simplification of logic systems. We will find that it is possible to generate many different ways to implement a specified logic function, but that one of these is usually to be preferred on the basis of some practical criterion, such as lowest cost, fewest number of logic gates or the availability of particular types of gate.

3.2 Boolean operators

The standard logic-diagram symbols for AND, OR and NOT were presented in Chapter 2. Each symbol implies a set of specific relations between the input and output states. The same logic operations can be represented by an algebraic notation. The algebraic signs used in this text for the Boolean operators are as follows:

$$\begin{aligned} \text{AND} &\quad \cdot \ \text{(dot)} \\ \text{OR} &\quad + \ \text{(plus)} \\ \text{NOT} &\quad ^- \ \text{(bar)} \end{aligned}$$

There is lack of uniformity between authors in the choice of symbols for the Boolean operators. The symbols used in this text are those commonly found in texts dealing with the application of Boolean algebra to digital logic and switching-circuit design. Figure 3.1 lists some of the equivalent names and signs used for the Boolean operators together with their Venn diagram representations. The Venn diagram derives from set theory, and allows the graphical represention and simplification of Boolean functions.

BOOLEAN OPERATION	ALTERNATIVE TERM	SYMBOLIC FORM	VENN DIAGRAM
AND	INTERSECTION OF SET A & SET B	$A \cdot B \quad AB$ $A \cap B \quad A \wedge B$	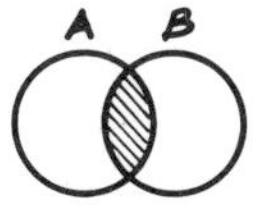
OR	UNION OF SET A & SET B	$A + B$ $A \cup B \quad A \vee B$	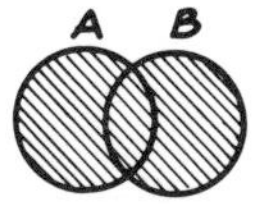
INVERT	COMPLEMENT OF SET A NOT A NEGATION	$\bar{A} \quad A'$ $\sim A$ $\neg A$	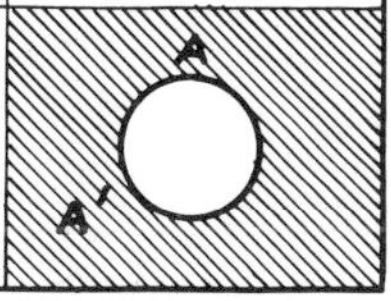

Figure 3.1. *Some alternative ways of representing the Boolean operators.*

Boolean functions have several important characteristics which help in their simplification and manipulation. In algebra, an expression is composed of variables, constants and operators. There are differences, however, between normal algebra and Boolean algebra. In Boolean algebra, a variable can have only two values, 1 or 0. For example, the Boolean variable A can have either the value 1 or 0, but nothing else. Similarly, there are only two Boolean constants, 1 and 0. As with variables and constants, the entire expression or Boolean function can only have the value 1 or 0. For example, the function $\{A + C \cdot (B \cdot C + D)\}$ can represent only one of two values, 1 or 0, depending upon the values of the variables A, B, C and D.

A Boolean function can be completely defined by listing the value (0 or 1) of the function for each combination of input conditions. Such a listing is the familiar truth table. When preparing truth tables, remember that, if there are N different variables involved, then the table will contain 2^N rows. For example, the expression $A + B \cdot C \cdot D$ contains four variables, and therefore its truth table will contain 16 rows. It is good practice to use some standard method for generating the combinations of values for the inputs of truth tables. In this text, binary counting is used. The first row of a truth table has the value binary zero, and the value of each succeeding row is incremented by one.

Figure 3.2 shows the logic-diagram symbol and truth table corresponding to each of the three basic Boolean operations. The basic Boolean operations may be combined to give more complex operations; for example, the AND operation may be combined with NOT to give the NOT AND or NAND operation, which gives a logic 0 output only when both inputs are at logic 1:

$$A \cdot B = \text{AND operation}$$
$$\overline{A \cdot B} = \text{NAND operation}$$

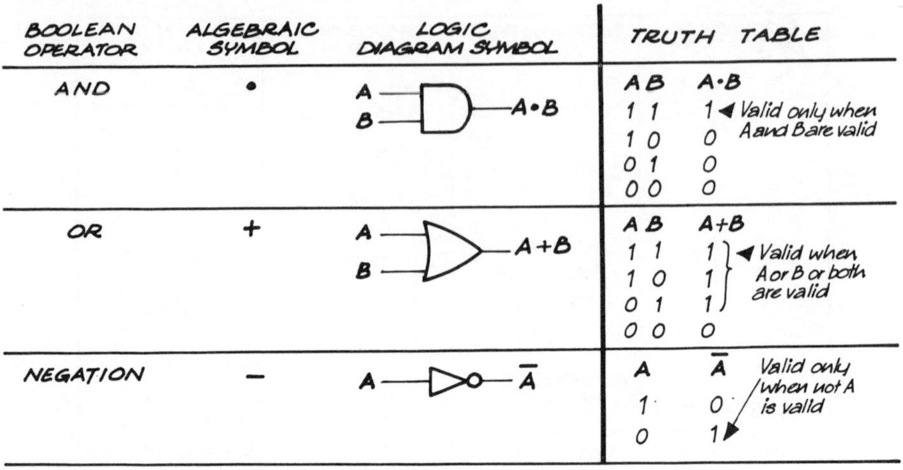

BOOLEAN OPERATOR	ALGEBRAIC SYMBOL	LOGIC DIAGRAM SYMBOL	TRUTH TABLE
AND	•	A ─┐ ⟩─ A•B B ─┘	A B A•B 1 1 1 ◀ Valid only when 1 0 0 A and B are valid 0 1 0 0 0 0
OR	+	A ─┐ ⟩─ A+B B ─┘	A B A+B 1 1 1 ⎫ ◀ Valid when 1 0 1 ⎬ A or B or both 0 1 1 ⎭ are valid 0 0 0
NEGATION	−	A ─▷o─ $\bar{A}$	A $\bar{A}$ Valid only 1 0 when not A 0 1 is valid

Figure 3.2. *Logic-diagram symbols and truth tables for the three Boolean operations.*

Negating the variables on either side of the OR operation is equivalent to a negated input OR operation:

$$A + B = \text{OR operation}$$
$$\bar{A} + \bar{B} = \text{negated input OR operation}$$

Combinations of the Boolean operations can be used to specify any new required logic operation. Figure 3.3 illustrates some of the logic operations which are commonly available in electronic form. Later in the chapter, we will discover that the first two combinations are logically equivalent, as are the last two combinations.

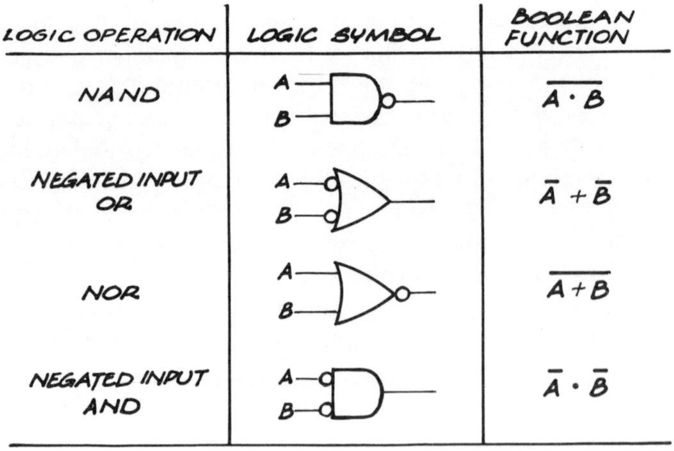

LOGIC OPERATION	LOGIC SYMBOL	BOOLEAN FUNCTION
NAND	A ─┐ ⟩o─ B ─┘	$\overline{A \cdot B}$
NEGATED INPUT OR	A ─o┐ ⟩─ B ─o┘	$\bar{A} + \bar{B}$
NOR	A ─┐ ⟩o─ B ─┘	$\overline{A + B}$
NEGATED INPUT AND	A ─o┐ ⟩─ B ─o┘	$\bar{A} \cdot \bar{B}$

Figure 3.3. *Logic functions often found in integrated circuits.*

3.3 Boolean laws

There are three basic laws of Boolean algebra:

(1) it is commutative, i.e. $A + B = B + A$
(2) it is associative, i.e.
$$A + B + C = A + (B + C) = (A + B) + C$$
$$A \cdot B \cdot C = A \cdot (B \cdot C) = (A \cdot B) \cdot C$$
(3) it is distributive, i.e.
$$A \cdot (B + C) = A \cdot B + A \cdot C$$
$$A + (B \cdot C) = (A + B) \cdot (A + C)$$

These laws can be derived intuitively by truth tables or by the use of Venn diagrams. Figure 3.4 shows a Venn diagram for the first part of the distributive law, and Figure 3.5 is a truth table for the second part of the distributive law. Care should be taken when applying the distributive law, because the second part is not valid in ordinary algebra.

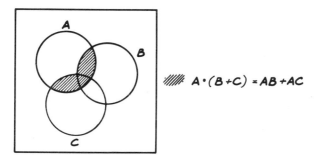

$$\text{////// } A \cdot (B + C) = AB + AC$$

Figure 3.4. *Venn diagram for the first part of the distributive law. The shaded area may be seen to represent either side of the equation.*

A B C	(B·C)	A+(B·C)	(A+B)	(A+C)	(A+B) · (A+C)
0 0 0	0	0	0	0	0
0 0 1	0	0	0	1	0
0 1 0	0	0	1	0	0
0 1 1	1	1	1	1	1
1 0 0	0	1	1	1	1
1 0 1	0	1	1	1	1
1 1 0	0	1	1	1	1
1 1 1	1	1	1	1	1

$$<=>$$

Figure 3.5. *Truth table for the second part of the distributive law.*

3.4 Boolean identities

There are nine basic Boolean identities, involving one variable, one constant and the AND, OR and NOT operators. They are as follows:

(1) $\bar{\bar{A}} = A$ the NOT identity

(2) $A \cdot 1 = A$ the AND identities
(3) $A \cdot 0 = 0$
(4) $A \cdot A = A$
(5) $A \cdot \bar{A} = 0$

(6) $A + 1 = 1$ the OR identities
(7) $A + 0 = A$
(8) $A + A = A$
(9) $A + \bar{A} = 1$

Each of these identities may be shown to be valid by means of truth tables or Venn diagrams. Truth tables for identities 1, 2 and 9 are shown in Figure 3.6.

In ordinary algebra, the writing of $A \cdot B$ is abbreviated to AB when no ambiguity is involved, and the same convention is adopted in Boolean algebra. Thus $A + B \cdot (C + A \cdot B)$ would normally be written in the form $A + B(C + AB)$.

Further Boolean identities involve two or more variables:

(10) $A + AB = A$
(11) $AB + A\bar{B} = A$
(12) $(A + B)(A + \bar{B}) = A$
(13) $A + \bar{A}B = A + B$
(14) $(A + \bar{B})B = AB$
(15) $AC + AB + B\bar{C} = AC + B\bar{C}$
(16) $(A + B)(B + C)(\bar{A} + C) = (A + B)(\bar{A} + C)$

Identity 10 may be derived as follows:

$$A + AB = A(1 + B)$$

from the distributive law. We know

$$1 + B = 1$$

from identity 6. Therefore
$$A + AB = A \cdot 1$$
$$= A$$

from identity 2.

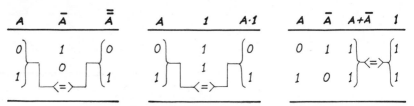

Figure 3.6. *Truth tables for identities 1, 2 and 9.*

A	B	$\bar{B}$	$A+\bar{B}$	LEFT SIDE $(A+\bar{B})\cdot B$	RIGHT SIDE $A\cdot B$
0	0	1	1	0	0
0	1	0	0	0	0
1	0	1	1	0	0
1	1	0	1	1	1

$\left.\begin{matrix}0\\0\\0\\1\end{matrix}\right\} <=> \left\{\begin{matrix}0\\0\\0\\1\end{matrix}\right.$

Figure 3.7. *Truth table for identity 14.*

A	B	C	A·C	A·B	$\bar{C}$	$B\cdot\bar{C}$	LEFT SIDE $A\cdot C+A\cdot B+B\cdot\bar{C}$	RIGHT SIDE $A\cdot C+B\cdot\bar{C}$
0	0	0	0	0	1	0	0	0
0	0	1	0	0	0	0	0	0
0	1	0	0	0	1	1	1	1
0	1	1	0	0	0	0	0	0
1	0	0	0	0	1	0	0	0
1	0	1	1	0	0	0	1	1
1	1	0	0	1	1	1	1	1
1	1	1	1	1	0	0	1	1

$\left.\begin{matrix}0\\0\\1\\0\\0\\1\\1\\1\end{matrix}\right\} <=> \left\{\begin{matrix}0\\0\\1\\0\\0\\1\\1\\1\end{matrix}\right.$

Figure 3.8. *Truth table for identity 15.*

The identities may be demonstrated by the truth-table technique. The method employed is to determine the value of the function on the left-hand side of the identity for all possible combinations of the values of the variables, and then to repeat this procedure for the function on the right-hand side of the identity. If the identity is true, then the two functions will have the same values for corresponding values of the variables. This procedure is shown for identity 14 in Figure 3.7 and for identity 15 in Figure 3.8.

The Venn diagram technique is somewhat less formal than the truth table technique, but does allow a rapid demonstration of the identities, as in Figure 3.9. Venn diagrams are useful for the simplification of Boolean functions of a

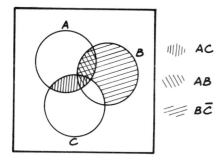

Figure 3.9. *Venn diagram for identity 15.*

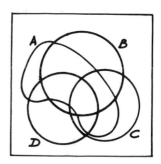

Figure 3.10. *Venn diagram for four variables.*

small number of variables. The technique becomes extremely unwieldy with more than four variables (Figure 3.10).

3.5 De Morgan's theorem

This is a powerful theorem which is often useful for the simplification of complex Boolean functions. The essence of de Morgan's theorem is given by the following equations:

(1) $\bar{A} \cdot \bar{B} = \overline{A + B}$
(2) $\bar{A} + \bar{B} = \overline{A \cdot B}$

The first equation asserts the equivalence of the negated input AND gate and the NOR gate; the second equation asserts the equivalence of the negated input OR gate and the NAND gate. These gates were explained in Figure 3.3. De Morgan's theorem may be demonstrated by the truth-table technique, as shown in Figure 3.11.

Repeated application of these equations often provides dramatic simplification of complex Boolean functions.
Consider the function

$$\overline{A \ \overline{AB} \ \overline{CD}}$$

Applying de Morgan's theorem once,

$$\overline{A \ \overline{AB} \cdot \overline{CD}} = \overline{A \ \overline{AB}} + CD$$

Applying it again to the first half of the OR function,

$$\overline{A \ \overline{AB}} + CD = \bar{A} + A\bar{B} + CD$$

Identity 13 gives the final simplification, and

$$\overline{A \ \overline{AB} \ \overline{CD}} = \bar{A} + \bar{B} + CD$$

Figure 3.12 converts the function to logic-diagram form.

A	B	Ā	B̄	ĀB̄	A+B	A̅+B̅	Ā+B̄	AB	A̅B̅
0	0	1	1	1	0	1	1	0	1
0	1	1	0	0	1	0	1	0	1
1	0	0	1	0	1	0	1	0	1
1	1	0	0	0	1	0	0	1	0

Figure 3.11. *Truth table for de Morgan's theorem.*

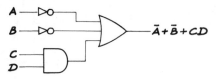

Figure 3.12. *Logic diagram for the simplified form of* $\overline{A \ \overline{AB} \ \overline{CD}}$.

3.6 Simplifying logic diagrams

Logic designers usually follow a definite sequence of operations when converting a required logic function to a simplified logic diagram. The first operation is to express the requirement in the form of a Boolean function. The function is then manipulated into a simplified form. For simple functions of a few variables, this may be done directly, in Boolean algebraic form, but, for more complex functions, specialized tabular procedures are generally used. Phister (1958) gives an account of the standard methods for simplification of Boolean functions.

The objectives of simplification depend upon the situation. An equipment designer working on a product which is intended for large-scale production will aim to minimize the final unit cost. He will probably evaluate alternative forms of the Boolean function on the basis of budgetary figures for the cost of various types of gate, together with a cost for each interconnection. An experimenter setting up logic equipment in the laboratory is in a rather different situation. His aim is usually to interconnect an existing set of laboratory equipment so that the required functions are carried out. It may be of little immediate interest that a different function might be implemented at lower cost if the required logic modules are not readily to hand and would have to be specially ordered. Simplification in this case means manipulating the function so that it can be implemented with the existing equipment. When the simplified function is determined, the apparatus should be interconnected according to the logic diagram, and tested with all combinations of inputs to verify that it operates in accordance with the truth table for the original Boolean function.

The following example demonstrates the translation of a logic requirement into three different but equivalent logic diagrams. In a reaction-time experiment, we might wish to generate a stimulus if the experimenter's control switch is on, the subject's finger is resting on the pushbutton and the data-recording equipment is not busy. Let us first represent each of these conditions by a Boolean variable:

$$A = \text{experimenter's switch on}$$
$$B = \text{subject's finger resting on pushbutton}$$
$$C = \text{data-recording equipment busy}$$
$$S = \text{stimulus signal}$$

The following equation defines the conditions under which a stimulus is to be generated:

$$S = AB\bar{C}$$

The logic diagram corresponding to this equation is given in Figure 3.13. In order to implement the diagram directly, a 3-input AND gate and an inverter are required. Even such a simple logic requirement can be implemented in a variety of ways. Suppose the AND gates which are available only accept two

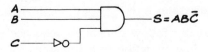

Figure 3.13. *Control of stimulus generation in a reaction-time experiment.*

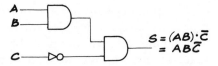

Figure 3.14. *Control of stimulus generation using two* AND *gates.*

inputs each. The associative law allows us to rewrite the function in the form

$$S = (AB) \cdot \bar{C}$$

Figure 3.14 shows the logic diagram using two input AND gates. If we have no AND gates available, but we do have inverters and OR gates, it is still possible to implement the requirement. We first transform the Boolean function by applying de Morgan's theorem:

$$
\begin{aligned}
S &= AB\bar{C} \\
&= (AB) \cdot \bar{C} \\
&= \overline{\overline{AB} + C} \\
&= \overline{\bar{A} + \bar{B} + C}
\end{aligned}
$$

Although this form of the function uses more logic elements (Figure 3.15) than the original, and would hardly be the preferred form for an equipment designer, it functions just as well, and would be the preferred form for an experimenter who found himself short of AND gates. In effect, de Morgan's theorem, with the help of inverters, allows us to replace AND gates by OR gates, and vice versa

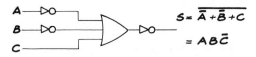

Figure 3.15. *An alternative form of Figure 3.13 using an* OR *gate in place of the* AND *gate.*

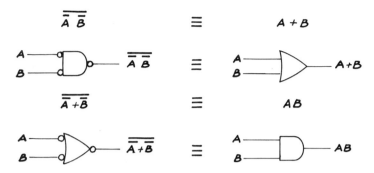

Figure 3.16. AND *and* OR *gates may be interchanged by the use of de Morgan's theorem.*

(Figure 3.16). This not only enables us to make the best use of an existing stock of logic elements, but has the consequence that, in general, only one of the Boolean operators AND and OR are strictly necessary. We could express any Boolean function using only the operators NOT and AND, or only the operators NOT and OR. One may persue this line further, and show that any of the three Boolean operations may be effected by combinations of only one type of gate, either the NOR gate or the NAND gate (Figure 3.3). Consequently, these gates are widely used in professional equipment. The basic Boolean gates are, of course, much simpler for non-professionals to use.

3.7 Summary

Boolean algebra provides a mathematical notation which, together with graphical and tabular techniques, facilitates the design and manipulation of systems built from 2-state devices. De Morgan's theorem is particularly useful when building logic systems from a restricted set of available elements.

CHAPTER 4

Modular Programming Equipment

4.1 Introduction

Modular programming equipment has been designed to provide flexible facilities for control and measurement in psychological experimentation and related fields. The early systems used electromechanical components, such as relays for logical operations and synchronous motors driving cam-operated switches for timing operations. Figure 4.1 shows the basic principles of relay operation, and the use of relays for the three logic operations NOT, AND and OR is illustrated in Figures 4.2 and 4.3. Logic 1 corresponds to a short circuit and logic 0 to an open circuit. Relay programming equipment used in psychology laboratories operates from 28 V d.c., and is designed to clip onto pairs of horizontal power rails mounted in a 19 in instrument rack. Interconnections are made using snap connectors, which are rather like press studs, and can be stacked one upon another. A useful introduction to relay programming equip-

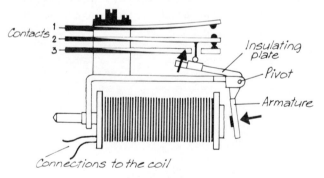

Figure 4.1. *A typical relay shown in its non-energized state. When current flows through the coil, the armature is attracted to the electromagnet, causing the normally open pair of contacts (1 and 2) to close and the normally closed pair of contacts (2 and 3) to open. Relays may be fitted with various contact arrangements.*

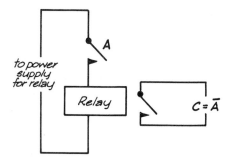

Figure 4.2. *A relay used as an inverter. Contact C is normally closed. When the input contact A is closed, current flows through the relay coil and contact C opens.*

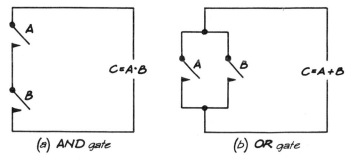

(a) AND gate (b) OR gate

Figure 4.3. *Relay contacts A and B on two different relays are connected to give the two logic functions (a)* AND *and (b)* OR. *Logic 1 is a short circuit (i.e. contacts closed to allow the flow of current), and logic 0 is an open circuit (i.e. contacts open giving no current flow).*

ment is the handbook published by the instrument manufacturer GenRad (1976)

Modern programming systems use solid-state circuits which allow an experimenter with no knowledge of electronics to connect up his own instrumentation systems. Typically, the modules are plugged into frames which distribute power to the modules. The user either makes the control interconnections between sockets on the front panels of the modules, or may use a removable program frame which connects to connectors at the rear of the modules. This latter facility allows the user to change rapidly from one program to another. The front-panel connections carry only low voltages, and are therefore safe to handle. They are also usually proof against accidental short circuits, facilitating their use by students and other experimenters with little technical knowledge. The layouts are usually arranged systematically to allow easy identification of the various functional modules, and inputs and outputs are usually coded by means of colours or symbols.

Each system of modular programming equipment has the voltage levels which correspond to logic 0 and logic 1 defined by the system designer. Modules are provided to convert external events, for example contacts opening or closing, to the standard logic levels of the system. Modules are also provided to convert logic levels to external events, such as relay operation or switching on a lamp indicator.

The outputs of modules should be capable of driving a large number of inputs with few restrictions on interconnections. This feature greatly affects the ease with which a non-technical experimenter can use the modules, and the various systems are highly variable in this respect. If the outputs are capable of driving at least 20 inputs, then loading rules can be virtually ignored in most behavioural experiments.

4.2 Some typical modules

The modules described in this chapter are typical of those forming the bases of solid-state modular programming systems offered by a number of manufacturers. They do correspond most closely, however, to the modular system manufactured by **BRD** (Electronics) Ltd. Although there are general similarities between the systems of different manufacturers, the detailed specifications, such as number of inputs on logic gates, or the range of operation of timers, will vary greatly. All the examples in this chapter will work with **BRD** modules.

In this chapter, we introduce some new logic operations, those which involve memory and time. We will continue to represent the basic Boolean operations by the logic diagrams used in the previous chapters, but we will represent new operations by a box with inputs and outputs. The conventions for the inputs and outputs are given in Figure 4.4.

A list of modules used in this chapter follows. When a new logic operation is introduced, the operation of the module will be described in detail.

4.2.1 AND *gate*

This is a 3-input gate of the type described in Chapters 2 and 3. Care is necessary when using the module as a 2-input gate, because the inputs in this

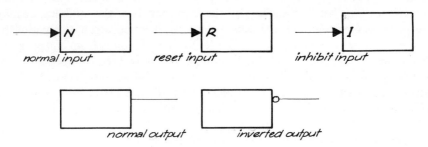

Figure 4.4. *Conventions employed for the representation of the logic inputs and outputs.*

logic system rest at logic 0 unless they are explicitly driven to logic 1. Therefore an unused input must be connected to logic 1 or to one of the other two inputs. AND gates with a greater number of inputs can be constructed by connecting two or more 3-input gates in cascade.

4.2.2 *D.C.* OR *gate*

This is a 3-input OR gate of the type described in Chapters 2 and 3. When this module is used as a 2-input gate, the unused input may be left disconnected. In a similar manner to the AND gate, higher number input OR gates may be constructed by connecting two or more OR gates in cascade.

4.2.3 *A.C.* OR *gate*

This is a special type of OR gate. When any one of the three inputs is subject to a change from logic 0 to logic 1, a pulse of logic 1 for 1 ms appears at the output socket. An example of the use of this module would be in counting the totals of various classes of events. The abbreviations d.c. and a.c. refer strictly to direct current and alternating current, but they are widely used to distinguish between circuits which operate under steady-state (d.c.) or transient-state (a.c.) conditions.

4.2.4 *Inverter*

This module provides normal Boolean negation. The symbols used for the modules described so far in this chapter are shown in Figure 4.5.

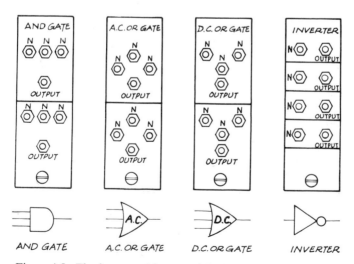

Figure 4.5. *The front-panel layouts of the basic logic modules, and the logic-diagram symbols used for one element from each module.*

36

4.2.5 *Input station*

This module is used to convert external events to the standard logic levels used in the remainder of the system. The input terminals are numbered, and convert non-standard signals into standard logic levels as follows:

input 1 operates on contact closure to earth
input 2 operates on a positive-going voltage
input 3 operates on a negative-going voltage
input 4 operates on any non-zero voltage, such as an a.c. waveform

A logic 1 to the inhibit input overrides the normal inputs, and prevents the occurrence of an output. The module is illustrated in Figure 4.6.

When mechanical switches operate, there is a period of intermittency as the contacts make or break. This is usually called contact bounce. Electronic equipment can operate so quickly that the series of makes and breaks during contact bounce may be recorded as separate responses (see also Section 10.1.1). The input station is designed to filter out contact bounce from a high-quality switch such as a microswitch or reed switch, but, if it is necessary to detect responses using devices with excessive contact bounce, or in situations in which the subject's response is accompanied by considerable tremor, further signal conditioning can be achieved by connecting a delay control after the input station. In most cases, the only time of interest when detecting responses is the instant at which the switch contacts are made, that is at the transition from logic 0 to logic 1 in the output of the input station. Accordingly, the resulting

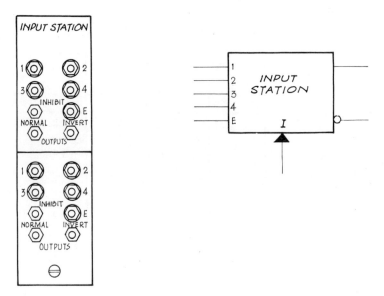

Figure 4.6. *Input station. Front panel layout and logic-diagram symbol.*
The earth terminal is labelled E.

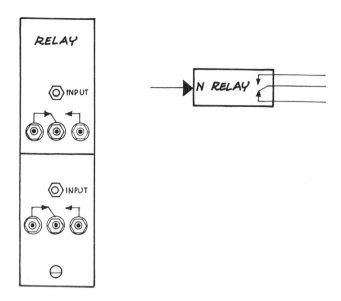

Figure 4.7. *Relay module. Front panel layout and logic-diagram symbol.*

standardization of the pulse length by the delay control is unlikely to present a problem.

4.2.6 *Relay module*

The relay module is fitted with changeover contacts. The legend on the front of the module (see Figure 4.7) shows the relay contacts in the normal state, that is the state when the input is at logic 0. A logic 1 on the input causes the contacts to change state.

4.2.7 *Lamp indicator*

This module is used to show the status of a logic line. The lamp glows when a logic 1 is applied to the input. The module is illustrated in Figure 4.8.

4.2.8 *Electromagnetic counter*

This module contains a solenoid-operated register which displays the number of operations which have occurred. The register can be reset to zero by a mechanical pushbutton. Electromagnetic counters are often used for counting the total number of responses. The counter increments by one whenever the input is at logic 1 for a period of 1 ms or longer. The maximum rate of counting is 25 s^{-1}. The module is illustrated in Figure 4.9.

In some types of electromagnetic counter, an additional register is provided

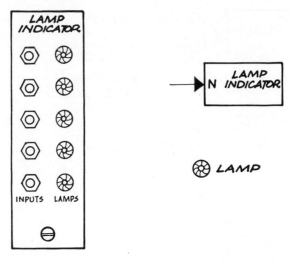

Figure 4.8. *Lamp indicator. Front panel layout and logic-diagram symbol.*

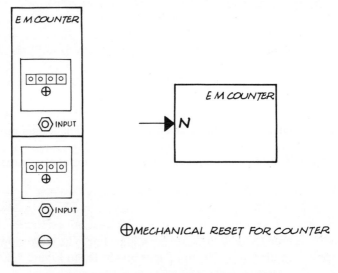

Figure 4.9. *Electromagnetic counter. Front panel layout and logic-diagram symbol.*

which can be set manually to some desired total. When the counter reaches the same value as the manual register, an output is generated. Thus, the device can be used to generate a control action after a predetermined number of events.

4.2.9 *Sequence counter*

This module is able to count events which occur at a higher rate than can be

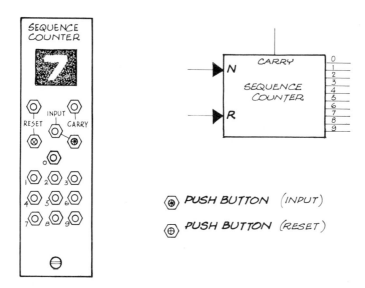

Figure 4.10. *Sequence counter. Front panel layout and logic-diagram symbol.*

registered on an electromagnetic counter. It can also be used to count in bases other than 10. The bistable (Section 4.2.10) is normally used to count in binary. The state of the counter is displayed by an electronic numerical indicator as well as being available at the logic outputs. When the sequence counter is in the reset state, the 0 output is at logic 1 and the 1 to 9 outputs are at logic 0. When the normal input is operated, the 1 output goes to logic 1 and the 0 output returns to logic 0. For each subsequent input, the logic 1 moves to the next higher labelled output, and so the number displayed on the indicator at any time corresponds to that output which is at logic 1. When the sequence counter is at 9, the next normal input moves the logic 1 to output 0, this transition being accompanied by an additional output in the form of a 1 ms duration logic 1 pulse at the carry output. The carry pulse is generated whenever the unit automatically reset on the tenth pulse, or at any time when the counter is reset either by the pushbutton or by a logic input. This carry pulse may be used to operate a further decade of counting. The module can also be used to count to bases less than 10 by patching from the appropriate output to the reset input; to count in octal, for example, one would patch from the 8 output to the reset input. The module is illustrated in Figure 4.10.

In addition to being used as simple counters, modules of this kind can be used to control the sequence of operations in an experiment. For example, in discrimination-learning experiments, the sequence in which stimuli are presented is usually chosen so that reinforcement will occur at only chance level if the subject responds on the basis of some strategy, such as position or alternation. Such a sequence is termed a Gellermann series (Gellermann, 1933). As an example of the use of a sequence counter to generate a Gellermann series,

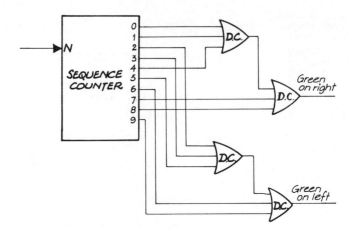

Figure 4.11. *Use of a sequence counter to generate a Gellermann series. The green-on-left signal could be derived more simply by inverting the green-on-right signal.*

let us consider a simultaneous red–green discrimination experiment. Suppose we wish to reinforce responses to the green light, using the following series for the position of the green stimulus on each successive trial:

$$\text{R R L R L L R R L L} \qquad (\text{R} = \text{right}, \text{L} = \text{left})$$

We simply OR together the 0, 1, 4, 7 and 8 outputs of the sequence counter for the green-on-right signal (the same signal indicates red-on-left), and OR together the 2, 3, 5, 6 and 9 outputs for the green-on-left signal (which also indicates red-on-right), as shown in Figure 4.11. The sequence counter should be incremented after each response. Note that the outputs of the sequence counter must be explicitly combined using an OR gate; they cannot be merely connected together, as this would produce an undefined logic condition.

Various kinds of solenoid-operated rotary switches are used in relay programming systems for similar purposes. They are often termed stepper switches or uniselectors.

4.2.10 *Bistable*

This is a device with memory which is frequently used to store information about past events when programming experiments. The bistable has three inputs; normal (or set), reset and divide by two. It has two outputs: normal and invert. When a module in the reset state, that is the state in which the normal output is at logic 0, receives a logic 1 at the set input, the output changes from logic 0 to logic 1. The module will remain in this state until a logic 1 signal is applied to the reset input, or the manual reset button has been operated.

If a logic 1 pulse is fed into the divide-by-two input, the bistable changes state. Thus, if the normal output is at logic 1, a transition from logic 0 to 1 on the divide-by-two input will cause the output to go to logic 0. The next transition from logic 0 to 1 on the divide-by-two input will cause the output to change back to logic 1. Thus, if the bistable is initially in the reset state, and a series of logic 1 pulses is applied to the divide-by-two input, then the output will be logic 1 after an odd number of pulses and logic 0 after an even number of pulses. We could use a bistable to provide the least significant bit of a binary counter for a series of input pulses. To give more bits to the counter, we need to generate a carry pulse from the existing stage. This should occur whenever the normal output of the bistable changes from logic 1 to logic 0, that is when the inverted output changes from logic 0 to logic 1. Thus, the inverted output of one bistable may be used to drive the divide-by-two input of another bistable. The process may be repeated for as many bits as are necessary to accommodate the maximum count. In practice, when using a counter of this type, all the bistables are initially reset, and the pulses to be counted are fed into the divide-by-two input of the first bistable. The carry pulses are transmitted along from the inverted output of each stage to the divide-by-two input of the next more significant stage. The accumulated binary count at any given time is represented by the state of the

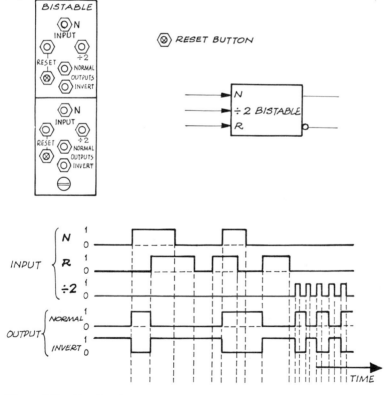

Figure 4.12. *The bistable. Front panel layout, logic-diagram symbol and operation.*

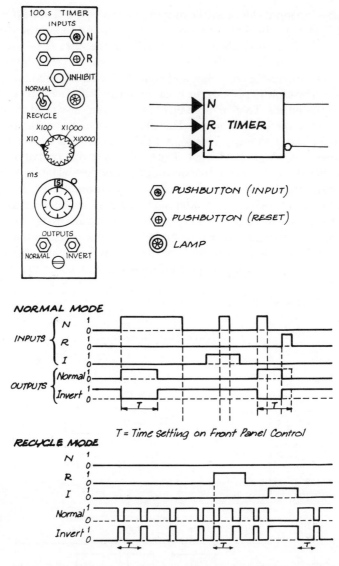

Figure 4.13. *100 s timer. Front panel layout, logic-diagram symbol and operation in the normal and recycle modes.*

normal outputs. The applications of counting circuits are discussed in Sections 4.3.2 and 6.5.

The module is illustrated in Figure 4.12, which also shows diagrammatically its mode of operation. Bistables are sometimes called latches, or flip–flops.

A relay can be used as a simple memory device by arranging that one pair of its contacts continues to hold the supply voltage connected to the relay coil after it has been energized. The relay will then remain in the energized state, even though the initial contact closure which energized the relay was of brief duration. The relay can be reset by breaking the supply to the holding contacts.

4.2.11 *Timer*

This module can produce logic levels for a predetermined period of time within the range 10 ms to 100 s. The time intervals are set by a range-selector switch and a continuous fine control. In its normal mode, the module starts timing after the application of logic 1 to the normal input or after the manual start button has been operated, provided that the inhibit input is at logic 0. At the end of the preset time interval, the unit resets ready for the next operation. The unit will reset immediately, however, if the reset or inhibit inputs receive a logic 1 during the timing period. The reset input is used to terminate timing period, but, while a logic 1 is on the inhibit input, the timer is additionally prevented from starting any further timing cycles.

In the recycle mode, the unit repeatedly produces a 1 ms duration logic 1 pulse at the end of each timed period. The reset and inhibit inputs function as in the normal mode. Figure 4.13 shows the front-panel layout of the module, and illustrates its mode of operation.

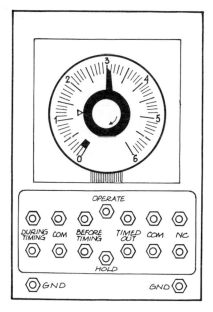

Figure 4.14. *A typical electromechanical interval timer. The timer can be set to any period between 0·3 s and 60 h. The smaller dial selects the range and the larger dial selects the interval within the range (Gerbrands model G4612).*

Interval timers in relay programming systems are usually based upon motor-driven process-control units (Figure 4.14), and can be set to give timed intervals over a range from the order of 1 s to a few hours. A typical timer is operated by connecting the input stud to the negative-supply rail (earth or ground). Outputs are provided to indicate the state of the timer (active or inactive) and the completion of the timed period (time out). It is usual to provide an input which allows the timing to be held (by switching off the timing motor) and also an input to reset the timer on demand.

The tape or filmstrip timer (Figure 4.15) is a versatile device for controlling programmed sequences of times, and is often used for variable interval schedules of reinforcement. The timer is programmed by punching holes into a loop of 16 mm film which is driven by a motorized sprocket wheel. When a punched hole passes over the sprocket wheel, a feeler arm drops into the hole and operates a microswitch. Further control equipment can be used to stop and start the drive motor and also to step on the filmstrip by fixed amounts, allowing quite complex sequences to be programmed.

4.2.12 *Delay control*

For many purposes, the sophisticated facilities provided by the timer module are unnecessary, and therefore a simpler and less expensive module known as a

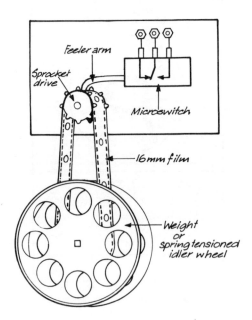

Figure 4.15. *A tape timer which will give programmed sequences of time intervals. The sprocket wheel is driven by a mains-operated motor, and gives a speed of 1 mm$^{s^{-1}}$.*

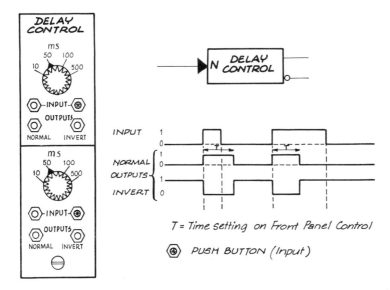

Figure 4.16. *Delay control. Front panel layout, logic-diagram symbol and operation.*

delay control is provided. This module generates a logic 1 pulse having a duration of 10, 50, 100 or 500 ms at the normal output when a change from logic 0 to logic 1 occurs at the input. The duration is selected by a switch on the front panel. The delay control is useful for setting the operating time for devices such as reinforcement dispensers. A device of this kind is sometimes called a one-shot, or monostable. In relay logic systems, the pulse former provides a similar function. The diagram for the delay control is shown in Figure 4.16. A similar module, known as a long delay, gives timed periods of 1, 2, 5 and 10 s duration.

4.3 Schedules of reinforcement

The following sections illustrate the use of programming modules for the generation of some commonly used schedules of reinforcement.

4.3.1 *Continuous reinforcement*

This is the simplest of the schedules, and provides reinforcement for every response. The logic diagram is shown in Figure 4.17. The response key is connected to the input terminals on the input station, and the normal output of this module operates the delay control. This module standardizes the pulse-width of the response, and therefore the relay is operated for a fixed time period selected by the switch on the front panel of the delay control. A further connection is made from the normal output of the delay control to the inhibit on the

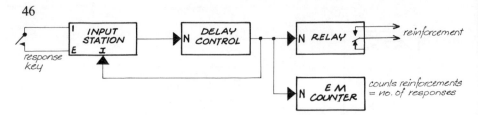

Figure 4.17. *Continuous reinforcement schedule.*

input station; this prevents the detection of further responses during the presentation of the reinforcer.

4.3.2 *Fixed ratio schedule*

The fixed ratio schedule is an extension of the technique used for continuous reinforcement, but, in this case, reinforcement is provided for every given number of responses. Figure 4.18a shows the logic diagram with the schedule programmed to give reinforcement for every ten responses. A sequence counter is interposed between the input station and the delay control. When the output is taken from the carry socket, the sequence counter acts as a divide-by-ten, that is it provides a logic 1 to the delay control after every ten responses. Other ratios between one and nine can be obtained by connecting the appropriate

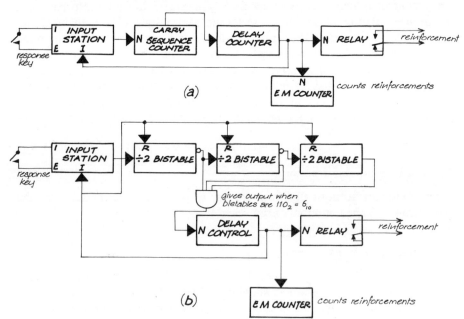

Figure 4.18. *Fixed ratio reinforcement schedules. (a) A sequence counter giving an FR10 schedule. (b) Bistables giving an FR6 schedule. For reliable detection of the selected count from such a series of bistables, additional logic should be included to allow completion of all binary carries before the AND gate can be enabled.*

output on the sequence counter to the reset socket. Two sequence counters can be connected in series to obtain ratio schedules up to 100. The sequence counter may be replaced by a series of bistables used as binary counters (Figure 4.18b).

4.3.3 *Probability ratio schedule*

This schedule provides a response-to-reward ratio based on a percentage probability. The program shown in Figure 4.19 gives a 20% probability of reward, but percentage probabilities from 10% to 90% can be programmed in steps of 10% by simply patching to the appropriate number on the sequence counter. One half of the input station is used to generate logic 1 pulses at a rate of 100 s^{-1}. A 50 Hz low-voltage a.c. supply connected to terminals 4 and E on the input station generates an output every 10 ms. The sequence counter therefore completes a cycle every 100 ms, each output remaining at logic 1 for 10 ms. The carry pulse from the sequence counter sets the bistable, which allows the AND gate to provide a path for the response, and therefore also the reinforcement, while the bistable remains in this state. The chosen output, in this case output 2, is used to reset the bistable, causing the AND gate to close, thereby preventing reinforcement during the remaining part of the cycle. Thus, the probability of reinforcement is given by the proportion of the cycle for which the AND gate is open, allowing a response to operate the delay control. If the inter-response time is longer than the cycle time (100 ms), the probabilities for successive responses will be substantially independent. As with most systems based on probabilities, the larger the sample of events taken, the greater is the likelihood that the observed proportion of reinforced responses approximates to the expected proportion.

4.3.4 *Fixed interval schedule*

This schedule provides reinforcement to the first response occurring after the elapse of a given time interval from the last reinforcement. The logic diagram is shown in Figure 4.20. The normal output of the input station is patched to a timer operating in the normal mode, the setting of the timer defining the time interval T. When a response is detected, the timer starts to operate. Immediately a logic 1 occurs at the timer output, the delay control and relay provide reinforce-

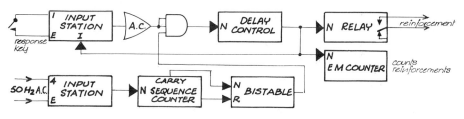

Figure 4.19. *Probability reinforcement schedule.*

48

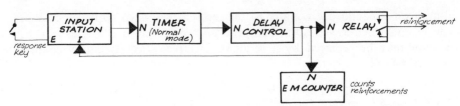

Figure 4.20. *Fixed interval reinforcement schedule.*

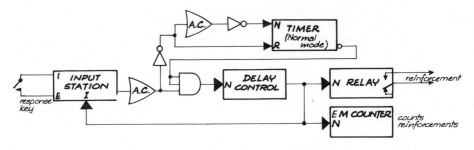

Figure 4.21. *Differential reinforcement of low rates.*

ment. If further responses are made during the period *T*, no reinforcement will follow, because the timer is still operating. When the timer has completed its operation, it will be triggered by the first response detected, and this response will be reinforced.

Logic diagrams for a further two commonly used schedules of reinforcement are given in Figure 4.21 and Figure 4.22. The differential reinforcement of low rates schedule (DRL) gives reinforcement only when the time interval between two successive responses exceeds a criterion level. With Sidman avoidance conditioning, a series of shocks is presented unless the subject responds within

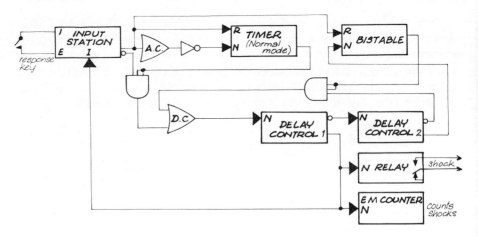

Figure 4.22. *Sidman avoidance procedure.*

a specified time, the shocks being terminated when the subject eventually responds. In both logic diagrams, an a.c. OR gate and an inverter are used to delay the propagation of an event by 1 ms. The undelayed event resets a timer, and the delayed event restarts it. In Chapter 12, computer programs are given for all the schedules of reinforcement included in this chapter.

4.4 Other applications

Modular programming equipment is, of course, often used to control experiments in areas other than operant conditioning. As an example of an experiment involving a human subject, we will suppose that an experimenter wishes to investigate the responses of a subject to near threshold stimuli. On each trial, the experimenter will select either an auditory or a visual stimulus. This should continue to be presented until the subject responds to one of two response keys. One key will indicate an auditory judgement and the other key will indicate a visual judgement. The apparatus should count:

(1) correct responses to light stimulus
(2) incorrect responses to light stimulus
(3) correct responses to auditory stimulus
(4) incorrect responses to auditory stimulus
(5) all responses

and also give a visual indication to the experimenter that the subject has made a response. The response latencies are to be measured on an electronic stopclock which is able to record the duration of a logic 1 signal.

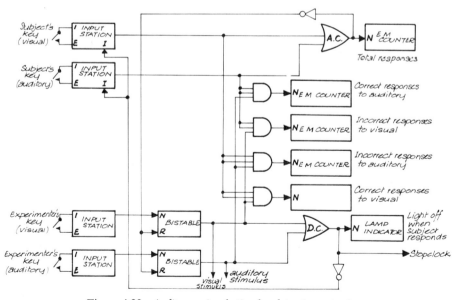

Figure 4.23. *Auditory–visual stimulus detection experiment.*

A possible configuration of modules to control this experiment is shown in Figure 4.23. Input stations are used to convert the key operations made by both the experimenter and the subject to logic levels. The stimulus selected by the experimenter is stored in a bistable. The subject's judgement is compared with the selected stimulus and categorized by four AND gates which drive electro-magnetic counters. An a.c. OR gate and an inverter delay the response signal for 1 ms before resetting the bistable, giving a 1 ms period during which the response and experimenter's selection are both present. The outputs of the bistables are ORed to provide a signal for the stopclock and also to drive a lamp indicator to give a visual signal to the experimenter. The same signal is inverted and used to inhibit the input stations used for the subject's response keys, so that only the first response occurring after the selection of a stimulus will be detected.

4.5 Summary

This chapter has presented a brief description of a typical solid-state modular programming system. The modules provide logical and timing functions at standard logic levels. Special interfacing modules are necessary to convert other input events, such as contact closures, and to drive external equipment, such as pellet dispensers. Examples have been given of typical applications of programming modules.

CHAPTER 5

Fundamentals of Electronic Circuits

5.1 Introduction

Although much experimental work can be accomplished without a profound understanding of electronics, an experimental psychologist needs some familiarity with the theory and practice of electronics in order to make the best use of electronic instruments in the laboratory. This knowledge is needed when comparing commercial instrument specifications to select the best instrument for a particular application. When no commercially manufacturing instrument is available, or when budgets do not allow its purchase, the experimenter will find that some acquaintance with electronics is a great help in communicating requirements to the technical staff responsible for the design and construction of apparatus. Whatever the source of his equipment, a technically informed psychologist is in a good position to design his experiments with an awareness of the limitations and advantages of the instruments which are available.

This chapter is intended as an introduction to the basic concepts of electronics. It may be omitted by readers with an understanding of solid-state electronics. It is not intended to give a rigorous or comprehensive treatment of the subject, such as would be appropriate in the training of an electronics engineer, but rather to treat the subject from the practical viewpoint of the psychologist as a selector, specifier and user of electronic instrumentation.

5.2 The electron and its relation to the atom

Modern ideas about electricity are based on the orbital model of the atom proposed by Niels Bohr in 1913. The Bohr model suggested that the atom of each chemical element was in the form of a miniature sun-and-planet system. The central sun is termed the nucleus, around which particles called electrons move (Figure 5.1). Experiments have shown that the nucleus itself consists of a group of particles called nucleons. The nucleons, which are held in a tight dense mass at the centre of the atom, are of two types: protons, which carry one unit of

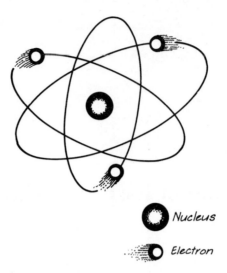

Figure 5.1. *The lithium atom.*

positive electric charge, and neutrons, which are electrically neutral. The positive charge of the protons is balanced by the negative charge of the electrons. Since each electron carries one unit of negative charge, the number of electrons will be equal to the number of protons in a stable atom.

Our main concern is with the groups of electrons which rotate around the nucleus in various-sized orbits. An electron is held in its orbit by the attraction between its own negative charge and the positive charge due to the protons in the nucleus. These electrostatic forces, which are known as Coulomb forces, follow the inverse-square law, and cause the electron to follow an elliptical orbit around the nucleus.

5.2.1 *Electron shells*

As already described, the electrons are held in their orbits by the attraction between their own negative charges and the positive charges on the nucleus. It appears that an electron can rotate in an orbit which corresponds with only one of seven shell sizes around the nucleus. Those electrons nearest to the nucleus are said to be in the K shell, those next closest to the nucleus are in the L shell, and so on to the outermost electrons, which occupy the Q shell. It has been established that there is a maximum number of electrons which can occupy each shell. Thus, no more than two electrons may occupy the K shell, no more than eight electrons may occupy the L shell and so on. As the number of electrons increases, atoms become rather unstable, and the largest known atoms have just over 100 electrons. Considering the smaller atoms first, we find that the electrons usually fill up each shell in turn, starting with the K shell and working outwards. After each shell is filled with its maximum number of electrons, a new shell is started.

Within each shell, the electrons can take up particular discrete energy levels. The outer shells and levels contain the more energetic, or faster-moving, electrons, and the inner electrons are less energetic. If an electron drops from one level to another, that is it moves inwards from a certain energy state to a lower energy state, then the surplus energy is emitted in the form of a quantum of light or some other kind of electromagnetic radiation. Atoms with only a few electrons in the outer shell tend to lose them and become positively charged, whereas atoms with a nearly complete outer shell tend to acquire electrons to complete the shell and become negatively charged. Charged atoms are termed ions. Sodium chloride (common salt) is composed of sodium ions and chloride ions. Sodium has an atomic number of 11; the two inner shells are complete, leaving only one electron in the outer M shell. The sodium atom can lose this and form a sodium ion, carrying a single positive charge. Chlorine has an atomic number of 17; again the two inner shells are complete, leaving seven electrons in the outer M shell. One more electron completes the shell to form a chloride ion with a single negative charge. Equal numbers of sodium and chlorine atoms will combine, transferring electrons to form electrically neutral sodium chloride. The capacity of atoms to combine with one another and form a molecule is known as valency; the electrons in the outer shell are, therefore, often termed valence electrons. Another way in which atoms can combine and achieve stability is to share their incomplete outer-shell electrons. Outer-shell electrons are important in electronics, for the development of the transistor is a consequence of an understanding of their action.

Before we embark upon the complexities of semiconductors, however, let us consider what constitutes an electric current in a conductor. Although copper is the most generally used electrical conductor, all metals are good conductors of both heat and electricity. These properties are explained by the free-electron theory, which considers metals to be constructed in the form of a crystal lattice of positive ions with the electrons occupying the space between the ions. It is rather as though the lattice is permeated by a gas of randomly moving electrons, which are only hindered by their collisions with the ions. As the electrons move in all directions, there is no net electron flow unless an electric field is applied across the metal to bias the movement of the electrons. If this field is generated by a source such as a battery which provides a complete circuit, then a continuous electric current will flow. Thermal conduction takes place by the spread of increased energy in the electrons. In the case of an insulator, the electrons are so tightly bound to the parent atoms that little electron flow is possible. The atom requires very few interchange electrons to complete its incomplete shell. When the outer shell is complete, it becomes difficult to dislodge electrons from it, and little electrical activity is observed.

The ratio of charge to mass of the electron is very high, and, as a consequence, the acceleration of an electron in the presence of an electric field is very rapid. Thus, electronic devices are able to respond at extremely high speeds.

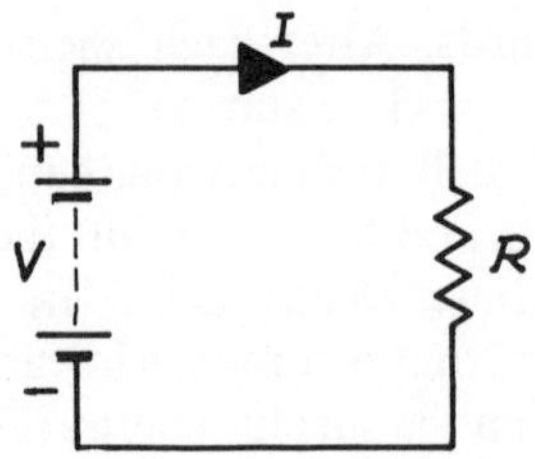

54

Figure 5.2. *A simple
electronic circuit comprising a battery of voltage V
and a resistor of value R.*

We will return to the topic of valence electrons when we discuss semiconductor materials in Section 5.9. First, let us consider large-scale movements
of electrons, or electric current flow.

5.2.2 *Electric current*

In order to describe the behaviour of electric current, comparisons are often
made with the flow of water in a pipe. The voltage of the battery or source of
electromotive force is analogous to the pressure developed by the pump or the
head of water in a storage tank. The current corresponds to the rate of flow of
water, and electrical resistance corresponds to the opposition generated to the
flow of water by the narrow pipes. These intuitive ideas are useful in visualizing
some of the more important points about current flow which will be introduced
in the next section.

One point of possible confusion should be cleared up at the outset. It is
conventional to designate the direction of electric current flow as being from the
positive pole of the voltage source, through the external circuit, to the negative
pole. Electrons, however, are negatively charged, and therefore flow in the
opposite direction. The arrow in a circuit diagram (Figure 5.2) always indicates
conventional current flow, unless it is explicitly labelled otherwise.

5.3 Ohm's law

If a current *I* supplied from a battery of voltage *V* passes through a resistance
R, as shown in Figure 5.2, the relationship defined by Ohm's law is

$$R = \frac{V}{I}$$

where *I* is the current in amperes (A), *V* is the electromotive force in volts (V)
and *R* is the resistance in ohms (Ω).

It can also be shown that the power *P* dissipated in the form of heat by the
resistance *R* is

$$P = VI$$

By applying Ohm's law, this may also be expressed in the form

$$P = I^2R \quad \text{or} \quad \frac{V^2}{R}$$

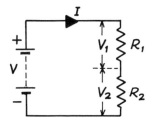

Figure 5.3. *Resistors in series.*

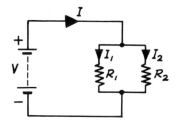

Figure 5.4. *Resistors in parallel.*

Power is the rate at which energy is developed, and is expressed in watts (W).

It can further be shown that, if two resistances R_1 and R_2 are connected in series, as in Figure 5.3, the total voltage is the sum of the voltages developed across the two resistors:

$$V = V_1 + V_2$$

It therefore follows that the total circuit resistance is given by

$$R = R_1 + R_2$$

and, in general,

$$R = R_1 + R_2 + \ldots + R_n$$

for n resistors in series.

If the resistors are connected in parallel, as in Figure 5.4, the current divides into two paths, and the values of I_1 and I_2 depend upon the values of resistors R_1 and R_2.

Thus, $I = I_1 + I_2$, and, as the voltage across both resistors is equal to the supply voltage V, it follows by Ohm's law that the total resistance R is given by

$$\frac{1}{R} = \frac{1}{R_1} + \frac{1}{R_2}$$

Therefore

$$R = \frac{R_1 R_2}{R_1 + R_2}$$

and, in general,

$$\frac{1}{R} = \frac{1}{R_1} + \frac{1}{R_2} + \ldots + \frac{1}{R_n}$$

5.4 The resistor

Resistors used in electronics are made from various materials, the commonest being carbon Most resistors have the value marked on the body of the compo-

Colour	First digit A	Second digit B	Multiplier C	Tolerance D
Black	0	0	1	–
Brown	1	1	10	–
Red	2	2	100	–
Orange	3	3	1,000	–
Yellow	4	4	10,000	–
Green	5	5	100,000	–
Blue	6	6	1,000,000	–
Violet	7	7	10,000,000	–
Grey	8	8	100,000,000	–
White	9	9	–	–
Gold	–	–	–	±5%
Silver	–	–	–	±10%
No Colour	–	–	–	±20%

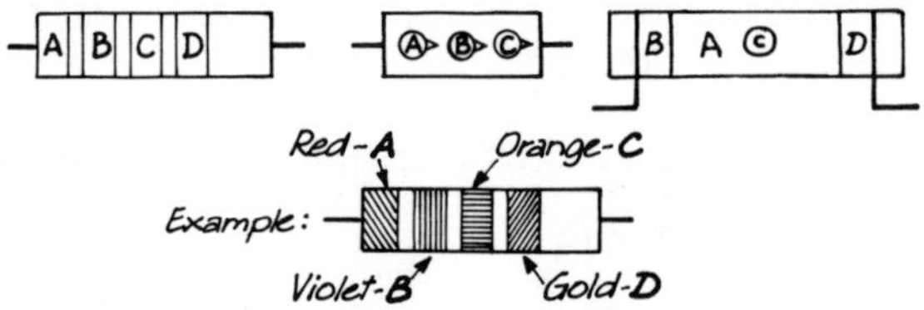

Example:

A Red	B Violet	C Orange	Total resistance	D Tolerance
2	7	000	27,000	±5%

Figure 5.5. *The resistor colour code.*

nent in the form of a colour code, as illustrated in Figure 5.5.

Resistors are usually manufactured with nominal values which are decimal multiples of the series 10, 12, 15, 18, 22, 27, 33, 39, 47, 56, 68, 82, 100, 120 etc. This approximately geometric series allows a 10% tolerance on each adjacent pair of values without any overlap.

Each style of resistor has a specified maximum power rating. This rating is related to the temperature rise above normal ambient level for which the style of resistor has been designed. In general, the larger the resistor, the greater the permitted power dissipation.

5.5 The inductor and transformer

When an electric current passes along a conductor, it produces a magnetic field. The magnetic lines of force form concentric circles around the conductor, producing a kind of sheath along the conductor. An inductor maximizes the effect of this magnetic flux by forming the conductor into a coil and keeping the windings close together. The practical unit of inductance is the henry (H); this is defined as the inductance of a circuit in which 1 V is induced (by magnetic

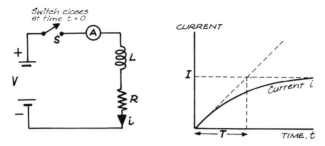

Figure 5.6. *Growth of current through an inductor. When the switch is closed, the initial increase in current causes a voltage to be generated across the inductor. This voltage is of opposite direction to the battery voltage, but is almost equal in magnitude to it. This back e.m.f. slows down the growth of current as it approaches the steady value I. T is the time constant of the circuit.*

flux linkages) when the current varies at the rate of 1 A/s. If a steady current flowing through an inductor is broken by a switch, the rapid cessation of the current can produce very high voltages (Sections 8.1.3 and 9.1).

The electrical properties of inductors are somewhat involved, and need advanced mathematics for a full treatment. We shall, therefore, only note that, as the inductance involves the rate of change of current, the relationship between current and voltage cannot be a simple linear one, such as Ohm's law for resistance, but must also involve time. The current in the circuit of Figure 5.6 is indicated on meter A. When the switch S is closed, the instantaneous current i grows from zero and follows the exponential law

$$i = I(1 - e^{-\frac{R}{L}t})$$

where I is the final current taken by the circuit. The constant L/R in the exponent of e is termed the time constant of the circuit. The resistor R is included, because all materials used to wind a practical coil have a finite resistance. This is represented as a lumped resistance R in series with the inductor.

A familiar practical example of the use of electromagnetism is the relay, which was discussed in connection with programming equipment in Section 4.1. When current flows in the coil of the relay, it causes the pole to become magnetized, and the magnetic force attracts the armature, operating an arrangement of switch contacts.

Another useful component utilizing electromagnetism is the transformer. Here, a magnetic circuit links the two coils through a common ferrous-metal path, as shown in Figure 5.7. The current changes occurring in the primary winding induce a voltage in the secondary winding through the mutual coupling provided by the transformer core. Transformers are used to change alternating-voltage levels in power supplies (Sections 5.9.6 and 6.6).

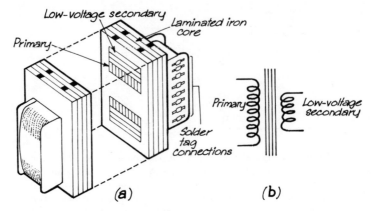

Figure 5.7. *The construction of a small mains transformer (a) of the type commonly used in simple power supplies. The circuit-diagram symbol is shown in (b).*

5.6 The capacitor

Consider two metal plates separated by insulating material and connected in series with a resistor R, as shown in Figure 5.8. An electrostatic force exists between the plates when the switch S is closed. In the case of an inductor, the flow of electrons along a conductor gives rise to a magnetic field. In this case, however, the buildup of electrons on one side of the insulator, and the removal of electrons from the other side, gives rise to an electric field. This imbalance of electrons is known as an electric charge, and is a form of stored energy.

The ratio of the charge on the plates to the voltage between the plates is termed capacitance, and the component is called a capacitor. Again the relationships involved are time-dependent, and the growth of voltage across the capacitor follows the exponential law

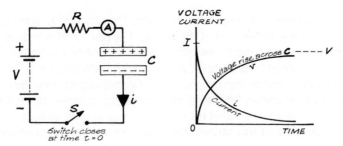

Figure 5.8. *The charging of a capacitor from a constant voltage V. The current is a maximum when C is uncharged, because the voltage across it is zero. As the capacitor becomes charged, the voltage across it increase. This reduces the voltage across R, causing the charging current to fall. The instantaneous voltage v across the capacitor gradually approaches V as the charging current i falls to zero.*

$$v = V(1 - e^{-\frac{1}{RC}t})$$

The current shown on ammeter A will fall with time:

$$i = Ie^{-\frac{1}{RC}t}$$

In this case, the time constant is given by RC.

When capacitors are connected in parallel, the areas of the plates are effectively combined, and therefore the value of the combination is simply the sum of the values of the individual capacitors:

$$C = C_1 + C_2 + \ldots + C_n$$

The unit of capacitance is the farad (F). It is a very large-value unit, and most capacitors used in electronic circuits have values in the microfarad (μF) or picofarad (pF) range.

If capacitors are connected in series, the thickness of the insulating layer is effectively increased, and the value of the resulting capacitance is reduced:

$$\frac{1}{C} = \frac{1}{C_1} + \frac{1}{C_2} + \ldots + \frac{1}{C_n}$$

The insulating layer between the plates is known as a dielectric. Commonly used dielectrics are mica, ceramics, paper and various kinds of plastic film. With these dielectrics, the working of the capacitor is unaffected by the direction of the applied voltage. Electrolytic capacitors, however, are constructed from thin aluminium foil separated by an electrolyte, and the dielectric is formed by electrolytic action. They must only be used with direct voltages applied in the direction marked on the case of the capacitor. Electrolytic capacitors give much larger values per unit volume than other types, but are less effective in retaining charge.

5.7 Types of current

There are two main types of electric current:
(1) direct current, or d.c. This is available from sources such as batteries and accumulators in which the direction of the current supplied does not change.
(2) alternating current, or a.c. In this case, the voltage varies sinusoidally with time (Section 1.4). This gives the type of electric power available from the public electricity supply or from an audio oscillator.

So far, only the effects of direct current have been considered. It is obvious that complications will arise when alternating current is applied to circuits containing time-dependent components, such as inductors and capacitors.

The public electricity supply in the United Kingdom is nominally 240 V alternating current, and its frequency is 50 cycle/s or 50 Hz. This is shown diagrammatically in Figure 5.9. In the USA and some other countries, 110 V and 60 Hz are used.

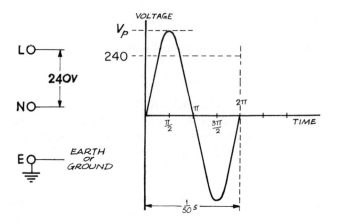

Figure 5.9. *The waveform of 240 V, 50 Hz public electricity supply.*

Note that the voltage is sinusoidal in time, and that the value of 240 V does not apply to peak voltage. The voltage *v* at any instant can be found from the general formula for a sine wave:

$$v = V \sin 2\pi f t$$

where *V* is the peak voltage, *f* is the frequency and *t* is the instantaneous time.

5.7.1 *The r.m.s. value of sinusoidal waveforms*

The 240 V figure indicates the effective value of the voltage. If the voltage were applied to a pure resistance, an alternating current would flow, and would dissipate power in the form of heat. The effective value of an alternating voltage is the value of direct voltage which, when applied to the same resistor, would dissipate an equal average amount of power. The average power may be calculated by integrating the expression for the instantaneous power dissipated. The result turns out to be the root-mean-square, or r.m.s., value of the sine wave. This is related to the peak value as follows:

$$V_{r.m.s.} = \frac{V}{\sqrt{2}}$$
$$= \text{approximately } 0.707 \text{ V}$$

Therefore, if the electrical supply voltage is 240 V r.m.s., the peak value is approximately 339 V.

5.7.2 *Resistors in a.c. circuits*

The waveforms shown in Figure 5.10 give the relationships between voltage, current and power in a purely resistive circuit. Note that the instantaneous

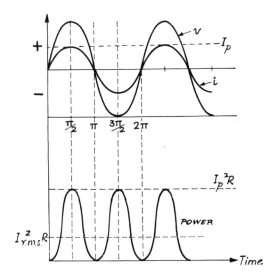

Figure 5.10. *Instantaneous voltage, current and power from an alternating voltage in a resistive circuit.*

voltage *v* and the instantaneous current *i* are in phase, and that the power dissipated may be calculated by using the r.m.s. values of current and voltage in the expressions given for d.c. conditions in Section 5.3. Similarly, by using r.m.s. values, Ohm's law can be applied in a purely resistive circuit:

$$R = \frac{V_{r.m.s.}}{I_{r.m.s.}}$$

5.7.3 Inductors in a.c. circuits

If we apply an alternating voltage across a coil of inductance *L* and negligible resistance, we obtain the waveforms of Figure 5.11. Note that there is now a phase difference between the applied voltage *v* and the current flowing through

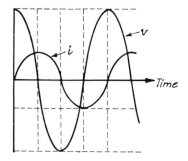

Figure 5.11. *Instantaneous voltage and current from an alternating voltage applied to an ideal inductor.*

the coil. The current is said to lag the voltage by $\pi/2$ radians (rad). It can be shown that, if the applied voltage v is given by

$$v = V \sin 2\pi ft$$

then the current i will be given by

$$i = \frac{V}{2\pi fL} \sin\left(2\pi ft - \frac{\pi}{2}\right)$$

It can be shown that the constant

$$\frac{V}{2\pi fL}$$

is equal to the peak current I, and therefore

$$I = \frac{V}{2\pi fL}$$

If this is compared with Ohm's law, it will be seen that the term

$$2\pi fL$$

has the same current-determining effect as R in the case of a purely resistive circuit. In the present case, however, it is not called resistance, but inductive reactance X_L. The main differences between reactance and resistance follow from the way in which reactance varies with frequency. In the case of inductive reactance, there is an increase in reactance with frequency. Another point to note is that resistance and reactance cannot be added together by straightforward summation. When a circuit contains both resistance and reactance, the total opposition to the flow of current must be calculated by vector arithmetic, and the result is then termed the impedance Z of the circuit:

$$Z = \sqrt{(X^2 + R^2)}$$

5.7.4 Capacitors in a.c. circuits

If we apply an alternating voltage to a capacitor, the voltage and current waveforms will be as shown in Figure 5.12. Note that the instantaneous current i

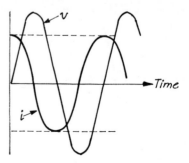

Figure 5.12. *Instantaneous voltage and current from an alternating voltage applied to an ideal capacitor.*

leads the applied voltage v by $\pi/2$ rad. It can be shown that, if the applied voltage v is given by

$$v = V \sin 2\pi f t$$

then the current i will be given by

$$i = 2\pi f C V \sin\left(2\pi f t + \frac{\pi}{2}\right)$$

The constant

$$2\pi f C V$$

is equal to the peak current I, and therefore

$$I = 2\pi f C V$$

If we relate this equation to Ohm's law, we find that the current determining term for a capacitor is

$$\frac{1}{2\pi f C}$$

This is called the capacitive reactance. Note that capacitive reactance decreases with frequency.

The basic properties of inductance and capacitance in a.c. circuits have now been outlined. We have found that these components affect the flow of alternating current in a manner rather similar to that of the resistor. Reactances, however, are complex, and produce a phase difference between the voltage across the terminals of a component and the current flowing through it. In the case of ideal inductors and capacitors, that is components having no resistive properties, this phase shift will be $\pi/2$ rad, and there will be no power dissipated.

5.8 Impedance

Resistors, inductors and capacitors can be connected together in series and parallel circuits. The resulting networks display an opposition to the flow of alternating current, known as the impedance of the circuit. This impedance is the vector sum of the reactances and resistances in the circuit. Because reactances are involved, the impedance will, as described earlier, depend on the frequency of the alternating current.

It is conventional to consider inductive reactance to be positive and capacitive reactance to be negative. Although vector addition is needed to find the result when reactance and resistance are combined, normal addition can be used for pure reactances as long as the signs are observed. Remembering that inductive reactance increases with frequency, whereas capacitive reactance decreases with frequency, it will be seen that, for any circuit which includes both inductors and capacitors, there will be one frequency for which the inductive reactance will equal the capacitive reactance, giving a result of zero reactance. This frequency is known as the resonant frequency of the circuit, and its application is important in the design of filters and oscillators. It is the basis of the tuned circuits used in radio and television receivers to select the channel frequencies of the various broadcasting stations.

5.9 Semiconductors

The semiconducting properties of germanium formed the basis of the first transistors. Although semiconductor diodes had been used many years earlier in the crystal set, the mechanism was not fully understood, and it was not until 1948 that the first semiconductor amplifying device, the transistor, was produced.

A very simple, but somewhat superficial, definition of semiconductors is that they are those materials whose resistivity lies between that of a perfect insulator and that of a good conductor. Thus, glass (resistivity about $2 \times 10^9 \ \Omega\text{m}$) is an insulator, copper (resistivity about $1 \cdot 7 \times 10^{-8} \ \Omega\text{m}$) is a conductor, but germanium ($0 \cdot 047 \ \Omega\text{m}$ at $27 \,^{\circ}\text{C}$) and silicon ($3000 \ \Omega\text{m}$ at $27 \,^{\circ}\text{C}$) are semiconductors.

Silicon and germanium are the best known semiconductor materials, and it is from these that the most common devices, transistors and diodes, are made. Silicon has a lower leakage current, and is less affected by temperature changes, than germanium. As a result, silicon devices are now preferred, and modern manufacturing techniques permit easy mass production of high-quality devices. Many other semiconductor materials are also in use, for example cadmium sulphide, cadmium selenide, gallium arsenide and indium antimonide, but these tend to be found mainly in specialized devices such as photoelectric cells.

5.9.1 *The crystal structure*

As was mentioned earlier in this chapter, the outer electrons of an atom are called the valence electrons. Silicon and germanium are tetravalent, that is their atoms have four electrons in their outer orbits (tetra = four). The silicon atom, which is simpler than that of germanium, is represented in Figure 5.13.

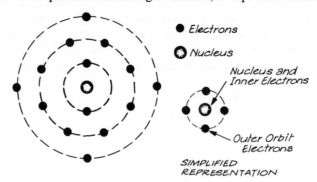

Figure 5.13. *The silicon atom.*

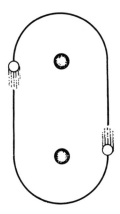

Figure 5.14 *Electron sharing.*

As in any atom, the nucleus is positively charged and the electrons are negatively charged, the positive charge on the nucleus being equal to the total negative charge of all the electrons. The complete atom is therefore electrically neutral. Since it is only the outer or valence electrons which take part in the flow of current, it is convenient to simplify the representation as shown.

When two atoms are close together, there is often a tendency towards electron sharing. As a simple example, consider the two hydrogen atoms shown in Figure 5.14. The hydrogen atom has only one electron, but, when two atoms come close together, the electrons are able to orbit both nuclei, and this electron sharing results in a bonding between the atoms that would not otherwise exist. This phenomenon is called covalent bonding. Figure 5.15 illustrates what happens in tetravalent semiconductor crystals. Each of the four valence electrons of any one atom is shared with four neighbouring nuclei, so that each

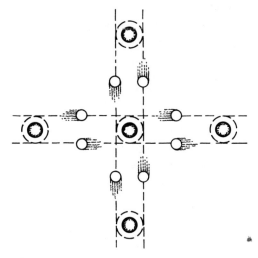

Figure 5.15. *Electron sharing in silicon and germanium crystals.*

66

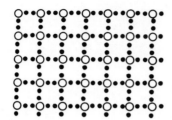

Figure 5.16. *Diagrammatic representation of germanium or silicon crystal.*

nucleus is, in effect, orbited by eight electrons, causing strong bonds to exist between neighbouring atoms in the crystal. As it is very difficult for such an electron to break away from its bonds to participate in current flow, such crystals tend to be rather poor conductors. In practice, however, pure silicon and germanium are perfect insulators only at a temperature of absolute zero, for, at room temperatures, thermal agitation causes the occasional electron to break away from the crystal lattice. This allows a small current to flow when a battery is connected across the crystal. This effect is more pronounced in germanium, for, as noted earlier, the resistivity of germanium is far less than that of silicon. Figure 5.16 illustrates, in a simplified 2-dimensional form, the crystal structure of such tetravalent semiconductor materials.

5.9.2 *P- and n-type semiconductors*

In order to obtain the controlled flow of current which is required for transistors, diodes and other devices, it is necessary to introduce minute traces of certain impurity elements into the intrinsic, or pure, semiconductor crystal. For instance, if impurity atoms of a pentavalent element such as antimony or arsenic are added (Figure 5.17), only four of the five outer electrons of the impurity atom can be accommodated in the existing lattice, and so the surplus fifth electron becomes free to act as a current carrier. There will, of course, be one free electron for each atom of impurity added. A crystal treated in this way is called *n*-type semiconductor material, because it contains free electrons which are negative-charge carriers. It should be noted, however, that the overall charge on the crystal remains zero, because each of the individual atoms present was originally electrically neutral, and, although the impurity atoms have released a negatively charged carrier electron, they have become posi-

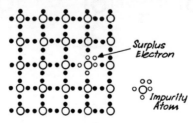

Figure 5.17. *N-type semiconductor material.*

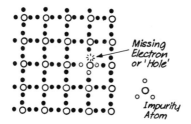

Figure 5.18. *P-type semiconductor material.*

tively charged. The effect of the impurity is to produce a large increase in electrical conductivity. The resistivity is reduced by addition of about one impurity atom to every 10^8 atoms of pure semiconductor. The pentavalent impurity atoms are called donor atoms, since each atom donates one free electron to the lattice.

If, on the other hand, pure semiconductor crystal is contaminated or doped with atoms of a trivalent element, such as aluminium or indium (Figure 5.18), a deficiency of electrons is introduced into the lattice. For each impurity atom, there is a deficiency of one electron. These deficiencies are called holes. Because a hole exerts an attractive force on neighbouring electrons in the lattice, it constitutes a virtual positive charge, and may be considered as a positively charged particle. A hole need not stay near the impurity atom which introduced it. An electron from a neighbouring atom can move in and cancel it, so that the hole moves to the neighbouring atom. A semiconductor crystal which contains mainly holes is called *p*-type (*p* for positively charged particles). Whilst the presence of holes increases the conductivity, *p*-type material is electrically neutral. The impurity atoms are called acceptors, because each atom can accept one electron from the lattice.

In future illustrations, we shall indicate only the free electrons and holes, as in Figure 5.19. The donor and acceptor atoms will be omitted for the sake of clarity. In practice, all semiconductor materials at room temperature contain some holes and free electrons. These are generated by thermal agitation; such thermal generations and recombinations are taking place continuously. Thus,

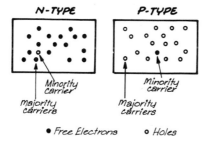

Figure 5.19. *Diagrammatic representation of p- and n-type materials.*

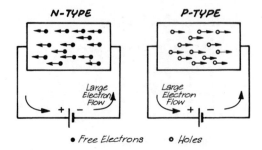

Figure 5.20. *Current flow in p- and n-type semiconductors.*

p-type material will at all times contain a few free electrons, and *n*-type material will contain a few holes. Of course these thermally generated electrons and holes are small in number compared with those introduced deliberately, which are called majority carriers. Figure 5.20 illustrates what happens when a battery is connected to *n*- and *p*-type semiconductors. In the *n*-type material negatively charged electrons are attracted to the positive terminal of the battery. The loss of electrons from the left-hand end of the crystal would cause the material to become positively charged, but the positive charge is cancelled by the electrons which flow into the right-hand end from the negative terminal of the battery. This action takes place continuously, and produces a flow of electrons or an electric current through the crystal, the net number of electrons within the crystal at any given instant remaining constant.

In the *p*-type material (Figure 5.20), holes reaching the right-hand side are neutralized by a flow of electrons from the negative terminal of the battery. This gain of electrons does not cause the crystal to become negatively charged, for equilibrium is maintained by a similar number of electrons being ejected from the left-hand end of the crystal to the positive terminal of the battery. A continuous flow of electrons results, the number of holes within the crystal at any instant remaining constant.

5.9.3 *The semiconductor diode*

Basically, the semiconductor diode consists of a piece of *n*-type and a piece of *p*-type semiconductor joined together (Figure 5.21). The two electrodes are the

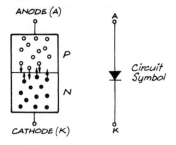

Figure 5.21. *P–n junction diode.*

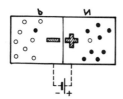

Figure 5.22. *Virtual battery across a p-n junction.*

anode (*p*-type) and the cathode (*n*-type).

Naturally, as soon as the junction is formed, there will be a drift of carriers across it. Holes move into the *n*-type material and electrons move into the *p*-type material. At first sight, it might be expected that all the electrons in the *n*-type material would move into the *p*-type material, and that all the holes would move into the *n*-type material, resulting in a total disappearance of all carriers. The first few electrons entering the *p*-type material, however, make it negatively charged (both regions were initially neutral). Similarly, the gain of holes by the *n*-type material makes it positively charged (Figure 5.22). Since like charges repel, the negative charge opposes the further flow of electrons and the positive charge opposes the further flow of holes, just as though there were a small battery across the junction. In Figure 5.22, the region near the junction has been shown, for simplicity, devoid of carriers. This carrier-free area is called the barrier, or depletion, region.

5.9.4 *Biasing the junction*

If a real battery is now connected across the junction in the same direction as the virtual battery (Figure 5.23), the barrier region is broadened, and no majority carriers can cross the junction. Only occasional minority carriers, those generated thermally, cross the junction, and therefore only a small flow of current, known as the leakage cirrent, results. The diode is now said to be reverse-biased. The leakage current in germanium diodes is far greater than that in silicon diodes.

If, on the other hand, a real battery with a larger voltage than the virtual battery is connected in opposition to it (Figure 5.24), a considerable flow of current results. Holes, attracted by the negative terminal of the battery, drift to the right towards the junction; on reaching it, they are cancelled by electrons

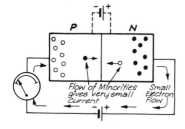

Figure 5.23. *Reverse bias.*

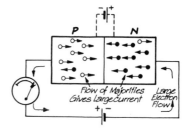

Figure 5.24. *Forward bias.*

from the *n*-type material. Simultaneously, more electrons are injected from the negative terminal of the battery, compensating for the loss of electrons from the *n*-type material. As holes from the *p*-type material are cancelled at the junction, electrons are simultaneously released from its left-hand side to the positive terminal of the battery. The small leakage current due to minority carriers adds to the main majority-carrier flow, and a large current flows. The diode is now said to be forward-biased.

5.9.5 *The diode characteristic*

Figure 5.25 illustrates the characteristic curve of the semiconductor diode. The virtual battery across the junction is of a low voltage, and so only a fraction of a volt need be applied in the forward direction to start a current. This so-called turnon voltage is of the order of 200 mV for germanium diodes and 600 mV for silicon diodes. Once this voltage has been reached, small changes in voltage will produce large changes in current. The curves become very steep, and are, in fact, exponentials. The forward current can quickly become large enough to damage the device, and, hence, in the test circuit, a limiting resistor R is added.

In the reverse direction, however, so little current flows that it is necessary to expand the $-I$ scale in order to see the current at all. The lower leakage current of silicon diodes is clearly shown by the reverse characteristics. There comes a point, however, when breakdown occurs, and a considerable current flow takes place. Below about 3 V, it is caused by electrons breaking away from their covalent bonds, and is known as the Zener effect. At higher voltages, it is caused by the minority electrons gaining sufficient velocity to dislodge other electrons from their atoms. These new electrons are then themselves acclerated, and, in turn, can produce more electrons. There is, therefore, a sudden buildup of current, and this is known as the avalanche effect. These breakdown effects are exploited in voltage-regulator diodes, usually known as Zener diodes. These diodes make use of the fact that, once the breakdown voltage has been reached, the characteristic is almost parallel to the *I* axis, and therefore the voltage across the diode is almost independent of the current flowing through it. The voltage at which breakdown occurs is determined by impurity levels and other physical factors.

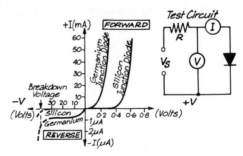

Figure 5.25. *Diode characteristic.*

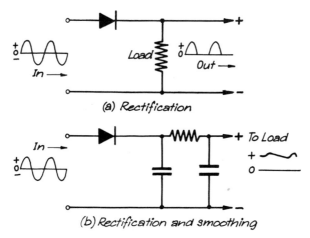

(a) Rectification

(b) Rectification and smoothing

Figure 5.26. Diode applications.

5.9.6 Diode applications

Semiconductor diodes are commonly used for rectification, modulation and demodulation. They are also used in logic circuits (Section 5.11). In the rectifier curcuit of Figure 5.26a, the diode allows current to flow only during the positive halfcycles of the input, and therefore the waveform across the load is a half wave rectified sine wave. This can be smoothed to obtain an almost steady direct voltage, as shown in Figure 5.26b. Circuits of this type are used in laboratory power supplies to generate low direct voltages from the a.c. public electricity supply. A mains transformer provides the low alternating voltage, and gives electrical isolation from the a.c. mains supply. In most laboratary power supplies, further circuits are included after the smoothing components. They are designed to stabilize the direct voltage against fluctuations in the voltage of the public electricity supply, and also to reduce the effects of variations in the current drawn by the load (Section 6.6).

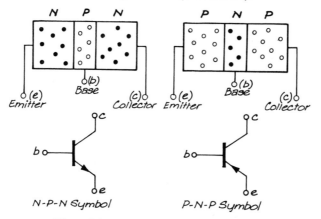

Figure 5.27. N–p–n and p–n–p transistors.

5.9.7 *The transistor*

The conventional transistor is a 2-junction, 3-layer semiconductor device capable of current, voltage and power amplification. Clearly, there are two possible configurations: *p–n–p* and *n–p–n* (Figure 5.27). A transistor has three electrodes: the base (b), emitter (e) and collector (c). Note that the arrow in the symbol for the *p–n–p* device points towards the base, whereas, in the *n–p–n* transistor, it points away from it. The arrow indicates the direction in which conventional current would normally flow in the device, electron flow being in the opposite direction to the arrows.

5.9.8 *Transistor action*

Figures 5.28 and 5.29 illustrate current amplification in an *n–p–n* silicon transistor. The base–emitter junction forms a forward-based diode, because it is connected by its *p*-type region to the positive terminal of the 600 mV supply. On the other hand, the *n*-type collector is 5·4 V (6 V less 600 mV) positive with respect to the base, and therefore the base–collector junction is reverse-biased. A large number of electrons enter the *n*-type emitter under the influence of the forward-biased base–emitter junction. The base region is very thin, and therefore the force due to the attraction of the positive collector potential is very strong. Consequently, most of the electrons from the emitter pass straight through the base into the collector. Of course the occasional electron meets a hole in the base, and combines with it, giving rise to a small base current. For a typical silicon transistor with an emitter current (I_e) of 1 mA, the collector current (I_c) might be 0·995 mA and the base current (I_b) only 0·005 mA (1 mA less 0·995 mA).

Suppose the base voltage is increased sufficiently to cause the emitter current

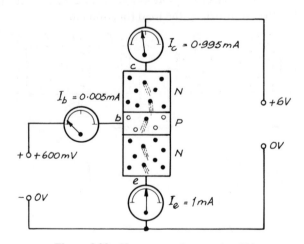

Figure 5.28. *N–p–n transistor action (1)*.

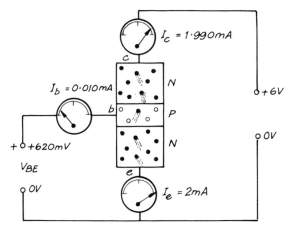

Figure 5.29. *N–p–n transistor action (2)*.

to be doubled to 2 mA (Figure 5.29). On referring back to the diode characteristic in Figure 5.25, we see that a large increase in forward current can be achieved by just a few millivolts change in forward voltage. Thus, an increase in base voltage from about 600 mV to 620 mV would typically produce a change of emitter current from 1 mA to 2 mA. The collector current doubles to 1·990 mA, and the base current rises to 0·010 mA, because there are now twice as many electrons per second entering the emitter, twice as many passing through to the collector and twice as many electron–hole combinations in the base.

Comparing Figure 5.28 with Figure 5.29, it can be seen that a change of 0·005 mA in I_b causes a change of 0·995 mA in I_c. Thus, the transistor has produced a current gain, or amplification, of

$$\frac{\text{change in } I_c}{\text{change in } I_b}$$

$$= \frac{0·995}{0·005}$$

or approximately 200.

5.9.9 *Voltage and power amplification*

In order to obtain a voltage output, a load resistor must be added. The base–collector junction is reverse-biased, making its resistance about 10,000 Ω or more. Therefore a load resistor of a few hundred ohms can be added in series with the collector without causing much change in I_c. In Figure 5.30, a load of 1 kΩ has been added. The voltage developed across this load is the output voltage (V_{out}). As we have seen, in a typical case, a change in the base–emitter voltage (V_{be}) of 20 mV causes a change of 0·995 mA in I_c; assuming that the presence of the load resistor will not significantly alter I_c, V_{out} will change by

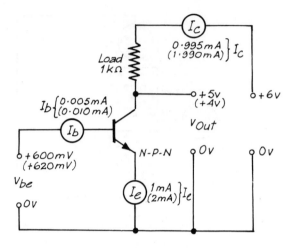

Figure 5.30. *Voltage amplification.*

0·995 mA × 1 kΩ ≈ 1 V. The change in output voltage is, therefore, about 50 times the 20 mV change in V_{be}. This represents a voltage gain of 50. In Figure 5.30, the conditions after the input has been increased to 620 mV are given in parentheses. Similarly, by calculating the changes in input and output power, we could show that the circuit gives a power gain of about 1000.

5.9.10 *A.C. amplification*

Figure 5.31 shows a basic circuit for an a.c. amplifier. An input signal of 20 mV peak-to-peak is applied, through a d.c. blocking capacitor C_1, to the base of the transistor. The a.c. input signal is superimposed on the d.c. base bias of 610 mV. Assuming that the same current transfer ratio applies as in

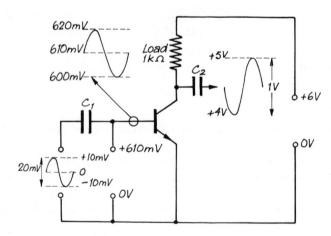

Figure 5.31. *A.C. amplification.*

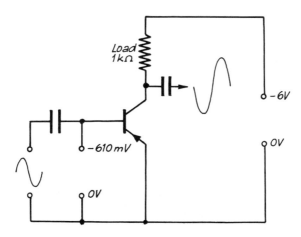

Figure 5.32. *P–n–p a.c. amplifier.*

Figure 5.30, the a.c. output waveform has a peak-to-peak value of 1 V. Note that a single stage of amplification inverts the waveform of the signal.

The principle of operation of *p–n–p* transistors is similar to that of *n–p–n* devices, but it is described in terms of holes which are considered to flow in the same direction as the electrons in *n–p–n* devices. Figure 5.32 is the circuit of a basic *p–n–p*-transistor a.c. amplifier. When using *p–n–p* transistors, the power supplies are connected in the opposite direction to that employed with *n–p–n* transistors. From the user's point of view, *n–p–n* and *p–n–p* transistors appear to be equally useful, and the reader may wonder why semiconductor manufacturers make both types. The short answer is that it is easier to mass-produce silicon transistors in *n–p–n* form than in *p–n–p* form, but, on the other hand, it is easier to mass-produce germanium transistors in *p–n–p* form than in *n–p–n* form. It is often advantageous to use both *n–p–n* and *p–n–p* types together in the same circuit, as is done in some audioamplifier circuits. Germanium transistors also require a lower forward base–emitter bias voltage than silicon transistors.

5.9.11 *Integrated circuits*

In recent years, there has been a tendency for electronic components to become smaller and smaller. This tendency has been accelerated by the invention of integrated circuits (ICs).

Some of these devices are shown in Figure 5.33, where it will be seen that the encapsulation and leads take up most of the space. Figure 5.34 shows the smallness of the piece of silicon crystal which forms the integrated circuit proper. This silicon chip is typically about 1 mm square and 0·2 mm thick; it contains many transistors, diodes, capacitors and resistors connected together to form the desired circuit configuration, for example the logic of a pocket

Figure 5.33. *An integrated circuit before encapsulation (top) and some encapsulated devices. The IC is the dark square in the middle of the unencapsulated device.*

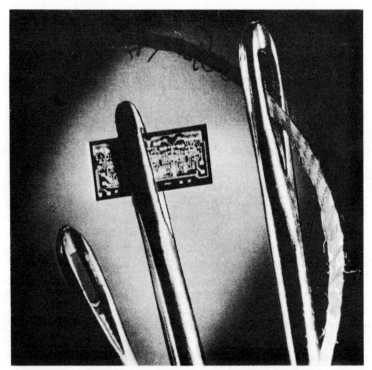

Figure 5.34. *An IC silicon chip is so small that this unencapsulated decade counter will pass through the eye of a number 5 sewing needle. The needle on the right is threaded with normal sewing cotton.*

calculator. Until the late 1950s, most electronic equipment was built using thermionic valves (vacuum tubes). To give some idea of the advances in miniaturization which have taken place since that time, a typical small valve had a volume roughly equal to that of ten integrated circuits, each of which could carry out circuit functions equivalent to that of many hundreds of valves and their associated components. The small size of integrated circuits is obviously an important feature, but there are other equally important factors; they are ultimately more reliable than circuits which use discrete components, and they simplify the mass-production of equipment, thus reducing its cost. Integrated circuits are to be found in every type of electronic apparatus, ranging from computers, satellites, hearing aids and portable instruments, where their small size is very important, to domestic television and radio receivers and laboratory and industrial equipment, where size is often of secondary importance compared with other factors, such as reliability and ease of assembly onto printed-circuit boards. In a small computer, it is now possible to replace many of the hundreds of discrete components, each requiring individual handling and hand-soldered joints, by just a few integrated circuits.

5.9.12 *Construction of integrated circuits*

The method used to manufacture integrated circuits is an extension of the techniques used to make transistors and diodes. Figure 5.35 (centre) is a sketch representing a tiny section of an integrated circuit. It shows an *n–p–n* transistor (a) and a resistor (b). Included in Figure 5.35, at (c), is a sketch of a metal–oxide–semiconductor transistor, or MOST, another type of transistor frequently used in integrated circuits.

The lowest plane of *p*-type silicon is the foundation, or substrate, of the integrated circuit. The next plane is the epitaxial layer, into which the various components are built. This layer is grown as a continuation of the substrate, and has the same crystal orientation. The word epitaxial refers to this type of crystal growth, and is a combination of the Greek words *epi*, meaning upon, and *taxos*, meaning arranged. The resistors and collectors of transistors are isolated from each other and from other components of the integrated circuit by the curved vertical columns of *p*-type silicon. Above the epitaxial layer are are the various layers of silicon oxides formed during the diffusion phase, and

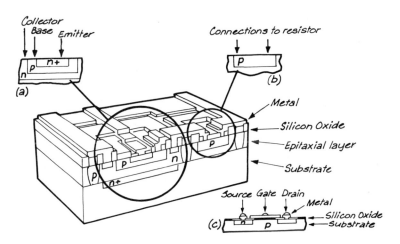

Figure 5.35. *Diagrammatic view of a section of integrated circuit containing (a) a transistor and (b) a resistor. One type of MOST is shown in (c).*

the metal areas, which make contact with the various electrodes and inter-connect the devices on the integrated circuit.

Isolated between components is achieved by reverse-biasing the junctions formed between the epitaxial n-type layer and the p-type isolation regions. Access to the isolation regions is gained in the same way as for the transistor electrodes; windows, which are not shown in the diagram, are cut in the oxide layer at convenient points for this purpose. The value of the transistor depends upon the dimensions of the p-type area and the amount of impurity which has been introduced as dopant. In practice, the impurity level is constant for all transistor bases and resistors on the integrated circuit, since they are diffused in a single operation. The epitaxial layer is a refinement, for it would be possible to diffuse the various components straight into an n-type substrate. The epitaxial layer, however, makes it possible to have an extremely thin collector. The underlying substrate acts simply as a mounting base which bears the mechanical stresses. A thin collector region is necessary to obtain a low satura-tion voltage. Another desirable feature is a high transistor-breakdown voltage. To achieve this, a high collector resistivity is necessary, and this is obtained by only slightly doping the epitaxial layer. The lighter the doping, the lower the conductivity and the higher the resistivity. Unfortunately, this also tends to increase the saturation voltage, and therefore areas of heavily doped n-type material ($n+$) are added. These areas short the lateral resistance of the epitaxial collector layer, thus reducing the saturation voltage.

Integrated-circuit diodes can be made by the same process as transistors, but omitting the emitter diffusion. The more usual method, however, is to use a transistor with its emitter and collecter shortcircuited.

Where capacitors are required, reverse-biased diodes are used. Diodes have a capacitance of a few picofarads, the precise value being dependent on the applied reverse-bias voltage. It is also feasible, but not common practice, to make capacitors by sandwiching a layer of silicon oxide between two layers of metal. These methods yield only very small values of capacitance, and, whenever possible, designers of integrated circuits avoid the use of capacitors. In those cases where large-value capacitors are necessary, they must be wired in externally to the integrated circuit by the user. Large inductors, too, must be added externally.

5.9.13 *Types of integrated circuit*

Digital-circuit designers have developed circuit configurations based on diode–transistor logic (DTL), transistor–transistor logic (TTL) and so on. These families of logic circuits are now available in integrated-circuit form.

A wide range of linear integrated circuits is also available (the use of the term linear is discussed in Section 5.10). This range includes preamplifiers for audio applications, operational amplifiers, audio output amplifiers, and radio and television receiver circuits. It is now also possible to make hybrid integrated circuits, for example ADCs and DACs.

The integrated circuits dealt with so far are those of the junction type of transistor. As already mentioned, there is another type of transistor which is commonly used in integrated circuits: the MOST. The MOST is a type of field-effect transistor (FET). The construction of one type of MOST is illustrated in the bottom right-hand corner of Figure 5.35. The flow of current between the drain and source is controlled by the voltage applied to the gate, which usually carries the input signal to the device. The gate is insulated from the substrate by a layer of silicon oxide, and so the input resistance is extremely large. The MOST is particularly useful in low-power integrated circuits, such as those used in the information-processing sections of computers. In such applications, due to its simple construction and very low input current, the MOST can be made extremely small. Some MOST integrated circuits currently being made have more than 1000 transistors on an area about 1 mm square.

FETs are also manufactured as individual transistors, and are used in a number of applications in preference to conventional or bipolar transistors. A common difficulty with bipolar-transistor circuits is that their input resistance is too low for many applications. Field-effect devices, on the other hand, have input resistances of 100 MΩ or more, and, for this reason, they are highly suitable devices for such applications as the input stages of biological pre-amplifiers, where a high input impedance reduces the attenuating effect of the often unavoidably high resistance of biological tissue and electrodes.

5.9.14 Photoelectric devices

When light falls on a semiconductor material, current carriers are liberated. This effect is exploited in photodiodes and phototransistors. Figure 5.36 shows a simple linear lightmeter which uses a silicon phototransistor. Variations in the intensity of light falling near the base–collector junction cause variations in the emitter–collector current, which is displayed on the meter.

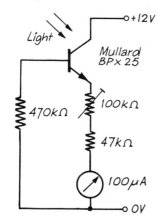

Figure 5.36. A phototransistor in a lightmeter circuit.

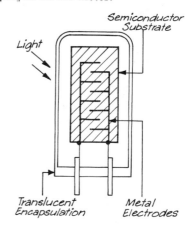

Figure 5.37. A photoconductive cell.

The photoconductive cell, or photoresistor (Figure 5.37), is manufactured from a light-sensitive semiconductor material. The resistance of the material between the electrodes decreases as the intensity of light falling on the substrate increases. Semiconductor materials commonly used for photoconductive cells are cadmium sulphide, cadmium selenide, lead sulphide, indium antimonide and copper-doped germanium. The material used determines the range of optical wavelengths to which the cell is sensitive. Cadmium sulphide is mainly suitable for visible light, whereas lead sulphide has its peak response in the infrared region; it is therefore used in infrared detectors. Cadmium selenide cells are often used in photoplethysmography (Section 10.3.2), because they have a good response in the near-infrared region and react fairly rapidly to changes in illuminance.

Other semiconductor photoelectric devices are photovoltaic or solar cells which generate a voltage increasing with the intensity of the incident light, and light-emitting diodes (LEDs) which emit infrared or visible radiation when a current flows through them. Light-emitting diodes are now widely used in alphanumeric displays (see Sections 8.1.4 and 8.7.3). Optoisolators are devices which contain a photocell and LED within the same light-tight package. They allow signals to be transmitted without a direct electrical connection, and are used to protect sensitive equipment or when the receiver and transmitter are at widely different potentials.

5.9.15 *Thermistors*

Thermistors are temperature-sensitive resistors made from semiconductor materials. The temperature change may be brought about by the direct application of heat, or by changing the current through the device. Thermistors are often used as temperature sensors in automatic-control systems. Because they are sensitive to temperature changes resulting from current flowing through them, they are also used for purposes such as controlling the amplitude of oscillators. Materials commonly used for the manufacture of thermistors are the oxides of nickel, zinc, copper and manganese. Most thermistors are of the negative temperature coefficient (NTC) type, in which case their resistance decreases with increases in temperature. Positive temperature coefficient (PTC) devices are also available. Very small bead-type thermistors are used as temperature transducers for respiration recording, and are discussed in Section 10.3.4. They have also been used to measure body-surface temperature.

5.9.16 *Silicon-controlled rectifiers*

The silicon-controlled rectifier (SCR or thyristor) is a 4-layer device with three electrodes: the gate, the anode and the cathode (see Figure 5.38). As the symbol suggests, the silicon-controlled rectifier behaves like an ordinary diode, but conduction between anode and cathode can take place only when

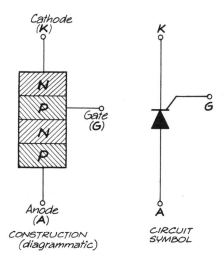

Figure 5.38. *The silicon-controlled recti-fier.*

the gate–cathode junction is adequately forward-biased. Thus, when the anode is positive with respect to the cathode, and sufficient gate current is flowing, conduction between anode and cathode is initiated. Once conduction has commenced, the gate loses control, and cannot be used to switch the device off. To switch the device off, the anode current must be reduced below its maintenance level. In practice, the anode–cathode supply is often the a.c. mains, and the silicon-controlled rectifier is turned on periodically by short gate pulses and turned off by the reversal of the mains supply, giving a controlled pulsating d.c. supply. Silicon-controlled rectifiers are used in apparatus such as d.c.-motor speed controllers, power supplies and a.c. inverters.

The triac has a further *n*-type layer, giving a symmetrical construction. Conduction can be triggered in either direction, allowing the device to control the duration of each halfcycle of a.c. power. The triac is widely used for low-power a.c. control in equipment such as lamp dimmers and a.c.-motor speed controllers.

5.10 Applications of electronic devices

There are, in general, two categories of application for electronic devices. The first is the controlled use of electical power, and the second is the manipulation of signals which represent information.

An example of the control of power is the high fidelity audio amplifier. The input signal from a tape head or gramophone pickup represents a power level in the microwatt region. In the audio amplifier, this signal is used to control the flow of current from a heavy-duty power supply to the loudspeaker. The output power will typically be around 20W, representing a very large power gain. An audio amplifier is an example of a linear electronic circuit; it is a circuit in which the output is ideally proportional to the input, whereas, in a nonlinear circuit, the output represents a more complicated function of the input.

This brings us to our second category, that of circuits for the manipulation of signals representing information. These may be of two types: analogue or digital. An example of an analogue circuit of this type is the instrumentation tape recorder. This device is used to record d.c. or slowly varying signals on magnetic tape. A normal audio tape recorder cannot handle frequencies below about 50 Hz, because, at lower frequencies, the rate of change of the magnetic field at the replay head is unable to produce a signal greater than the noise level. This frequency limitation is quite acceptable for the reproduction of audio signals, but it is unacceptable for signals representing such slowly changing physiological parameters as, for example, blood pressure or skin resistance. The instrumentation tape recorder overcomes this difficulty by generating a frequency which is proportional to the input voltage, and recording this varying frequency on the tape. Conversely, on replay, a circuit is used which converts the frequency signal back to a voltage form. Recorders of this type are discussed more fully in Chapter 11, and it is sufficient here to note the application of signal conversion circuits.

The second subcategory is that of digital circuits for signal manipulation. Applications of digital logic in psychology are numerous, one of the simplest being the fixed ratio reinforcement schedule, which provides an output signal for every so many input signals. At the other end of the scale, we may consider the example of a general-purpose digital computer being used to control an experiment. In such cases, the overall purpose is not primarily that of power amplification, but some form of complex control. In a digital computer, the power needed to read input, such as punched cards or paper tape, may be comparable to that needed to operate the output printer, but, in general, there will be no simple relationship between the input and output signals. This is quite different from the earlier example of the audio amplifier.

5.11 Logic circuits

Although circuit designers now normally use integrated circuits for logic operations, it is still useful to have some idea of the kind of circuit configurations which give the standard logic operations. It should be emphasized that, in any fully engineered system, many more components would be required for reliable operation than are shown in the simple circuit examples considered here. The professional circuit designer must consider such requirements as noise immunity and fanout or the ability of any one circuit to drive a specified number of inputs. In realizing a practical logic system, it is also necessary to define carefully the voltage levels which correspond to the logic levels 0 and 1. In this section, we will content ourselves, for descriptive purposes, with defining logic 0 as around 0 V and logic 1 as approximately $+ 12$ V.

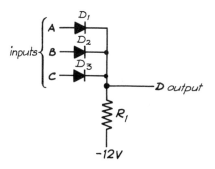

Figure 5.39. OR *gate*. $D = A + B + C$.

5.11.1 OR *gate*

A simple diode–resistor circuit for an OR gate is shown in Figure 5.39. A, B and C represent inputs and D an output. It is, therefore, a 3-input OR gate. Consider the state when all inputs are at logic 0, that is in the region of 0 V. The diodes are connected so that, under these circumstances, current will flow through them to the − 12 V line. The resistor R_1 has a value which is large compared with the forward resistance of the diodes, and therefore output D approaches the value of the inputs, that is logic 0. If input A goes to logic 1, that is to around + 12 V, diode D_1 will still conduct, making the output also rise to logic 1. Even if inputs B and C remain at logic 0, they will not affect the output, because diodes D_2 and D_3 are now reverse-biased and offer a very high resistance. Similar arguments follow when logic 1 signals are applied to inputs B and C, and therefore the circuit follows the truth table for an OR gate. One practical point to note is that the circuit does not incorporate any power-amplifying devices, such as transistors or other active components. There is, therefore, some degradation of the logic levels when they pass through this circuit, consisting of only passive components. If many stages of logic gates are used, some at least must contain active devices to maintain the integrity of the logic levels. Integrated-circuit logic gates incorporating one stage of an active inverter are therefore usually NAND or NOR gates (see Section 3.2).

5.11.2 AND *gate*

The corresponding circuit for an AND gate is shown in Figure 5.40. In this case, the diodes are biased to the positive supply, and they are connected in the opposite direction. Again with all inputs at logic 0, the diodes conduct, offering a low resistance, and the output is again at logic 0. When any one input, say A, goes to logic 1, it causes the corresponding diode D_1 to be reverse-biased, because the output is still at logic 0. This causes diode D_1 to become effectively a very high resistance. The output is unaffected, and remains at logic 0. Only when all three inputs go to logic 1 will the output change and follow the inputs.

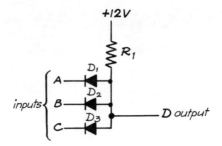

Figure 5.40. AND *gate.* $D = ABC$.

The circuit, therefore, follows the truth table for an AND gate. Note that this is again a passive circuit, and the signals suffer a power loss.

5.11.3 *Inverter*

The simple circuit for a transistor amplifier (Figure 5.41) behaves as an inverter. When A is at logic 0, no base current will flow, and the transistor is cut off, that is no collector current will flow. D is, therefore, at the potential of the + 12 V line, that is at logic 1. When A is at logic 1, base current will flow, and the transistor conducts. Resistor R_2 is chosen to be of higher value than the effective emitter–collector resistance of the transistor. Thus, the output voltage approaches zero, that is D is at logic 0. The circuit, therefore, follows the truth table for an inverter. Because this circuit uses a transistor, power gain is possible.

5.11.4 *Bistable*

Two inverters can be connected to form a bistable circuit, as shown in Figure 5.42. When the circuit is in the state in which TR_1 is conducting, output Q is at logic 0. The output is also connected to the base of TR_2 by R_2, and therefore TR_2 does not conduct. $\bar{Q}$, the output of TR_2, is therefore at logic 1, as we

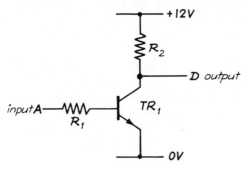

Figure 5.41. *Inverter.* $D = \bar{A}$.

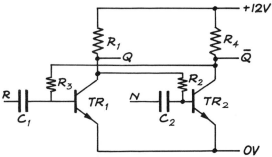

Figure 5.42. *A bistable. N and R are the normal and reset inputs. Q and Q̄ are the normal and inverted outputs. When provided with suitable gating circuits on the inputs, the bistable can be used for binary counting, as in the module described in Section 4.2.10.*

would expect for a bistable in the reset state. The output of TR_2 is also connected to the base of TR_1 by resistor R_3. This causes TR_1 to conduct, and so completes the circle. Thus, we have a stable state. Because the circuit is symmetrical, it follows that we could have started the description equally well with TR_2 as the conducting device; this would have given a stable state with TR_1 not conducting. The outputs would then be Q at logic 1 and Q̄ at logic 0, and the bistable would be in the set state. The inputs are coupled to the bases of the two transistors by capacitors which allow only the a.c. components of the input signals to reach the transistors. Consider the case when the bistable is reset, that is TR_2 is not conducting. If a transition from logic 0 to logic 1 occurs at the normal input N, the positive-going signal will cause the transistor TR_2 to conduct, thereby changing the state of the bistable. Similarly, a transition from logic 0 to logic 1 occurring at the input R will return the bistable to the reset state.

A version of this circuit which incorporates capacitors in the coupling between the two transistors can provide timing functions. A circuit which gives a logic pulse for a defined period of time is known as a monostable, and a circuit which gives a train of such pulses at a defined rate is known as a multivibrator. These functions were provided in the timer module described in Section 4.2.11.

5.12 Summary

Some understanding of electronics is helpful in making the best use of laboratory instruments. This chapter has given a brief introduction to electric circuits and semiconductor electronics. If a more thorough introduction is required, the reader should consult a text on electronics for the scientist. Olsen (1968) and Brophy (1972) have written suitable texts. In addition to giving an extensive introduction to solid-state electronics, these books also describe valve circuits, which were used in older equipment.

Some readers might care to try building their own apparatus. Zucker (1969) gives constructional hints and circuits for psychology applications, and, in this context, the monthly electronics hobby magazines should not be ignored.

They often publish articles of interest to the technically disposed psychologist, and it may be a worthwhile educational exercise for the reader wishing to gain some practical experience with electronics to build one of the many kits advertised in these magazines.

CHAPTER 6

Electronic Instruments

6.1 Moving-coil multimeter

Some electronic instruments are found in almost all laboratories and electronics workshops. In this chapter, the six kinds of electronic instrument which are likely to be encountered by any psychologist who is at all involved with electronics will be described.

The simplest and most widespread electronic instrument is the multimeter. This is an instrument which is able to measure two or more of the following electrical quantities: direct voltage, alternating voltage, direct current and resistance.

Both analogue and digital multimeters are manufactured (Figure 6.1), the difference being in the type of display. Digital multimeters use alphanumeric displays (Section 8.7.3), and are of fairly recent introduction. In this section, we will only describe the more common analogue multimeter, which uses a

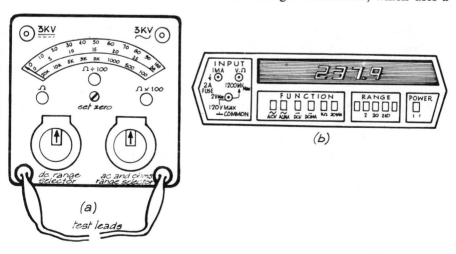

Figure 6.1. *Typical (a) analogue and (b) digital multimeters.*

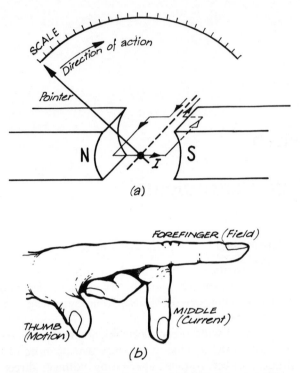

Figure 6.2. *Principle of the moving-coil meter. (a) When current flows through the coil, motor action causes it to rotate against the restoring torque of a light spring. The direction of movement is predicted by Fleming's left-hand rule (b) for the force acting upon a current-carrying conductor in a magnetic field.*

moving-coil meter (Figure 6.2) for the display. The face of the meter often has a different scale for each function, the various scales being marked to indicate the functions for which it is to be used.

The moving-coil, or d'Arsonval, meter is basically a direct-current measuring device. Its action depends upon electromagnetism, and it consists of a pivoted coil mounted in the field of a permanent magnet. When current flows through the coil, motor action in the direction indicated by Fleming's left-hand rule causes the coil to rotate against the restoring torque of a light spring. The movement is magnified by a long pointer and displayed against a scale. The coil has a fairly low resistance, and therefore the voltage drop across the meter terminals produces little error when the meter is inserted in series with most electronic circuits. The movement may be as sensitive as 10 μA for full-scale deflection. To measure larger values of current, the meter is shunted by low-value resistors (Figure 6.3a). In a typical multimeter, the maximum direct-current range would be about 10 A for full-scale deflection.

A basic moving-coil meter is converted to direct voltage by the inclusion of

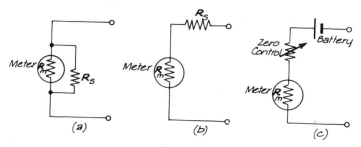

Figure 6.3. *With some additional components, the moving-coil meter may be used to measure various ranges of (a) direct current, (b) direct voltage and (c) resistance.*

a series resistor R_s (Figure 6.3b). The direct voltage to be measured is applied across the resistor–meter combination. From a knowledge of the full-scale sensitivity of the meter I and the values R_s and R_m, the voltage which will give full-scale deflection can be calculated by applying Ohm's law:

$$V = I(R_s + R_m)$$

Different values of series resistors are switched in to give various voltage ranges, typically 2·5 to 1000 V.

If a battery B (Figure 6.3c) is included in series with a meter and a variable resistor, the circuit will measure resistance. In use, the meter leads are first shorted together, and the zero control is adjusted to give full-scale deflection, which corresponds to zero resistance on the meter scale. The leads are then connected across the unknown resistor, and the value of the resistor is indicated by the resulting pointer deflection. Because the current flowing in a circuit is inversely proportional to resistance, the scale is nonlinear.

A facility for the measurement of alternating quantities is usually available on a multimeter. This is provided by circuits which rectify the alternating voltage or current, and then display the resulting d.c. signal on the moving-coil meter. Particular care is needed when making a.c. measurements. At low voltages, the diodes used for rectification cause nonlinearity in the pointer deflection, and a separate scale is often provided for a.c. measurements. Meter rectifiers generally only operate correctly up to about 20 kHz, and therefore high-frequency measurements cannot be made on a multimeter. Although the scale is traditionally calibrated in r.m.s. values, the actual value measured is usually the average value corrected to r.m.s. on the assumption that the waveform is sinusoidal. If non-sinusoidal waveforms are measured, the readings will be in error. Some sophisticated multimeters are capable of measuring true r.m.s. values. An oscilloscope (Section 6.4) may be used to inspect waveforms, and also allows the measurement of peak values.

Some general points concerning the use of instruments with meter displays are worth noting. When measuring an unknown quantity, the range-selector switch should always be set initially to the position of minimum sensitivity. This protects the meter movement against unintentional overloads. The range switch should then be used to select the range which gives maximum deflection without exceeding the full-scale calibration of the meter.

Moving-coil meters have a mechanical zero-adjusting mechanism which should be set with the meter in the orientation in which it is to be used. The balance of a moving-coil system may be such as to give different readings if the orientation is changed. If the selector switch of a multimeter has a position marked OFF, this position should always be selected when the meter is not in use or is to be transported. If there is no OFF position, care should be taken not to leave a resistance range selected, otherwise accidental shorting of the test leads will result in the battery quickly becoming discharged. All instruments using batteries should be regularly tested, and any discharged batteries replaced, preferably by sealed batteries, before leakage of electrolyte damages the instrument. Batteries should be removed if the instrument is to be put into long-term storage.

Moving-coil meters either use a taut-band suspension or jewelled pivots, as in a watch. In the latter type, friction at the pivot can affect the accuracy of readings, and gentle tapping on the meter case will reduce this source of error. Parallax errors can occur in reading instrument scales, because the pointer and the scale are not in the same plane. This produces an apparent displacement of the pointer when the position of the observer's head changes. The effect is eliminated in precision meters by the use of the antiparallax mirror (Figure 6.4).

6.2 High-impedance voltmeter

A limitation of the simple voltmeter is the finite internal resistance across its terminals. The resistance of a voltmeter should be as high as possible, in order to minimize the load imposed by the instrument on the circuit being tested. Psychologists sometimes use the term backward action to describe

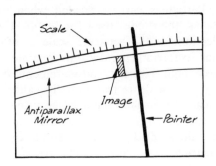

Figure 6.4. *The mirror scale. To eliminate parallax in meter readings, the observer aligns the pointer with its image in the mirror.*

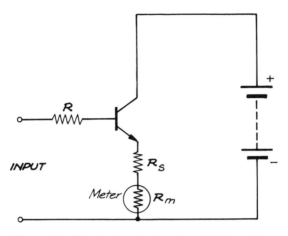

Figure 6.5. *The basic circuit of a high-impedance voltmeter.*

changes which take place in a phenomenon as a result of an attempt to measure it. In the most sensitive meters, this loading is around 100 kΩ/V of full-scale deflection. If we wish to measure voltages in a circuit containing fairly high resistances, say around 50 kΩ, the resistance of the voltmeter will greatly affect the reading. Transistor-operated voltmeters are available with input impedances of many megohms.

A very simple circuit for a high-impedance voltmeter is shown in Figure 6.5. This type of circuit is known as an emitter follower. It gives current amplification, but no voltage amplification. The output voltage, however, follows the input voltage very precisely. The circuit presents a very high impedance at its input terminals, and, in this application, the resistor R adds to this input impedance, different values being switched in to change ranges. By the in-

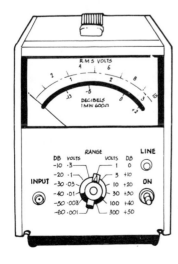

Figure 6.6. *A typical high-impedance (10 MΩ) a.c. voltmeter with ranges from 1 mV to 300 V full-scale deflection. The instrument covers a range from 10 Hz to 10 MHz (Hewlett–Packard model 3400A).*

clusion of suitable circuits, alternating voltages can be measured with greater accuracy, and to much higher frequencies, than with a simple multimeter. Amplification also allows the measurement of very small currents and voltages. Circuits giving these facilities are often included in digital multimeters. A typical high-impedance voltmeter is shown in Figure 6.6

6.3 Signal sources

An oscillator with a sine-wave output is the traditional standard signal source to be found in almost all electronics design laboratories and workshops. Oscillators are used when a periodic signal is required, and the main control is therefore scaled in terms of frequency. A somewhat different type of source is the pulse generator, which provides square pulses of precisely controlled duration, either singly or at a repetition interval which can be controlled independently of the pulse duration. Although many oscillators have a square-wave output, it is of fixed form, with the negative-going part of the wave equal in duration to the positive-going part.

Oscillators are classified according to the intended application and the circuit techniques which have been used in the instrument:

(1) Audio oscillators covering a frequency range from about 20 Hz to about 30 kHz with sine-wave and often also square-wave output (see also Section 7.7).
(2) Radio frequency signal generators covering a frequency range from about 30 kHz to 30 MHz, and often incorporating a means of modulating the output to give signals suitable for testing radio receivers.
(3) Wide-range oscillators, similar to (1), but covering a wider range of frequencies, perhaps from 1 Hz to 1 MHz.
(4) Function generators are very wide-range sources (about 0·001 Hz to 1 MHz) of sine, square and triangular waves.
(5) Specialist VHF, UHF and microwave signal generators for frequencies above 30 MHz.

Additional terms referring to the mode of generating the signal are sometimes used, for example, BFO (beat frequency oscillator), LC oscillator (inductor–capacitor oscillator) and RC oscillator (resistor–capacitor oscillator). The terms used by different manufacturers vary greatly, and so particular care is required when reading descriptions of commercial oscillators.

Most instruments generate the basic frequency signal as a sine-wave in an oscillator circuit utilizing positive feedback. The frequency-determining components are usually a resistor–capacitor or inductor–capacitor combination. In either case, one of the elements will be variable and its control brought out to the front panel of the instrument. Figure 6.7 shows a block diagram of a simple oscillator. The output of the oscillator circuit is passed through a buffer amplifier, the purpose of which is to reduce the effect of external circuits on the oscillator circuit. The output stage incorporates a level control, often in the

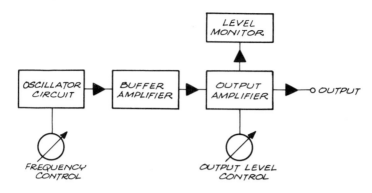

Figure 6.7. *Block diagram of a simple oscillator.*

form of an attenuator (see Sections 7.6.3 and 7.7). A meter is sometimes provided to allow the output level to be monitored. Figure 6.8 shows the front panel arrangement of a typical wide-range oscillator.

Function generators differ from other oscillators in not having a sine-wave oscillator circuit as the basic frequency source. Audio oscillators may have a square-wave output, but this is derived from the sine-wave oscillator circuit. The frequency source in a function generator is a type of multivibrator (Section 5.11.4) which produces both triangular and square waves (Figure 6.9). Sine waves are derived from the triangular signal by shaping circuits which alter the slope of the triangular wave at a number of points (Figure 6.10). The sine wave produced by a function generator may not be as pure as can be produced by a conventional oscillator. Shaping circuits with many breakpoints, however, can give a very good approximation to a sine wave.

The front-panel layout of a typical function generator shown in Figure 6.11 gives some idea of the range of facilities available on these instruments. VCF is an abbreviation for voltage control of frequency. This allows the frequency to be

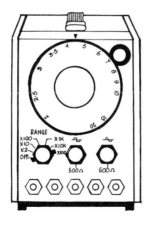

Figure 6.8. *The front-panel controls of a typical wide-range oscillator, covering a frequency range from 4 Hz to 2 MHz. The large control dial is turned by the knob in the centre for coarse setting of frequency. The knob in the top right corner gives fine adjustment. The lower controls are the frequency range selector and the amplitude controls for the square- and sine-wave outputs (Hewlett–Packard model 209A).*

94

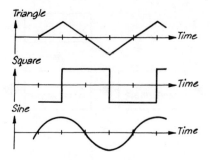

Figure 6.9. *Basic function-generator waveforms.*

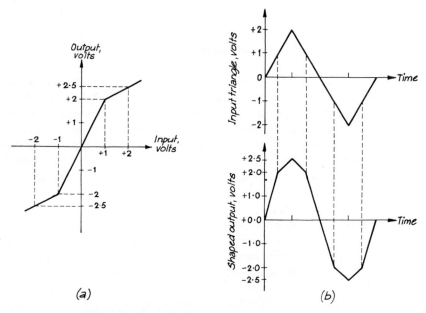

(a)

(b)

Figure 6.10. *The action of a simple sine-wave shaping circuit, (a) amplifier characteristic, (b) shaping process.*

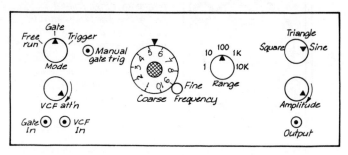

Figure 6.11. *A typical front-panel layout for a function generator.*

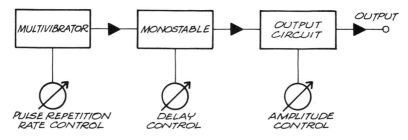

Figure 6.12. *Block diagram of a simple pulse generator.*

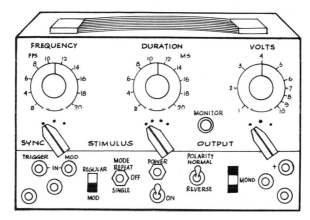

Figure 6.13. *A typical pulse generator designed for use as a physiological stimulator (Grass Instruments model S9).*

controlled by an externally applied voltage in addition to the normal front-panel controls. The gate control allows the production of tone bursts containing an integral number of cycles (Section 7.7).

A block diagram of a simple form of pulse generator is shown in Figure 6.12. The multivibrator controls the pulse repetition rate. Its output triggers a pulse from the monostable with variable delay. The output circuit provides control of the pulse amplitude. Specialized pulse generators are used as stimulators in physiological work (Figure 6.13).

6.4 Oscilloscope

The oscilloscope is built around the cathode-ray tube (Section 8.7.4), and is used to plot a graph of the waveform under investigation. The visual form of the display facilitates measurement and detailed analysis of the waveform. Measurements may be made directly on the screen if the waveform is repetitive or if a storage oscilloscope is used; otherwise the display may be photographed (Section 11.1.3). In addition to the cathode-ray tube, an oscilloscope contains at

96

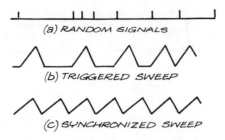

(a) RANDOM SIGNALS

(b) TRIGGERED SWEEP

(c) SYNCHRONIZED SWEEP

Figure 6.14. *The effects of a random signal
(a) on the generation of a time base by (b)
a triggered oscilloscope and (c) a synchronized oscilloscope. With the triggered
oscilloscope, the generation of a sawtooth
is always linked to the occurrence of an
event.*

least one vertical, or *Y*, amplifier for the signal, and a timebase generator to
provide the sweep signal to the *X* plates of the oscilloscope.

There have been two basic approaches to the design of oscilloscopes. The
first resulted in the development of the synchronized oscilloscope, which is
suitable only for the display of uniformly repetitive waveforms. In this instrument, the horizontal signal is a sawtooth waveform of a frequency equal to a
precise submultiple of the frequency of the waveform under investigation.
Many phenomena occur randomly or are of very short duration, making them
difficult to display on the synchronized oscilloscope. Accordingly, most modern
instruments are of the type known as triggered oscilloscopes. These are capable
of detecting the start of an event and triggering a single sawtooth sweep for the
timebase (Figure 6.14).

The block diagram of a basic triggered oscilloscope is given in Figure 6.15.
The vertical amplifier usually has a switched input attenuator calibrated in
volts per centimetre of deflection. There may also be a switch to select a.c. or d.c.

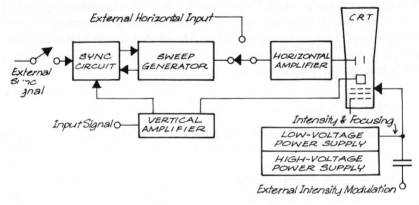

Figure 6.15. *Block diagram of a typical oscilloscope.*

amplification. The triggered oscilloscope often incorporates a delay line in the Y amplifier in order to allow time for the sweep to start. On oscilloscopes of this kind, the leading edge of pulse waveforms can be closely examined.

The brightness, or Z, axis of the display is modulated by a signal which is derived from the timebase circuit, so that the display is blanked during the return of the X sweep.

Modern oscilloscopes have many front-panel controls, often two or three beings ganged onto a common coaxial shaft. The instruction manuals should be fully studied before the instrument is used. Most instruments have the related controls grouped together in clearly marked areas on the front panel (Figure 6.16). Thus, the controls for focus, intensity and astigmatism, which are concerned with the appearance of the display, are normally grouped together. The controls for the vertical amplifier, including vertical position and vertical sensitivity (volts per centimetre), are also normally grouped together.

The horizontal section of a triggered oscilloscope has the largest number of controls. For example, the trigger generator usually has controls which allow triggering from negative or positive slopes, with slow or fast risetimes, automatic synchronization etc. The horizontal amplifier usually has controls which provide magnification and fine positioning of the vertical sweep.

Many instruments use a plug-in facility which allows amplifiers and timebase generators of diverse characteristics to be used. Dual-trace oscilloscopes allow two signals to be displayed with the same timebase. This is particularly useful for comparing, say, the input and output signals of an amplifier. Oscilloscopes with a storage display tube are frequently used for investigating transient phenomena, such as electrophysiological signals. Sometimes storage scopes have a variable persistence facility which is useful for the display of low-frequency events.

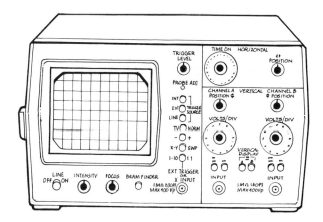

Figure 6.16. *Front panel layout of a typical dual-trace oscillo-scope (Hewlett–Packard model 1220A).*

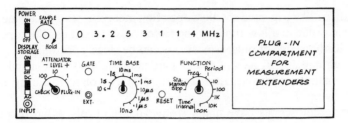

Figure 6.17. *Typical front panel layout of a universal counter.*

6.5 Timer/counter

Electronic counters are widely used, not only for counting separate events, but also for the measurement of frequencies and time intervals of electrical events. Non-electrical phenomena are easily converted into electrical signals by the use of switches or more sophisticated transducers. Most electronic counters are based upon decimal counting circuits, and may be considered, from the user's viewpoint, as a collection of sequence counters (Section 4.2.9) housed in a single instrument case together with some additional control logic.

When using the instrument for time measurements, a precise frequency signal is gated internally to the counting circuits for the time duration to be measured. When frequency is measured, each cycle of the input signal is counted during a precise interval of time.

Electronic counters have become widely accepted for such measurements because high resolution and accuracy are easily obtained in routine use, and the digital display enables unambiguous readings to be made.

For most applications in psychology, the microsecond resolution and capability for frequency measurement provided by general-purpose timer/ counters (Figure 6.17) are not required. Such instruments also require voltage

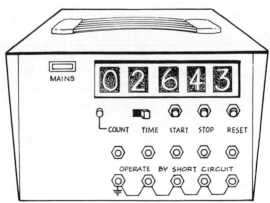

Figure 6.18. *Front panel layout of a millisecond stopclock designed for use in psychology (BRD (Electronics) Ltd. model MSIIA).*

levels for the control inputs, which is inconvenient for elementary instrumentation requirements, where contact closures are widely used. These problems are solved by the use of instruments specially designed for psychology laboratories, such as the millisecond stopclock and counter shown in Figure 6.18. This instrument uses a frequency source of 1 kHz, and displays time intervals over a range from 1 ms to 99·999 s on five numeric indicator tubes, without the need to change ranges. The instrument may be controlled either from the pushbuttons on the front panel or by contact closures between 4 mm sockets. A changeover switch allows the unit to be used either to count contact closures at the count input, or to measure elapsed time. The reset control operates in either mode. The instrument will measure the time interval between momentary contact closures at the start input and the stop input, and also the duration of contact closure at the time input. Thus, a simple reaction-time experiment might use the instrument in the time mode, with a pair of contacts which close at the time of stimulus presentation connected to the start input, and the subject's response key connected to the stop input. The front panel reset pushbutton would be used to zero the display after each reaction time had been recorded. Figure 6.19 shows a circuit diagram for such an experiment using the time input of the stopclock.

Sophisticated timer/counters often have facilities for the transfer of the display contents to data-recording instruments, such as digital printers, digital tape recorders, laboratory computers etc. This is usually done in binary-coded decimal (Section 1.4) rather than the one-out-of-ten code used by the sequence counter. Unless the timer/counter and recording equipment have been designed

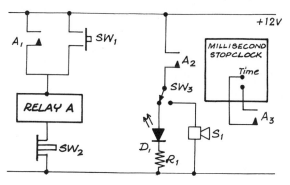

Figure 6.19. *Circuit diagram for simple reaction time.*
The experimenter presents a stimulus by brief operation of
pushbutton SW₁ which is normally open. This causes
relay A to operate, making contact A₁ and holding the
relay energized until the subject operates the response key
SW₂ and breaks the circuit. While the relay is energized,
contacts A₂ and A₃ will be made, presenting the stimulus
and operating the electronic stopclock. SW₃ allows the
experimenter to select a visual or auditory stimulus. D₁
is an LED (Section 8.1.4) and S₁ is an electronic buzzer.

for use together, some interfacing circuits will usually be necessary to control the transfer of data.

6.6 Stabilized power supply

Two main classes of stabilized power supply are manufactured: subunits for building into electronic equipment, and self-contained instruments for use in the laboratory. In this section, we will be mainly concerned with the latter type, which have front panels with controls and screw terminals for the output. They also usually have meters to monitor the output current and voltage.

A simplified diagram of a stabilized power supply is shown in Figure 6.20. This figure is basically similar to Figure 5.26, but additionally it includes a mains transformer and a series stabilizing circuit. In most power supplies, a bridge rectifier is preferred to a single diode, because a bridge rectifier allows current to flow during both the positive and negative halfcycles of the alternating voltage, making the smoothing more effective.

The series stabilizer is a transistor circuit which compares the actual voltage at the output terminals with the desired voltage. It adjusts the resistance of a series transistor in such a manner that the output voltage is kept nearly constant, in spite of changes in load resistance and fluctuations in the mains supply voltage. A front-panel control allows the output voltage to be adjusted over a wide range, typically from 0 to 48 V. On many power supplies, the front panel has separate terminals which sense the output voltage for the regulating circuit. The sensing terminals are normally strapped to the output terminals, but, if very long leads are used between the power supply and the load, the straps can be removed to allow the sensing terminals to be connected separately to the load. When this is done, the stabilizing circuit will compensate for the resistance of the lead between the power supply and the load.

Laboratory power supplies usually have efficient protection circuits. In many instruments, a front panel control is fitted which allows a maximum level to be set for the output current. As well as giving a measure of protection to any external equipment connected to the supply, this feature protects the instrument

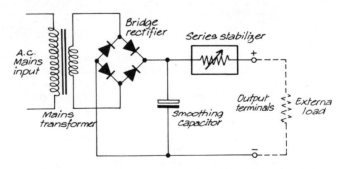

Figure 6.20. *Simplified diagram of a stabilized power supply.*

against short circuits across its output terminals, and also allows the instrument to be used as a constant-current power supply.

6.7 Summary

In this chapter, we have described some of the more common general-purpose laboratory instruments. A useful source of more detailed reading is the handbook on electronic instruments edited by Coombs (1972).

CHAPTER 7

Auditory Stimuli

7.1 Introduction

Auditory stimuli are very widely used in psychological experimentation, and often no instrumentation at all is involved. Subjects are frequently asked questions or are presented with lists of items spoken directly by the experimenter. It is well known that, under such conditions, the experimenter may unintentionally provide cues which could bias the results, and therefore stimuli of this type are often carefully prerecorded on magnetic tape to give improved control of the experimental conditions. Some workers have used synthesized speech to standardize their experimental stimuli (for example Cohen and Massaro (1976)). In the present state of the art, this is not at all widespread, and most of the discussion in this chapter will relate to techniques which are appropriate for the presentation of natural speech and pure tone stimuli.

7.2 Microphones

The function of a microphone is to translate an acoustic signal into its equivalent electrical signal. The basic types of microphone differ in the methods by which this translation is achieved. They also have various directional characteristics, which may be used to favour a wanted against an unwanted sound, for example distant traffic. The wanted sound may range in intensity from a faint whisper to the roar of a jet aircraft at takeoff, whilst the unwanted sound may range from low-level room reverberations to the clatter of heavy machinery. For high-quality sound reproduction, it is also necessary for the microphone to be uniformally sensitive to sound over a frequency range wide enough to encompass all the audible components of the original sound.

Each type of microphone has its own particular characteristics, and these should be used as the basis of selection for a particular application. In addition, there are certain basic requirements for a microphone whatever its intended application:

(1) The sensitivity of a microphone to the wanted sound should be high in

relation to its sensitivity to mechanical shock or noise generated by handling. The electrical-output level should also be high in relation to any self-generated noise, such as that arising from the basic thermal agitation of the molecules. (2) The microphone should be sensitive to transient sounds at all frequencies over its operating range, and should be free from resonances, which add a characteristic colouration to the reproduced sound. (3) The output of the microphone should be unaffected by adjacent magnetic or electrostatic fields. (4) Finally, the microphone should be of sufficiently robust construction to withstand a reasonable degree of handling. This is especially important for, say, a teaching laboratory, in which a microphone may be exposed to a variety of inexperienced users.

The following sections describe the types of microphone which are in common use. Because the various types of microphone exemplify some of the basic principles of converting mechanical signals to electrical signals, and these are common to a variety of other transducers, we will give this topic a fairly detailed treatment. The various types of microphone are not arranged in an order of merit, because the characteristics of the microphones determine the most suitable type for a particular application.

7.2.1 *The crystal microphone*

The piezoelectric effect is a phenomenon which is exhibited by certain crystals and ceramics. When these materials are subjected to mechanical strain, an electric charge appears across opposing faces of the crystal; the intensity of this charge is directly proportional to the applied strain. In the crystal microphone, this property is used to produce an output voltage which is proportional to the applied sound pressure.

Figure 7.1 shows the basic principles of operation of a simple crystal micro-

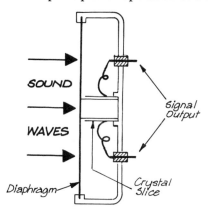

Figure 7.1. *A simple crystal micro-phone.*

104

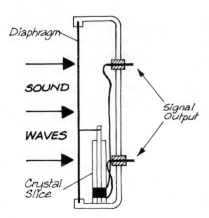

Figure 7.2. *A cantilever crystal micro-phone.*

phone. A thin circular diaphragm is clamped at its periphery. The sound waves induce movements in the diaphragm which are transmitted directly to the crystal slice. Leads are connected to silvered surfaces on the two opposing faces of the crystal slice.

In practice, such a microphone would be very insensitive, because the stiffness of the crystal would impede the movement of the diaphragm. It is more usual to employ a lever arrangement (Figure 7.2) to couple the diaphragm to the crystal. This produces a bending strain instead of compression.

In order to obtain an electrical output from this bending movement, two slices of crystal are cemented together; when the combination is deflected, one of the slices will be in tension and the other in compression. By suitable connection to the surfaces of the crystal slices (Figure 7.3), a voltage can be produced which is proportional to the applied pressure. Such crystal combinations are known as bimorphs.

The piezoelectric effect was first observed in quartz crystals, but later Rochelle salt was found to show a much greater piezoelectric effect than quartz, resulting

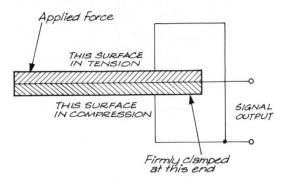

Figure 7.3. *A crystal bimorph.*

in a greater output. Because Rochelle salt is also cheaper and more readily available than quartz, it has been widely used in the manufacture of bimorphs for crystal microphones.

The main advantages of the crystal microphone are its high sensitivity, simplicity of construction and light weight. Because it is operated by sound pressure, it has an omnidirectional response. Its frequency response is fairly uniform up to about 7 kHz, and this, together with its high output, make it a useful microphone for communications applications.

Since the crystal element is basically a capacitor, the output impedance of a crystal microphone in high, and therefore the cable which connects the microphone to the amplifier must be kept fairly short to maintain sensitivity. The amplifier must also have a high input impedance, or the high-frequency response will be severely restricted. The cable between the microphone and the amplifier must be well screened in order to reduce the interference from stray magnetic fields, such as those arising from a.c. power lines.

The crystal element is fragile, but it is so light that breakage is unlikely in normal use. Rochelle salt, however, is affected by extreme humidity, and is unstable at high temperatures, being permanently damaged at temperatures above 40 °C.

Certain ceramic materials, such as barium titanate, exhibit the piezoelectric effect; they are widely used in the manufacture of crystal microphones and the cheaper forms of gramophone pickup, which are also used in the laboratory to detect the responses of fish and other small animals (Section 10.1.1). The construction of ceramic microphones is similar to that of crystal microphones; they have similar electrical characteristics, but are less affected by extreme temperature and humidity. Ceramic microphones are commonly supplied with the lower-priced domestic tape recorders.

7.2.2 The carbon microphone

The carbon microphone consists of loose carbon granules sandwiched between two plates. One of the plates is fixed, and the other is coupled to a diaphragm, so that the sound pressure waves cause the moving plate alternately to compress and release the granules. Pressure on the granules causes the electrical resistance between the plates to decrease, and, when the pressure is released, the resistance increases again. When a current flows through a microphone, its resistance will cause a voltage to be developed across the terminals. Variations in this resistance will cause corresponding variations in the voltage, and so the sound pressure variations acting upon the diaphragm will be translated into voltage variations.

Because the carbon microphone acts as a control valve for electric current, a form of amplification of the signal takes place, and the electric output of the carbon microphone can be higher than that of other types of microphones which generate an electrical voltage directly from the sound energy.

The carbon microphone can be manufactured very cheaply, and is usually

106

of very rugged construction. Its output impedance is low, and almost wholly resistive, so that long cables may be used with every little loss of signal. For these reasons it is used in almost all telephone systems, and is probably manufactured in greater quantity than any other type of microphone.

The carbon microphone suffers several disadvantages which make it unsuitable for high-quality applications. It produces a considerable amount of noise, due to random movement and local heating of the carbon granules. It introduces distortion of the signal, and, for this reason, its frequency response is often deliberately limited to between 300 and 3000 Hz, for example in telephone systems. This frequency range is adequate for the transmission of speech, and, as the microphone is placed only a few centimetres from the speaker's lips, the signal is large compared with the self-generated noise of the microphone.

There is also a tendency for the granules to cohere when the polarizing voltage is removed or when a steady signal is present. This produces a marked reduction in sensitivity until the granules are loosened by shaking or some other form of mechanical shock. Fortunately, the rugged construction of the carbon microphone usually permits such rough treatment.

7.2.3 *The moving-coil microphone*

Figure 7.4 shows the basic construction of the moving-coil, or dynamic, microphone. The thin circular diaphragm is suspended at its periphery, in such a way that the coil, which it supports, can move freely in the gap between the poles of a permanent magnet. Sound waves impinge on the diaphragm, and cause the coil to move through the magnetic field in the gap, thus inducing in the coil an alternating voltage which is directly proportional to the sound signal. Because this is the basic principle of the dynamo, the moving-coil microphone is often referred to as a dynamic, or electrodynamic, microphone.

The moving-coil microphone has a low output impedance and a low level of self-generated noise; these features make it suitable for a wide variety of applications. It has, therefore, been the subject of much development work. As a result, the moving-coil microphone exists in many forms, each being suitable for a particular application. It can be made fairly robust, for use as a

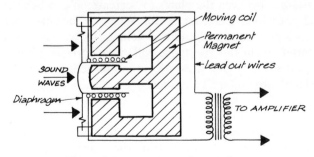

Figure 7.4. *A moving-coil microphone.*

general-purpose microphone, or may be given an extended frequency response to make it suitable for high-quality use. Its directional characteristics may be developed for specialized purposes, both highly directional and noise-cancelling types being available.

To enable the moving-coil microphone to reproduce high-frequency or transient sounds, the mass of the moving parts must be kept to a minimum. This limits the number of turns of wire which may be used in the coil, and so the output impedance and sensitivity of the moving-coil microphone are relatively low. A step-up transformer is often used to connect the microphone to the amplifier, because this gives a better impedance match and also increases the signal voltage. The transformer may be mounted at the amplifier, allowing the use of long cables from the microphone while reducing the mains hum picked up by the cable. For general-purpose applications, however, it is quite common for the step-up transformer to be mounted in the microphone casing, along with a switch which allows either high or low impedance to be selected. When high quality is not of vital importance, larger coils may be used, producing an increase in sensitivity and rendering a step-up transformer unnecessary. Low-priced moving-coil microphones of this type are superseding carbon microphones in some telephone systems.

Because the moving-coil microphone is a magnetic device, hum and noise will be introduced by a strong electromagnetic field. The microphone is, therefore, well screened to minimize these effects. Careful design of the case is also necessary to prevent any ferrous-metal particles, which are attracted by the permanent magnet, from entering the moving-coil assembly.

7.2.4 *The condenser microphone*

The condenser, or capacitor, microphone (Figure 7.5) basically consists of a thin circular metal diaphragm, tightly clamped at its edges and held under tension. The diaphragm is separated by a small airgap from a fixed metal backing plate. Together the diaphragm and backing plate form an air-dielectric

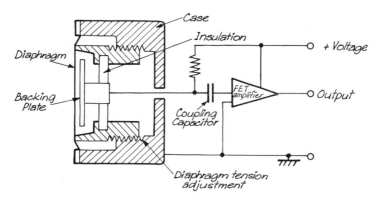

Figure 7.5. *A condenser microphone.*

capacitor. This capacitor is polarized by a high voltage applied through a high-value resistor, so that the charge across the capacitor remains substantially constant despite the small movements of the diaphragm caused by sound pressure waves. Since the voltage across a capacitor is equal to the charge divided by the capacitance, any change in capacitance due to movement of the diaphragm will produce a change in voltage across the capacitor. In order to make use of these voltage changes, it is necessary to derive an output voltage from the capacitor while maintaining the high resistance, which is necessary to keep the electrical charge constant. This is done by connecting the capacitor directly into a high-impedance amplifier, such as a field-effect transistor circuit.

The simple construction of the condenser microphone allows it to be manufactured to close tolerances, and therefore the performance of this microphone is both predictable and stable over time. It also has an excellent frequency response, and is consequently found in broadcasting studios and in other high-quality applications. Condenser microphones are employed as a laboratory standard, and are used whenever high-precision measurements are required.

The condenser microphone is fundamentally omnidirectional, because it is pressure operated. As in the case of the moving-coil microphone, its directional response may be modified for certain applications without unduly affecting its other characteristics.

Because the condenser microphone is connected directly into a high input impedance amplifier which is usually housed in the microphone casing, the microphone cable supplies the operating voltages necessary for the amplifier as well as carrying the output signal. The expense and complication of this special equipment tends to restrict the use of the condenser microphone to professional applications. Recently, however, mass-produced condenser microphones termed electrets have been developed. These use metallized plastic diaphragms which have been specially treated to give them a permanent electric charge, thereby removing the need to supply the high operating voltage. Electrets are now frequently built into cassette recorders, but, when used independently, they still require a high input impedance preamplifier in the microphone housing.

7.2.5 *The ribbon microphone*

All the microphones described in the preceding sections have depended for their operation upon the pressure difference between the front and rear of a diaphragm. The ribbon microphone, however, does not employ a diaphragm. As in the case of the moving-coil microphone, the principle of operation of the ribbon microphone is based upon the movement of a conductor in the field of a permanent magnet. In this case, the conductor is not a coil, but a narrow strip or ribbon of thin aluminium foil. It is suspended in the path of the sound waves (Figure 7.6), and forms both the moving element and the conductor.

The ribbon is open to the air on both sides, and therefore the sound pressure

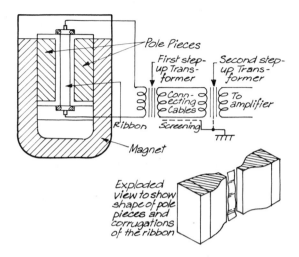

Figure 7.6. *A ribbon microphone.*

will normally be equal on both sides of the ribbon. The velocity component of an incident sound wave causes the ribbon to move, as it tends to follow the particle velocity of the air. The ribbon microphone is, therefore, often described as a velocity-operated microphone. Since the ribbon presents its greatest area to sound waves at both the front and the rear of the microphone, it is most sensitive to sound from these directions, and therefore has a highly directional response. The electrical output from the ribbon is dependent upon both the rate of movement of the ribbon and the intensity of the magnetic field. In order to obtain an adequate electrical output from the single ribbon conductor, the pole pieces of the magnet are specially shaped to concentrate the magnetic flux around the ribbon.

Because the impedance of the ribbon is very low, a step-up transformer is usually built into the microphone casing. This serves to increase the voltage output as well as to raise the output impedance to a more convenient level. The combination of ribbon microphone and transformer is often designed to have electrical characteristics similar to those of a moving-coil microphone.

In a well designed ribbon microphone, the force available to drive the ribbon from the velocity component of the sound wave can be made independent of frequency. Because of this excellent frequency response, it adds very little colouration to the reproduced sound, and therefore the ribbon microphone is widely used for the high-quality reproduction of music. Relatively inexpensive forms are also available for semiprofessional use.

As with the moving-coil microphone, the performance of the ribbon microphone is adversely affected by adjacent magnetic fields. Some electromagnetic screening is provided by housing the microphone in a metal case, but care should be taken not to use the microphone close to mains transformers and electric motors. The ribbon itself is very fragile, and may be blown out of the gap or even broken by the force of the wind. For this reason, the ribbon is generally protected by layers of fine gauze at the front and rear. Even so, the ribbon microphone is very susceptible to wind noise, and is therefore generally unsuitable for outdoor use.

7.3 Auditory sources

Although a loudspeaker is often a convenient stimulus source, its use poses a number of difficulties. The sound waves are reflected around the room, giving rise to complex resonances and reverberations; these affect the intensity and quality of the sound, and make precise specification of the proximal sound stimulus very difficult. It should also be realized that the intensity of the proximal stimulus will be affected by the position in the room of both the source and the subject and by the frequency of the stimulus being employed. Sometimes it is necessary to present auditory stimuli in this manner; experiments with young children and unrestrained animals are typical examples. In these cases, the experimental rooms should be acoustically treated and the sound system calibrated. In cases requiring precise control of the stimulus intensity, or high-quality reproduction, headphones should be employed. They can be carefully calibrated, and also provide a high degree of isolation from extraneous noises.

For many experiments, the intensity of the auditory stimulus is not crucial. It need only be in the normal hearing range, somewhere between the absolute threshold and the threshold of feeling. In such cases, the use of loudspeakers is more convenient than headphones. When faithful reproduction of a sound is required, commercial high-fidelity loudspeaker systems may be used. These generally consist of a multispeaker system mounted in a specially designed enclosure. For many applications, however, all that is required is an auditory signal with distinctive characteristics; in such cases, a low-cost loudspeaker of the type used in domestic radio or television receivers may be mounted on a wooden board near the subject.

7.3.1 *The loudspeaker*

A loudspeaker operates as a transducer in two stages. In the first stage, electrical energy is transformed into movements of the loudspeaker diaphragm, and, in the second stage, this mechanical energy is transformed into acoustical energy. The majority of loudspeakers operate on the electrodynamic, or moving-coil, principle. Electric current, flowing through a conductor situated in a magnetic field, gives rise to a force acting upon the conductor. Figure 7.7 shows a cross-sectional view of a typical moving-coil loudspeaker. The relationship between the current and force is linear, and so the transfer of energy is fundamentally free of distortion.

Another important type of operation which may be employed in a loudspeaker is that of electrostatics. This method is based upon the fact that a force exists between the plates of a charged capacitor. Although such a system

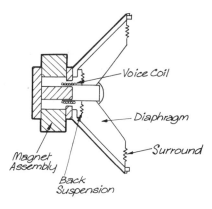

Figure 7.7. *A moving-coil loudspeaker.*

is not inherently linear, it can be made to behave in an essentially linear manner by biasing the capacitor with a direct voltage and arranging perforated fixed plates at either side of the diaphragm, as shown in Figure 7.8.

At low frequencies, the wavelength of the sound wave is large compared with the physical dimensions of normal loudspeaker units; for example, at 100 Hz, the wavelength is 3·4 m. The radiation from the rear of the loudspeaker is out of phase with respect to the radiation from the front. Therefore, unless means are adopted to prevent interaction between the front and rear radiation, severe attenuation will occur at those frequencies for which the difference in path length is small in comparison with the wavelength. For loudspeakers intended for purposes other than high-fidelity reproduction, it is usually adequate to mount the loudspeaker on a wooden board in which a hole of the same diameter as the loudspeaker cone has been cut. Such a board is known as a baffle, and the larger the baffle the better will be the low-frequency reproduction. For high-quality reproduction, say down to 30 Hz, the loudspeaker must be housed in an enclosure which has been specifically designed to prevent this cancellation of front and rear radiation.

When we consider operation at the middle frequencies, several other factors become important. The wavelengths of the radiated sound at these frequencies are comparable with the dimensions of the unit, giving rise to diffraction

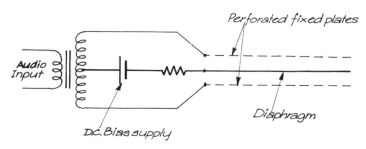

Figure 7.8. *An electrostatic loudspeaker.*

effects which make the pattern of radiation from the loudspeaker more directional in character. In moving-coil loudspeakers, the inductance of the voice coil causes the impedance of the unit to increase with frequency, thereby reducing the current flow. Because the dimensions of the diaphragm are comparable with the wavelength of the sound, standing waves are set up in the diaphragm. In low-cost units, standing waves may cause parts of the diaphragm to move in opposite directions, producing a very uneven frequency response. This effect, known as cone break-up, is reduced in high-quality loudspeakers by constructing the cone from a light, but very rigid, material.

As the frequency is raised still further, these problems become even more severe. For high-frequency reproduction, a small, light diaphragm is required, and the inductance of the voice coil causes the impedance to increase further. It is, therefore, difficult to design a single loudspeaker unit which will give high-quality reproduction over the whole audio frequency range. The requirements at various parts of the frequency spectrum differ so greatly that, in high-fidelity systems, two or more units are employed, each designed to operate over only one particular band of frequencies. The audio signal is divided between the units by electrical filters, known as crossover networks.

Sensitivity is not usually an important consideration in loudspeakers. Features which reduce distortion and improve frequency response usually cause a loss of efficiency. Thus, low-cost units will often produce adequate levels of sound in an average room when driven by an amplifier of about 1 W r.m.s. rating, whereas a high-quality loudspeaker system may require an amplifier of about 10 W r.m.s. rating to produce an adequate sound level in a similar room.

7.3.2 Headphones

The main advantage of headphones is that they provide an environment in which a wide variety of auditory stimuli can be presented in a closely controlled manner. Headphones provide a high degree of isolation from ambient noise. With a good seal between the headphone cup and the ear, an attenuation of 40 dB is possible, but bone conduction from the rest of the head makes higher levels of attenuation difficult to achieve. Because the sound radiator in a headphone is closely coupled to the ear, much lower levels of electrical power are needed to give the same sound-pressure level at the ear than when a loudspeaker is used. Hence, lower levels of distortion can be achieved, and, owing to the small size of the radiator, a much better dynamic response is possible.

The simplest type of headphone is that which is used in a telephone receiver. It is known as the moving-iron earphone. The radiator is a thin ferrous diaphragm which is driven by a fixed electromagnet carrying the audio signal. This type of headphone is often used in communications applications, but it is not suitable for high-quality reproduction.

A high-quality headphone in common use is the moving-coil type, which employs a drive mechanism similar to that of the moving-coil loudspeaker in

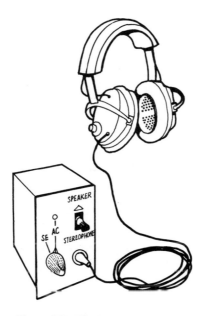

Figure 7.9. *Electrostatic stereophones with a self-energizer. When used with low-level signals, the energizer may be operated from the mains supply. Each pair of headphones is supplied with a calibration curve (Koss model ESP-9).*

Figure 7.7. Headphones are now often used for the domestic reproduction of stereophonic music, as well as in laboratory and studio work. This increased demand has resulted in considerable effort being applied in recent years to the development of high-quality headphones. One outcome of this work has been the development of electrostatic headphones based on methods used for electrostatic loudspeakers (Figure 7.8). Such headphones provide high-precision wide-range reproduction, and are well suited to psychoacoustic research (Figure 7.9).

7.4 Fundamentals of acoustic measurement

Sound waves are variations in pressure which result from mechanical disturbances in a material medium; they are usually oscillatory in nature. The simplest form of oscillation is simple harmonic motion (Section 1.4), and the sound which results from pressure variations of this form is described as a pure tone, because only one frequency is present.

If we consider the simple harmonic or sinusoidal variation of a plane surface in air or some other medium (Figure 7.10), it is apparent that movement of the surface will cause slight variations in pressure close to the surface. The

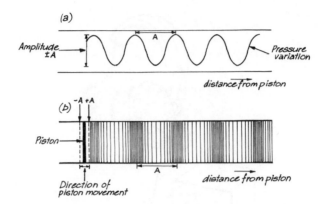

Figure 7.10. *The effect of vibrating a plane wave by $\pm A$ on the molecular distribution of a tube of air. The pressure variations at an instant in time are shown in (a). The corresponding variations in density are shown in (b). In practice, there is a tendency for the wavefront to become spherical, unless the piston is infinitely large.*

pressure variations will be transmitted through the medium at a particular velocity, in a somewhat similar manner to the spread of ripples when the surface of still water is disturbed. If the propagation takes the form of a plane wave, then the variation in pressure at a point distant from the source will also be sinusoidal. The properties of the wave are illustrated in Figure 7.11 and Figure 7.12. Figure 7.11 shows the situation at a given instant in time in the sound field, whereas Figure 7.12 shows the situation at a given point. The sound pressure varies through a complete cycle in time T, and, during this time, the wavefront will move a complete wavelength λ. Thus, the velocity of propagation V is given by λ/T, or, alternatively, $V = v \times \lambda$, where v is the frequency, or the number of complete periods in unit time. The velocity of propagation of sound waves in air at 0 °C is 332 m s^{-1}. The strength of the pressure wave may be expressed in terms of the amplitude of the local pressure variations from mean atmospheric pressure.

Although this description has been given in terms of a plane wave, similar concepts apply to spherical waves, the differences being that, as the wave

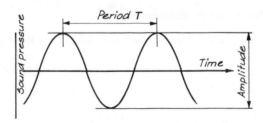

Figure 7.11. *The time properties of simple harmonic oscillation.*

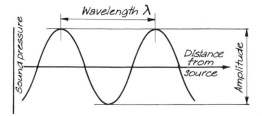

Figure 7.12. *The distance properties of simple harmonic oscillation.*

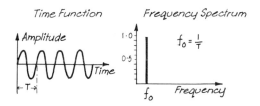

Figure 7.13. *The frequency spectrum of a pure tone.*

progresses, the area over which the energy of the source is spread becomes enlarged. Thus, the intensity, or the average power per unit area, is reduced.

The great majority of common sounds are more complex than pure tones, because they have components at several frequencies in the audio range. When sounds are produced by musical instruments, one fundamental frequency predominates for each note which is sounded, although other higher frequencies are present. These harmonics are related to the frequency of the fundamental, and they give a characteristic sound quality to the instrument. When analysing such sounds, the frequency spectrum is usually employed. This is a graph which illustrates the sound-pressure amplitude at various frequencies. A pure tone appears on the graph as a line at a particular frequency. The length of the line is proportional to the amplitude of the sound pressure, as in Figure 7.13. A more complex sound has a frequency spectrum which shows a number of lines at discrete frequencies (Figure 7.14), and consequently spectra of this type are known as line spectra. Many common sounds, however, are non-periodic, and have components spread over a wide range of frequencies, showing a continuous spectrum of the kind illustrated in Figure 7.15. Examples of everyday sounds with a continuous spectrum are the hiss of an air jet or the background noise of a room in busy building.

The decibel is the most widely used unit of acoustic intensity. It is defined as

$$10 \times \log_{10} \frac{x}{r}$$

where x is the measured power and r is a reference quantity in the same units.

Time Function
Frequency Spectrum
Amplitude
Time
←T→
1·0
0·5
f₀ = 1/T
f₀ 3f₀ 5f₀ 7f₀
Frequency

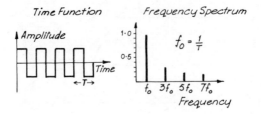

Figure 7.14. *The frequency spectrum of a square wave.*

Time Function
Amplitude
Time
Frequency Spectrum
Frequency

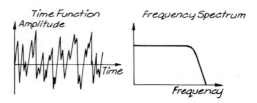

Figure 7.15. *The frequency spectrum of a non-periodic signal.*

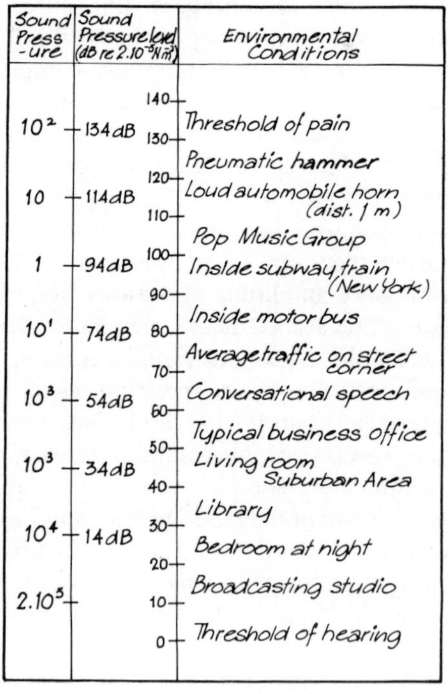

Sound Press -ure
Sound Pressure level (dB re 2.10⁻⁵N/m²)
Environmental Conditions
140
10² 134dB 130 Threshold of pain
Pneumatic hammer
120
10 114dB Loud automobile horn (dist. 1 m)
110
Pop Music Group
100
1 94dB Inside subway train (New York)
90
Inside motor bus
10' 74dB 80
Average traffic on street corner
70
10³ 54dB Conversational speech
60
Typical business office
50
10³ 34dB Living room
Suburban Area
40
Library
10⁴ 14dB 30
Bedroom at night
20
Broadcasting studio
2.10⁵ 10
0 Threshold of hearing

Figure 7.16. *The sound pressure levels of some common sounds.*

Thus, a tenfold increase in power would give 10 dB, and a hundredfold increase in power would give 20 dB. Because the decibel is a logarithmic unit, it gives an approximate indication of the perceived effects of changes in the intensity of sound at different levels. International standards specify the reference quantities for acoustic measurement:

$$\begin{array}{lll}
\text{sound power} & 10^{-12} & \text{watts} \\
\text{sound intensity} & 10^{-12} & \text{watts per square metre} \\
\text{sound pressure} & 2 \times 10^{-5} & \text{newtons per square metre}
\end{array}$$

Such commonly used terms as sound-power level (PWL), intensity level (IL) and sound-pressure level (SPL) are decibel ratios of the appropriate reference quantities; for example, the scale of the sound-pressure level in decibels (dB) referred to 2×10^{-5} N m^{-2} is added to the pressure scale of Figure 7.16. Note that it is of the utmost importance to state the reference quantity for the parameter being measured, because the decibel itself is simply the expression of a ratio.

The phon and sone are loudness scales which take account of the variation in loudness of sounds with frequency (Figure 7.17). Other scales commonly

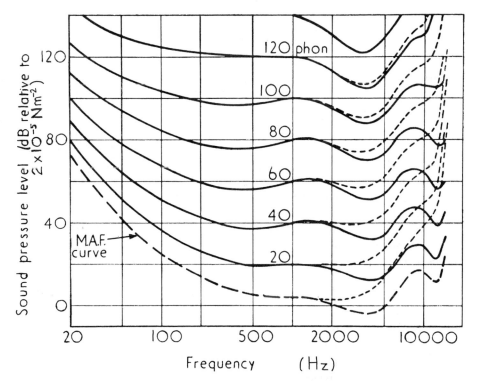

Figure 7.17. *Equal-loudness contours for subjects aged 20 years (solid line) and 60 years (broken). The curve labelled M.A.F. represents the threshold of hearing (minimum audible field). From Robinson and Dadson (1956).*

N-value	Environment in which this value is acceptable
15	Sound broadcasting studio
20-25	Television studio, theatre, large conference room, lecture room
25-30	Bedroom, hospital, living-room, church, cinema, small office
30-40	Larger office, department store, shop, quiet restaurant
40-50	Larger restaurant, secretarial office, gymnasium
50-60	Large typing office
60-70	Workshops

Figure 7.18. *Generally acceptable noise ratings for ambient levels in various types of room.*

used for specifying environmental noise are the noise rating system, or *N* curves (Figure 7.18) and the dBA, dBB, dBC and dBD frequency rating curves used on sound level meters.

7.5 Tape recorders

The modern audio tape recorder provides a convenient and widely used means for the controlled presentation of verbal stimuli. Tape recorders are manufactured in a variety of forms, which may be classified as follows:

(1) Low-cost cassette recorders, usually monophonic and battery-powered.
(2) High-quality mains-powered cassette recorders, with better tape-transport systems and special electronic processing of the audio signal for improved signal-to-noise ratio.
(3) Low-cost reel-to-reel mains-powered stereophonic and monophonic tape recorders, generally using 4-track recording.
(4) Semiprofessional 2- and 4-track stereophonic and quadraphonic tape recorders, with means for monitoring the signal on the tape during the recording process, heavy-duty tape-transport systems and often including a means for remote control of the tapedeck.
(5) Specialized tape recorders, designed to control an automatic slide projector by means of synchronizing pulses recorded on a separate track from the auditory material. These are often based on a recorder in group 1. They may be used in experimental work to operate equipment other than a slide projector.
(6) Professional-quality tape recorders, with multichannel facilities and able to use tape wider than 1/4 in.

The tape recorders found in the laboratory are usually from groups 1 and 4. Monophonic cassette recorders are widely used as electronic notebooks, but

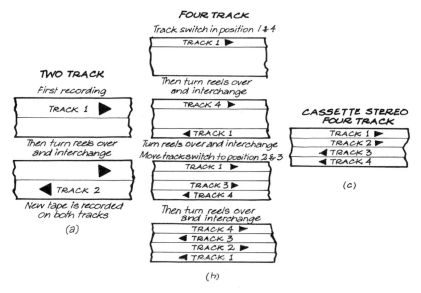

Figure 7.19. *Recording-track arrangements for (a) 2-track and (b) 4-track reel-to-reel monophonic tape recorders. 4-track stereophonic machines put the two channels of one recording on tracks 1 and 3, and the two tracks of a second recording on tracks 4 and 2. The arrangement of tracks for a stereophonic cassette recorder is shown in (c). Tracks 1 and 2 are used for the two channels in one direction, and then the cassette is turned over to record on tracks 4 and 3. Monophonic cassette recorders use tracks of double width, and are therefore compatible with stereophonic recorders.*

they may also be used for stimulus presentation when the audio quality is not critical. Details of the various recording-track arrangements are given in Figure 7.19. Although recorders are manufactured in a wide variety of forms, the basic recording and replaying process is the same in all types of machine. The early recording systems were severely limited by the materials and techniques available at that time. In the 1940s, steel tape was used as a recording medium, and the tape was magnetized by electromagnets placed laterally either side of the tape. The modern tape recorder uses as its medium a thin plastic tape coated on one side with a layer of fine ferromagnetic particles. The recording head is a toroid with a narrow gap in the core. This allows the magnetic flux to pass through the coated side of the tape which is in contact with the surface of the head. For ease of manufacture, the head usually has two gaps (see Figure 7.20), although the gap at the back is kept as small as possible.

The audio signal is stored on the tape in the form of induced magnetic elements in the ferromagnetic coating. The magnetism which remains in this material is not linearly related to the inducing field, and therefore a special high-frequency bias signal is added to the recording signal to produce a linear recording characteristic. The theory of magnetic recording is somewhat complex; for our purpose, it is sufficient to imagine the magnetic flux varying at the bias frequency, which is well above the audio range. The magnetic elements pass

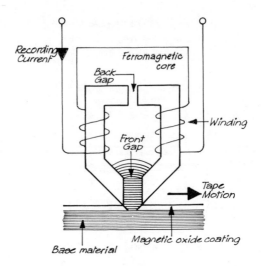

Figure 7.20. *The ring-type magnetic recording head.*

through this flux around the gap in the tape head, and undergo a series of magnetic cyclings. When the elements leave the area of the flux fringe, the magnetic intensity is reduced, and, if no recording signal is present, they stay in a demagnetized state. If a recording signal is present, some flux will remain induced in the element. The recording process, therefore, takes place at the edge of the flux rather than in the gap itself, and, for this reason, a sharp, well defined edge to the flux is more important than a narrow gap. When a tape is replayed, the moving magnetic elements induce a voltage in the coil as they pass through the gap in the replay head. In this case, a narrow gap is important for high-quality reproduction. Low-cost tape recorders use one head for both record and replay, but, in high-quality machines, separate specially designed heads are employed.

Tape recorders are also fitted with an erase head over which the tape passes before reaching the record head. The erase head is supplied with a higher power signal at the same frequency as the recording bias signal. Although the erase head will remove most of any previously recorded material, it is good practice to use a separate bulk eraser when reusing old tapes, otherwise traces of the previous material may be audible, particularly during quiet interstimulus intervals.

Some experience is necessary to obtain good results from a tape recorder. The setting of the record level is critical. If it is too low, then the signal-to-noise ratio on replay will be poor; if it is set too high, the recorded signal will be distorted. Although a recording-level meter is provided, the fundamental variations in level of the sound being recorded make interpretation of the indicated levels rather difficult. Also, on most tape recorders, the level indicator responds only to the average value of the signal, making setting for the peak levels of the signal rather difficult. In the case of machines which have separate record and replay heads, it is possible to monitor the signal from the tape a fraction of a second after it has been recorded. This makes it easier to find a recording level which provides a good signal-to-noise ratio without over recording on the peaks.

Care should be taken that no even slightly magnetized implements such as steel tools are brought close to the tape heads, or the recorded quality will suffer. To guard against this, it is good practice to periodically demagnetize the heads with a special instrument. It is also important to preserve the head geometry, for, if any appreciable damage or wear occurs to the tape guides or heads, the record–replay process will suffer. The various brands of recording tape have somewhat different recording characteristics, and the optimum level of bias signal varies from brand to brand. The setting of bias level is usually an internal adjustment on a tape recorder, and so it is good practice to have a machine adjusted by a technician for best performance with a specified brand of tape.

Stereophonic tape recorders are widely used for the preparation of dichotic stimulus materials. There are considerable problems in preparing tapes with precisely controlled presentation rates and well synchronized pairs of items. The preparation of even a short tape can involve many hours of work. A detailed method for the preparation of dichotic tapes has been described by Leong (1975).

7.6 Audio amplifiers

7.6.1 Preamplifiers

The term preamplifier is applied to amplifiers which are designed to amplify low-level signals in such a manner as to have minimal effect upon the signal-to-noise ratio and with output power not a primary consideration. A preamplifier may also modify the frequency spectrum of the input signal and provide a calibrated means of controlling the gain or degree of amplification. It should also have a wide dynamic range and introduce very little harmonic distortion.

There are several sources of noise in any practical amplifier system. Consider a resistor of value R at an absolute temperature T. The thermal energy of the electrons in the resistor will cause small fluctuations in the voltage across the resistor, the average value being zero. This noise voltage has a continuous frequency spectrum, and is termed white noise, by analogy with light. The open-circuit r.m.s. noise voltage V_n across the resistor increases with the temperature and the resistance as follows:

$$V_n^2 = 4kTBR$$

Where

k = Boltzmann's constant
B = bandwidth over which the measurement is made

Noise originating in this manner is often called Johnson noise.

Another type of noise is found in electronic devices. This has been variously called flicker noise, $1/f$ noise and current noise. It originates from the statistical fluctuations in the flow of electrons around control electrodes in electronic devices, and, with this type of noise, the power per unit bandwidth varies inversely with frequency.

Recording media such as discs and tape do not provide the best overall performance when recordings are made using a uniform frequency response. This is because of practical limitations in the materials and the associated electromechanical systems. For example, disc recordings are made with a rising frequency response above the middle audio frequencies and a falling response below. Such a modification of the spectrum of the signal is termed a recording characteristic. During the evolution of the gramophone, many recording characteristics were in use. At the present time, most recordings conform to a standard characteristic, and modern audio preamplifiers provide equalization in accordance with this standard. The preamplifier modifies the frequency spectrum of the audio signal from the gramophone pickup to give a flat frequency spectrum for the combined record–replay process.

In the case of tape recording, the playback characteristic is defined instead of the recording characteristic. The designer of a tape recorder must ensure that the recording characteristic is such that tapes recorded on his machine will produce a flat frequency response when played on a machine having the standard playback characteristic. The tape playback characteristics in common use are the subject of internationally agreed standards.

Most audio preamplifiers are provided with one pair of bass (or low-frequency) and treble (or high-frequency) tone controls. Usually these are continuously variable controls which produce characteristics within the limits indicated by Figure 7.21. This type of control does not vary the frequency at which cutoff starts to operate, but varies the rate of cutoff above or below a fixed frequency. The circuits normally used allow a maximum slope of 6 dB per octave.

In addition to tone controls, filters are often provided in preamplifiers to

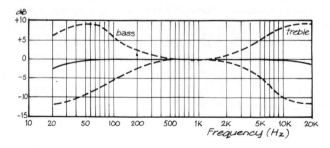

Figure 7.21. *The frequency response of a typical preamplifier, with the tone controls set at zero (solid line), and at their maxima and minima (broken lines).*

123

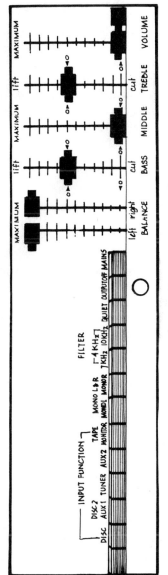

Figure 7.22. *A typical preamplifier (Radford Audio model SC-24).*

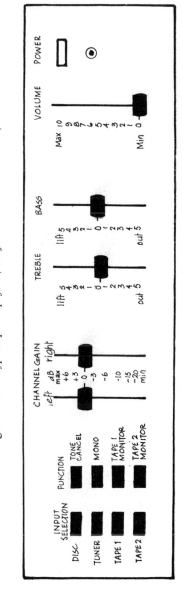

Figure 7.23. *A typical integrated stereophonic amplifier (Radford Audio model HD250).*

124

reduce the effects of extraneous noise in the system at the extremes of the audio range. For example, turntable rumble occurs at low frequencies, and recording distortion is often present in the high frequencies. Most audio preamplifiers incorporate a permanent rumble filter, that is they have been designed to provide a very rapid falloff in frequency response below about 25 Hz. If high-frequency filters are provided, there is usually a choice of cutoff frequencies, typically 5 or 10 kHz.

It is sometimes convenient to build the preamplifier as a separate unit with its own power supply, and use it remotely from the power amplifiers (Figure 7.22). If headphones are to be used in an experiment, then power amplifiers may be unnecessary. At other times, it is more convenient to have the preamplifier and power amplifier integrated into the same mechanical assembly (Figure 7.23).

7.6.2 *Power amplifiers*

The audio power amplifier is connected between the preamplifier and the loudspeaker in the audio reproduction chain. As its name implies, it provides power to drive the loudspeaker in response to input signals in the form of an alternating voltage of varying amplitude.

A power amplifier is required to represent the input signal faithfully in the power produced at its output terminals. Since the active devices used, either valves or transistors, have nonlinear characteristics, special measures must be taken to ensure that the amplifier has a linear response. Other important characteristics are freedom from distortion, a wide power bandwidth, a good signal-to-noise ratio, freedom from instability and a high degree of loudspeaker damping.

The forms in which specifications for power amplifiers may be presented differ greatly, and there is no universally adopted standard of minimum acceptable performance for an audio power amplifier of a given power rating. The amplifier power rating describes the amount of power available. This figure, usually expressed in watts, is subject to a number of qualifications. In the audio industry, various methods of expressing the power rating have been introduced. These refer to particular operating conditions, and have little meaning without further clarification. The best way of describing the output power of an amplifier is in terms of the maximum r.m.s. level of continuous sine-wave output which the amplifier is capable of producing. Alternatively, it may be acceptable to quote the intermittent maximum power rating, often termed the music power. This is equivalent to the peak level of the positive or negative halfcycle of the alternating output signal. More rarely, the term peak power is used. This is twice the music power, and corresponds to more than 2·8 times the r.m.s. level. Figure 7.24 gives a rather simplified representation of the relationship between these various ratings. For audio signals which are not pure sine waves, the r.m.s. value is not 0·707 of the zero-to-peak value. Some specifications use the term peak level for the zero-to-peak

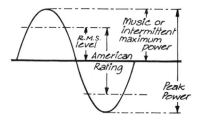

Figure 7.24. *A diagrammatic comparison of power-rating specifications.*

value, and not for the peak-to-peak value, as might be expected. The method termed American rating gives a power rating which is twice the r.m.s. rating.

Although the r.m.s. rating indicates the maximum safe level of continuous sine-wave output, an amplifier can usually supply a higher level of power for brief periods without serious levels of distortion. This is possible because the capacitors of the power supply provide a reserve of stored energy. Because audio signals are not usually continuous sine waves, the music-power rating gives additional useful information. Clearly, for laboratory use with sine waves, the amplifier should be limited to its r.m.s. rating. To give some idea of the power levels required to drive high-quality loudspeakers, it is usually considered that, for an average-sized domestic room, the r.m.s. output power rating should be at least 10 W for monophonic and 6 W per channel for stereophonic reproduction.

One of the best known parameters of amplifier performance is the frequency response. It is also the least important, because modern amplifiers can easily cover the whole audio spectrum. The frequency response specifies the upper and lower frequency limits of the useful response of the amplifier. Upper and lower tolerances are usually quoted in decibels, but, in the absence of an explicit statement, it may be assumed that the response quoted refers to a permissible deviation of ± 3 dB. The frequency at which the response drops by 3 dB is sometimes termed the half-power point.

In the case of a power amplifier, the input signal has usually been equalized and the level controlled by the preamplifier. The power amplifier is required to translate the signal into faithful power deviations for driving the loudspeaker. The input impedance of a power amplifier is normally high, in the region of 100 kΩ. The output is designed to drive a low impedance, usually in the range 3–16 Ω, in order to match a loudspeaker. Negative feedback is often employed to provide a linear response. When an output transformer is fitted, usually in a valve amplifier, its design greatly affects the performance of the amplifier at the extremes of the audio spectrum. The core of the transformer must be of generous size to handle the lower frequencies, and the windings must be closely coupled for a good high-frequency response. The frequency response of an amplifier is often measured at a very low power level. At low levels, the amplifier is not overstrained, and can easily provide an adequate response. It is important to ensure that an adequate frequency response is also maintained when the output power approaches the maximum.

Active components introduce some degree of harmonic distortion, because of their nonlinear operation. The distortion factor is the ratio of the various components of the 2nd- , 3rd- , 4th- , 5th- etc. harmonic distortion to the fundamental, and is usually expressed as a percentage:

$$D = \frac{100}{E} \times \sqrt{(D_2{}^2 + D_3{}^2 + D_4{}^2 + \ldots + D_n{}^2)}$$

where

D = distortion content
D_n = distortion at the nth harmonic
E = signal output

The distortion figure varies with output power, and therefore it is customary to plot the distortion factor against power output. An amplifier should give a low distortion factor (less than 0.1%) over its operating range. Distortion increases rapidly as the maximum power level is exceeded.

High-fidelity amplifiers often have a wide power bandwidth, that is they can deliver their rated power over a wide range of frequencies. This can lead to problems with loudspeakers which are not designed to handle high power levels at very low or very high frequencies, and may even result in damage to the loudspeakers.

The damping factor is another important parameter of an audio amplifier. When a loudspeaker cone is driven, some of the energy remains in the cone. If the signal is suddenly removed, this energy is usually dissipated in the form of decaying oscillations. These oscillations are undesirable as they add colouration to the reproduced sound. During the oscillations, a back e.m.f. is produced in the speech coil, driving a current back through the output circuit of the amplifier. If the source impedance of the amplifier is high, a long time will elapse before the power from the cone is absorbed, thus damping down the oscillations. A lower source impedance allows more current to flow, resulting in a more effective damping of the oscillations. The damping factor is the ratio of the load impedance to the source impedance, and so a high damping factor indicates a desirable low source impedance.

The intermodulation distortion of an amplifier specifies the extent to which spurious frequencies are produced when amplifying two or more different input frequencies. Intermodulation distortion is not entirely predictable from the commonly specified harmonic distortion factor, although, for high-quality reproduction of complex sounds, it is more critical. If the input to an amplifier contains two or more frequencies (that is the input is other than a pure tone), the nonlinearity in the amplifier causes the production of frequencies which are the sum and difference of the input frequencies. Such distortion is particularly unpleasant, because the sum and difference frequencies do not generally bear a harmonic relationship to each other or to the input frequencies. Negative feedback is used to reduce intermodulation distortion.

To measure intermodulation distortion, two known frequencies are fed into the amplifier. These are then filtered from the output and the remaining signal is measured. The output level is then expressed as a percentage of the total output. For high-quality reproduction, the intermodulation distortion should not exceed 3%. The frequencies selected and their amplitude ratios greatly affect the value of intermodulation distortion. Consequently, a standard procedure is necessary when making comparisons between various amplifiers.

Audio amplifiers should have a high signal-to-noise ratio. All amplifiers add some noise to the signal, but modern amplifiers should have signal-to-noise ratios of at least 50 dB. A more serious problem in many audio systems is mains frequency hum, that is interference at the electrical supply frequency. In order to reduce hum, interconnecting leads should be screened by an earthed metal braid. Trial and error methods are usually best for arranging the earth connection between items of audio equipment to give the minimum hum level.

7.6.3 Attenuators and filters

Variation in the level of an audio signal is best accomplished by means of variable attenuators. These allow the ratio of the output to input voltage to be changed manually, without introducing the changes of impedance which follow from the use of a simple potential divider circuit. Audio attenuators for use in signal lines normally have an impedance of 600 Ω, and those used between power amplifiers and loudspeakers have an impedance around 10 Ω. Although it is possible to make variable attenuators by combining potentiometers on a common shaft, switched decade attenuators are usually employed for precision work. A 3-decade attenuator will allow an attenuation range of 0–111 dB in 0·1 dB steps. Each decade (0·1 dB, 1 dB and 10 dB intervals) is additive when working in decibels (see Section 7.4). Programmable attenuators are also available which can be controlled by logic levels from solid-state programming modules or laboratory computers.

In Section 7.4, we introduced the use of frequency analysis for the description of continuous sound. To carry out a frequency analysis, the energy levels are measured between a series of frequency intervals. In building up the frequency analysis, the range of interest may be examined using either bands of constant frequency or bands whose width is proportional to the midfrequency of the interval.

An ideal filter will pass a particular range of frequencies, known as its passband, with zero attenuation, and reject frequencies outside this passband with infinite attenuation. Although the lower and upper limiting frequencies of the passband, f_1 and f_2, respectively, fully define the characteristics of such an ideal filter, a filter normally is specified by its centre frequency and its bandwidth. The centre frequency f_c is the geometric mean of the passband:

$$f_c = \sqrt{(f_1 \times f_2)}$$

and the bandwidth is given by

$$B = f_2 - f_1$$

Filters used for acoustic measurement may be either of the constant band-width or constant percentage bandwidth type. The bandwidth of a constant percentage bandwidth filter is proportional to its centre frequency, and so the bandwidth of a 6% bandwidth filter would be 6% of the particular centre frequency to which the filter was set. The widest bandwidth filter commonly used for acoustic measurement is the octave-band filter, the name being taken from the field of music and corresponding to a doubling of the frequency. Thus, the octave-band filter is a constant bandwidth filter in which

$$f_2 = 2 \times f_1$$

and therefore

$$f_c = \sqrt{(f_1 \times 2 \times f_1)}$$
$$= (\sqrt{2}) \times f_1$$

and

$$B = 2 \times f_1 - f_1$$
$$= f_1$$
$$= \frac{f_c}{\sqrt{2}} \quad \text{or approximately } 70\% f_c$$

In a practical filter, the transition from the passband to the stopband is not absolutely sharp, and the passband is usually specified to the 3 dB or half-power points.

Filters with other characteristics are commonly used for signal conditioning. High pass filters attenuate frequencies below a specified value, and low pass filters attenuate frequencies above a specified value. In these cases, it is often desirable for the filters to have more gradual transitions in attenuation between the passband and stopband. Signal-conditioning filters commonly have slopes in the region of 6–12 dB per octave. High pass and low pass filters are often incorporated in physiological preamplifiers, to allow the frequency response of the amplifier to be matched to that of the wanted signal. When a signal is filtered before being sampled by an analogue–digital converter, the filter should remove as much as possible of the signal at frequencies higher than half the sampling rate (Section 1.4). The filter used for this purpose should have a very rapid transition from its passband to its stopband, about 48 dB per octave is desirable.

7.7 Audio oscillators

Pure tone stimuli are, of course, widely used in psychoacoustic research. Also, because tones of different frequencies and waveforms can be produced with precise timing, they are often used in other areas of psychology, for example in reaction-time studies.

Instruments which provide audio signals are given various names, such as audio oscillators, test oscillators, function generators and so on. The names chosen depend on the mode of operation of the instrument and on its intended use. The oscillator circuit is basic to all the sources; it generates sine waves of known frequency and amplitude. In more recent instruments, the term test oscillator is used to describe an oscillator having a calibrated attenuator and a meter on which the output can be monitored. The term signal generator is usually reserved for an oscillator which provides signals at radio frequencies rather than in the audio spectrum. The function generator is a source which provides sophisticated control of the frequency and waveform of the output signal. It usually also allows the generation of a series of complete cycles of the selected waveform, starting and stopping at the zero crossing point. Function generators are thus a convenient source of clickless audio stimuli. In this section, we are mainly concerned with instruments which can be used as a source of auditory stimuli. A discussion of the various electronic instruments which are used as general signal sources in electronics is given in Section 6.3.

When selecting an oscillator, the main criterion is its frequency range. For audio stimuli, a basic range of 20 Hz to 20 kHz is required. Commercial audio oscillators usually have a range well in excess of this requirement. The second concern is usually the available output voltage or power. Some applications require large amounts of power. The instrument may, for example, be required to drive a loudspeaker directly. If it is merely providing a signal to drive a power amplifier, only microwatts will be required. Commercial oscillators are available to suit any likely laboratory application.

In addition to the frequency range and power output, other important considerations are the precision with which the controls can be set to a required value, the stability of the frequency and amplitude, the distortion in the output waveform and the amount of mains hum and noise in the output signal.

When the dial of the oscillator is set to a particular frequency, the oscillator should ideally deliver that frequency at all times. The dial accuracy of most oscillators is around $\pm 2\%$. In some cases, the dial has a vernier scale, which enables the main scale markings to be interpolated with accuracy. Some modern oscillators have digital control of frequency and amplitude, and can be set to an accuracy of about 1 in 10^4.

The frequency stability of an oscillator is a measure of its ability to maintain a selected frequency over a period of time. Stability is affected by such factors as:

(1) long-term changes in the values of components over time,
(2) sensitivity of some components to changes in temperature,
(3) the effects of fluctuations in power-supply voltage levels.

Good design practices, such as large amounts of negative feedback and careful choice of components in the frequency-determining networks, are important for good long-term stability. Amplitude stability is also important in many applications. A particularly troublesome defect which is found in many poorly designed oscillators is a marked change in the amplitude of the output when the frequency is changed.

Distortion in the output waveform is undesirable, because harmonics of the required frequency will be included in the signal. In most cases, however, the devices used to convert the electrical signal to an acoustic form will produce far more distortion than the source, and therefore the small amount of distortion produced by an oscillators can usually be neglected.

Mains frequency hum and noise may be introduced at a variety of points in an oscillator circuit, but it is usually produced by the final power amplifier. The amount of hum and noise is usually negligible in comparison with the maximum signal level, but problems can arise when generating low-level signals if the output control is on the input side of the power amplifier. For this reason, many oscillators have their amplitude control on the output side of the power amplifier, thus ensuring that hum and noise are reduced in proportion to the signal.

When presenting a tone to a subject for a finite period of time, it is necessary for the signal to start and to stop. If this is done by simple electromechanical switching, then clicks will be heard at the start and stop of the signal, due to the introduction of transients at the arbitrary switching points. There may be more than a single start or stop transient caused by the contacts bouncing and the uncertainty of contact at the instant of switching. There are two basic methods for producing clickless switching of audio signals. One is to use electronic circuits to switch the signal rapidly at an instant when it crosses the zero axis, thereby producing an integral number of cycles in the tone burst. This is the method used by the function generators discussed earlier in this section. The second, and older, technique is to use a special circuit to increase or decrease the level of the signal smoothly at the beginning or end of the tone burst. A combination of tungsten lamp and photocell is often used for this purpose.

7.8 Summary

In this chapter, we have discussed the main components in the audio recording and reproduction chain. The various types of microphones have different characteristics, and these should be borne in mind when selecting a microphone for a particular application; the directional characteristics are particularly important. A loudspeaker is a convenient acoustic source, but headphones provide better control of the stimulus, and should be used when possible. The acoustic properties of an auditory stimulus are specified in terms of its frequency spectrum and intensity. The unit of intensity is the decibel.

Speech stimuli are normally prerecorded on magnetic tape, but tone stimuli can be generated by an audio oscillator during the course of an experiment. Special switching techniques are used to minimize transient clicks at the start and stop of the tone.

CHAPTER 8

Visual Stimuli

8.1 Light sources

Light is a form of electromagnetic radiation belonging to the same class of physical phenomena as radio waves, X rays and cosmic rays (see Figure 8.1). Simultaneously, it exhibits the apparently contradictory properties of particles of energy and of waves propagated in a medium.

According to the particle theory, radiant energy is emitted from a source in the form of individual light quanta, or photons, which travel with a constant velocity in a vacuum, but which may differ in energy. When they are travelling through a transparent substance, the velocity of the particles is lower, so that a particle may change velocity when it passes from one medium to another. Particles may also undergo a change of direction (refraction) when passing between media. Opaque substances may convert the particles into other forms of energy, and some surfaces have the property of reflecting particles by changing their direction of movement, while leaving the characteristic energy of the particles unchanged.

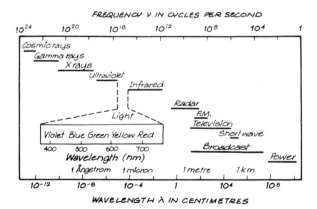

Figure 8.1. *The electromagnetic spectrum. From IES (1959).*

The energy E and frequency v of a photon are related to each other by the equation

$$E = hv$$

where the constant of proportionality h is known as Planck's constant. Visible light occupies only the narrow limits of the electromagnetic spectrum indicated in Figure 8.1. The wavelength λ of a photon is inversely proportional to its frequency v:

$$\lambda = \frac{c}{v}$$

where c is the velocity of light. In a vacuum, this is $2 \cdot 998 \times 10^8$ m s^{-1}.

There are two main ways in which energy is made available for the production of photons. Incandescence involves the emission of photons as a result of the motion of molecules at a high temperature. Molecules are constantly in motion, and this motion increases as the temperature rises. Incandescent radiation contains a fairly wide and continuous range of frequencies, regardless of the nature of the source. The other process is luminescence, which involves the excitation of electrons within atoms, and produces light with a wavelength which is characteristic both of the substance and the energy level of the electron which gave rise to the radiation.

8.1.1 Tungsten filament lamp

Incandescence is the high-energy discharge of photons from thermally agitated molecules. The energy of the photons so released does not have discrete values, as in the case of luminescence, but varies continuously from a lower to an upper limit which varies with the temperature.

Substances differ in their ability to radiate energy by incandescence, the ideal being termed a black-body radiator. In practice, this is approximated

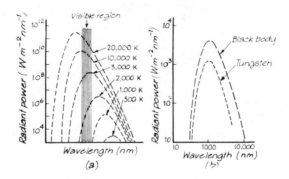

Figure 8.2. (a) Black-body radiation curves for various temperatures, (b) black-body and tungsten radiation curves at 3000 K. From IES (1959).

by a hollow chamber which may be raised to the desired temperature (Figure 8.2a). A selective radiator, such as a tungsten filament (Figure 8.2b), produces a spectrum of similar form to that of a black body, but with somewhat less radiation, particularly at the longer wavelengths. For the purposes of describing the visual characteristics of a continuous spectrum, it is usually possible to find a black-body temperature such that the balance of red and blue light in the spectrum so produced matches that in the source to be described. The absolute temperature of such a black body gives the colour temperature of the source to be described. The colour temperature for the spectrum of the 3000 K tungsten filament in Figure 8.2b is about 2700 K.

Tungsten filament lamps are widely used as light sources in visual research. Although the characteristics of such lamps are fairly stable over short periods, they are subject to long-term changes. Evaporation of the tungsten filament causes changes in its electrical resistance and hence in its operating temperature. The evaporated tungsten is also deposited on the glass envelope, causing a reduction in the light output.

When tungsten lamps are operated from an a.c. supply, the light output includes a flicker component at twice the supply frequency. If this is unacceptable, as for example in flicker-fusion work, the lamp should be operated from a smoothed d.c. supply. If it is necessary to switch tungsten lamps frequently, steps should be taken to reduce the magnitude of the thermal shock, or the life of the lamps will be considerably shortened. This may be done by allowing some current to flow through the lamp when the switch is off, or by providing means of slowly raising and lowering the operating voltage.

8.1.2 Gas discharge tube

Luminescence can best be described in terms of atomic theory. As we discussed in Section 5.2, electrons are grouped into shells according to their energy level in relation to the nucleus. If anything causes an electron to be displaced from one energy level to another of lower energy, there is a release of energy in the form of a photon. An electron will drop from a higher shell to fill up a lower shell if a vacancy has been caused by the displacement of an electron from the lower shell. This may occur as a result of a collision with another free electron travelling at high velocity. The collision could either knock the electron free from the atom or move it into a higher energy level. The energy of the photons released by this mechanism has one of several fixed values, depending upon the particular rearrangement which occurs. Electron displacements between adjacent levels give rise to lower-energy photons (redder light) than those between levels which are further apart. Thus, the luminescent spectra of different substances contain lines at characterisic wavelengths.

If the two energy levels are respectively E_1 and E_2, the frequency v of the emitted photon is given by

$$Hv = E_1 - E_2$$

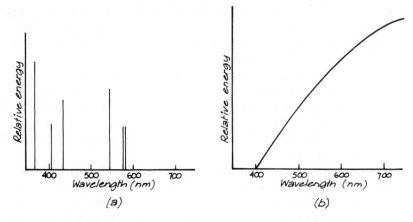

Figure 8.3. *(a) The line spectrum of a mercury-vapour lamp, (b) the continuous spectrum of an incandescent source at 2854 K (CIE Illuminant A).*

Both neon and mercury discharge tubes are frequently used in optical research to provide sources of known wavelength. For visual research, however, the continuous spectrum of a tungsten filament lamp is usually preferred to that of a line spectrum from, for example, a mercury-vapour lamp (Figure 8.3). Glow discharge tubes, sometimes called cold-cathode tubes, form the basis of many electronic alphanumeric displays (Section 8.7.3).

8.1.3 *Fluorescent tube*

Fluorescence is a type of luminescence in which high-frequency photons excite a substance causing it to emit photons of lower energy. The spectrum of a mercury-vapour lamp (Figure 8.3) contains a high proportion of invisible ultraviolet light. In the conventional fluorescent tube, part of this energy is absorbed by phosphors on the inner surface of the tube, and this causes the release of photons in the visible region. Thus, the coating transforms invisible radiation into visible light, and, by a suitable choice of phosphors (typically calcium tungstate, zinc sulphide, zinc silicate), the light from the lamp can be given a wide variety of colours. Figure 8.4 shows in diagrammatic form the excitation of a typical fluorescent lamp and its emission spectrum.

Fluorescent lamps are normally operated from the a.c. mains supply and require special control gear (Figure 8.5). This includes an inductor which is connected in series with the lamp. The main function of the inductor is to limit the current which can flow through the lamp, but it also plays a part in initiating the discharge. The starting of the lamp is controlled by a small auxiliary glow lamp provided with a thermal contact and connected in parallel with the fluorescent tube. When the supply is first switched on, the bimetallic thermal contact is open, and the glow lamp conducts. This causes the bimetallic strip to heat up and close the contact, allowing current to flow through the fluorescent

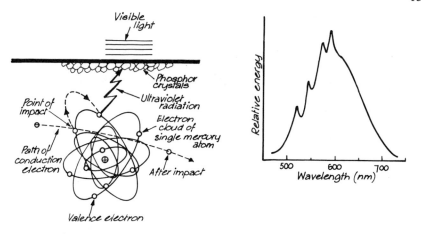

Figure 8.4. *Excitation in a fluorescent lamp. From IES (1959).*

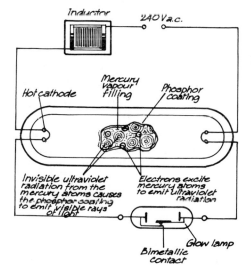

Figure 8.5. *Control gear for a fluorescent lamp.*

tube heaters and also shorting out the glow lamp. The bimetallic strip quickly cools and breaks the contact, interrupting the current flowing through the inductor. The sudden interruption of the current flowing through the inductor causes a voltage surge (Section 5.5) which establishes the discharge in the fluorescent tube. Since the glow lamp strikes at a higher voltage than is maintained across the operating fluorescent tube, it ceases to function. The heaters of the fluorescent tube are kept hot by the ionic bombardment, and so the lamp continues to function as long as the supply is maintained.

The main advantage of the fluorescent lamp is that, because nearly all its output is within the visible range, it is very efficient. It is also widely used for room lighting, because its large emitting area produces soft shadows. When fluorescent tubes are operated from a direct-current supply, an inductor cannot be used to limit the operating current, and so a different type of control circuit is required (Section 8.5).

8.1.4 *Light-emitting diode*

Silicon and germanium are the best known semiconductors, but they are not the only semiconductor materials. During investigations into the properties of other substances, it was found that some semiconductors emit radiation when current flows through them. The light-emitting diodes (LEDs) which are currently manufactured have $p-n$ junctions (Section 5.9.2), and are made from gallium phosphide (GaP) or gallium arsenide phosphide (GaAsP). They emit red or green light when they are forward-biased. This light is produced by the recombination of electrons and holes in the region of the junction.

The materials and fabrication processes involved in the manufacture of light-emitting diodes are expensive, but they are similar to those involved in the manufacturer of transistors and integrated circuits. Consequently, manufacturers have concentrated their effort into the mass production of small indicator lamps and assemblies of LEDs in the form of miniature numeric displays (Section 8.7.3), such as are used in pocket calculators and digital watches.

The luminous flux from a light-emitting diode is low, making it unsuitable for illumination of other objects, but, because the source is small, it has a high luminous intensity when viewed directly. LEDs operate on low voltages, and are electrically compatible with integrated circuits. They are very reliable devices, and can be switched very rapidly, because the light output is unaffected by thermal inertia.

8.1.5 *Electroluminescent panel*

Electroluminescent panels glow with luminance levels similar to a surface illuminated by normal ambient lighting, and are useful when a large area of even luminance is required. The light is emitted by direct electrical stimulation of a phosphor, usually doped zinc sulphide, which is sandwiched between a transparent conducting coating and a metal backing plate. The phosphor is a poor conductor, making the panel behave rather like a capacitor. Therefore, to make current flow through the panel, it must be driven by an alternating voltage. There is a maximum value of voltage which may be applied to any type of electroluminescent panel before it will be damaged by electrical breakdown of the phosphor, and so, if the luminance is too low when the panel is driven at mains frequency, the current through the panel should be increased by driving it from a higher-frequency source. Early types of panel were rather dim, and had a short working life. Although modern panels are quite bright and reliable, the device has a bad reputation, and is not widely used.

Because the panels are quite cool when operating, they provide a convenient way to display photographic transparencies. Gregory (1969) has used electro-luminescent panels in a tachistoscope, control of luminance being provided by variable transformers of the Variac type.

8.2 Photometry

The four standard photometric units are the candela, the lumen, the lux the candela per square metre. The candela is a basic SI unit, like the metre, kilogram and second. These four photometric units relate to the following four quantities:

(1) Luminous intensity, which corresponds physically to the brightness of a point source of light.
(2) Luminous flux, which is the rate of flow of light from a source into a solid angle over which the measurement is made.
(3) Illuminance, which is the luminous flux per unit area falling upon a surface.
(4) Luminance, which corresponds physically to the brightness of an illuminated surface.

Luminous intensity is roughly equivalent to the popular term candle power. Since 1948, the standard unit has been the candela (cd), which is defined in terms of the luminous intensity of a black-body radiator at the solidification temperature of platinum. For practical purposes, secondary standards, in the form of specially designed tungsten filament lamps, are used. Calibration services for such lamps are provided by national standards laboratories.

A point source will emit light in all directions. If we visualize a sphere with the point source at its centre, then luminous flux is the light flowing through a defined section of the sphere. The unit of luminous flux is the lumen (lm), which is defined as the light energy emitted per second within a solid angle of 1 steradian (sr) by a point source of 1 cd luminous intensity.

The steradian is defined as follows. If a sphere of radius r has an area equal to r^2 marked on its surface, then the solid angle subtended by this area at the surface of the sphere is 1 sr. Because the surface area of a sphere is $4\pi r^2$, the complete sphere subtends 4π sr, and so the total luminous flux from a point source of 1 cd is 12·57 lm. The term unit solid angle is sometimes used in preference to steradian.

When the luminous flux falls on the inner surface of the sphere, it is illuminated. Illuminance is defined in terms of luminous flux and the area of the surface. The unit of illuminance is the lux (lx), which is the illuminance produced by 1 lm falling perpendicularly on an area of 1 m². Thus, a point source of 1 cd at the centre of a sphere of radius 1 m will produce a luminous flux of 1 lm m^{-2} at the sphere, and hence an illuminance of 1 lx on the inner surface. Most photometry is concerned with luminous flux falling on flat surfaces, and, for small angles, the difference between flat and spherical surfaces can often be ignored. When large angles are subtended, the appropriate geometrical corrections are necessary.

Luminance is a measure of the light actually emitted per unit area of an illuminated or self-luminous surface. The standard unit of luminance is the candela per square metre (cd m^{-2}). A perfectly diffuse white surface with unity reflectance will have a luminance of $1/\pi$ cd m^{-2} when it is illuminated at 1 lx. Freshly deposited magnesium oxide has a reflectance of about 98%. Non-preferred units of luminance which are still in common use are the lambert (lumen per square centimetre) and the foot-lambert (lumen per square foot). Figure 8.6 shows typical luminance values for a wide range of stimuli.

Although photometric units are expressed in terms of light, they assume a spectral response curve, the CIE standard observer, which is typical of human vision. Individual visual systems do not have an unchanging spectral response curve. Real observers differ one from another, and also change with varying levels of luminous flux. Photometric units are appropriate for human visual work, but, if the work has no application to human vision, then radiometric units should be used. These are based on the radiated power, and do not assume the response curve of human vision. The relationship between radiometric and photometric units is explained very clearly by Tyler (1973).

Some nonpreferred photometric units which are still in common use may be converted to SI units as follows:

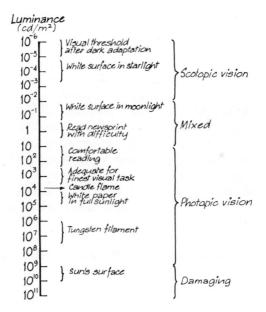

Figure 8.6. *Typical luminance values for a range of stimuli.*

Illuminance:
1 phot (lm cm^{-2}) $= 10^4 \text{ lx}$
1 foot–candle (lm ft^{-2}) $= 10\cdot76 \text{ lx}$

Luminance:
1 stilb (cd cm^{-2}) $= 10^4 \text{ cd m}^{-2}$
1 candela per square foot $= 10\cdot76 \text{ cd m}^{-2}$
1 apostilb (lm m^{-2}) $= 0\cdot3183 \text{ cd m}^{-2}$
1 lambert (lm cm^{-2}) $= 3183 \text{ cd m}^{-2}$
1 millilambert (mL) $= 3\cdot183 \text{ cd m}^{-2}$
1 foot–lambert (lm ft^{-2}) $= 3\cdot43 \text{ cd m}^{-2}$

The nit is an obsolete term for candela per square metre. A standard text on photometry has been written by Walsh (1958).

In visual work, it is often desirable to define the stimulus in terms of the light reaching the retina. The light arriving at the receptors is not a constant fraction of the light radiated by a visual stimulus. A fairly constant loss takes place in the optic media, but a major problem results from the constriction of the pupil. As the light passing through a lens is proportional to the area of its aperture, the product of luminance and pupillary area can be used as a unit of retinal stimulation. The troland is defined as the product of luminance, in candelas per square metre, and pupillary area, in square millimetres. A difficulty in the use of the troland is that the pupil size is quite variable. For some experiments, atropine, or some other drug, may be used to dilate the pupil to a constant size, but a more usual method is to use an artificial pupil, which is smaller than any constriction which the subject is likely to generate. This is done by using an aperture or the Maxwellian view (Section 8.7). Light entering the marginal zones of the pupil is less effective in receptor stimulation than light entering the central region. This is known as the Stiles–Crawford effect.

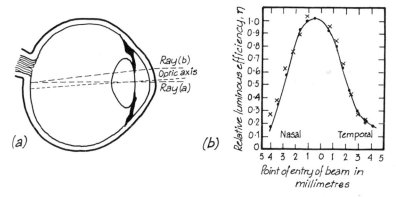

Figure 8.7. (a) The eye in horizontal section to show the Stiles–Crawford effect, (b) the relative luminous efficiency of light entering a pupil at various points in a horizontal plane through the centre of the eye. From Stiles and Crawford (1933).

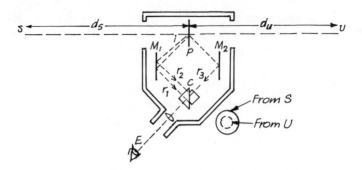

Figure 8.8. *Principle of the Lummer–Brodhun photometer.*

Figure 8.7 shows that marginal rays may be one third as effective as central rays. The effect is minimized by the use of a small central aperture.

A typical device for the measurement of luminous intensity is the Lummer–Brodhun photometer shown in Figure 8.8. Light from a standard source S illuminates one face of a magnesium oxide diffusing plate P. The other side of the plate is illuminated by the unknown source U. Rays r_1 and r_2 from one side of the plate reach the eye E by reflection in mirror M_1 and total reflection from the diagonal outer uncemented surfaces of glass cube C. Ray r_3 is reflected in mirror M_2, and passes through the cemented central portion of cube C. Thus, the visual field from E consists of an inner circular disc flooded with light from U, and an outer annulus flooded with light from S. The observer moves the unknown lamp along a track until the annulus matches the disc in luminance, that is until the two sides of the plate P are equally illuminated. From a knowledge of the luminous intensity I_s of the standard source, the distance d_s of the standard source and the distance d_u of the unknown source from the plate, the luminous intensity I_u of the unknown source may be calculated by the inverse-square law (Figure 8.9):

$$\frac{I_u}{I_s} = \frac{d_s^2}{d_u^2}$$

The Macbeth illuminometer (Figure 8.10) is a typical instrument for precise measurement of illuminance and luminance. In this device, rays from a white test plate of known reflectance pass directly through the centre of the Lummer cube. Rays from source S illuminate a diffusing screen D which is viewed in the annulus of the field of view. The distance of S from D is varied by the rack-and-pinion gear R to give a match between the disc and annulus. A scale on the rack and pinion gives a direct reading of illuminance if the instrument has been calibrated by the use of a standard lamp.

Measurement of illuminance may also be made by the use of instruments based on photoelectric cells. Such instruments use a moving-coil meter calibrated directly in units of illuminance when the cell is placed on the illuminated

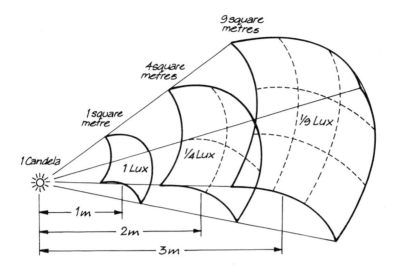

Figure 8.9. *Diagram showing the effect of the inverse-square law on illumination. The source of 1 cd produces a flux of 1 lm in the solid angle shown of 1 sr. At a radius of 1 m, the angle encloses a spherical surface of 1 m² and an illuminance of 1 lx results. At a radius of 2 m, the area is 4 m², and so the illuminance must be reduced to 1/4 lx. Similarly, at 3 m, the illuminance will be 1/9 lx. Thus, the illuminance from a point source varies inversely as the square of the distance.*

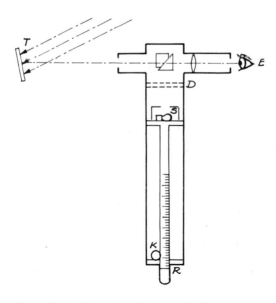

Figure 8.10. *Principle of the Macbeth illuminometer.*

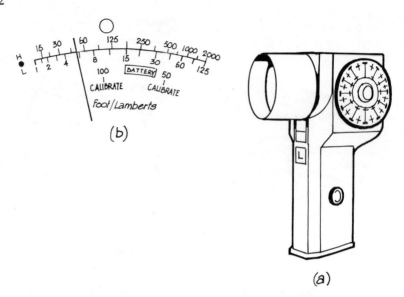

Figure 8.11. *A typical narrow-angle reflected-light luminance meter (a). The view through the eyepiece shows the scene in front of the meter. The circle indicates the area of measurement, with the meter scale and pointer superimposed (b) (Pentax Spotmeter model FL).*

surface. Filters are fitted to give the instrument spectral characteristics similar to those of the human eye. Photographic incident-light exposure meters are of similar design, and can be used to make rough measurements of illuminance. If the meter is set for a film speed of 100 ASA and an aperture of $f/16$, the illuminance will be given by the approximate formula

$$\text{lux} = \frac{2000}{T}$$

where T is the exposure time indicated by the meter in seconds. Thus, if an exposure of 1/50 s is indicated, then the illuminance is about 100,000 lx. Photographic principles are discussed in Section 8.7.1.

The more usual photographic exposure meters are of the reflected-light type, and provide a robust and convenient means for measurement of approximate values of the luminance of stimuli. Sometimes such meters are available scaled in luminance units (Figure 8.11), otherwise exposure times may be converted to luminance units by the approximate formula

$$\text{candelas per square metre} = \frac{150}{T}$$

Again the film speed should be set to 100 ASA and the aperture to $f/16$. Coren and Miller (1973) have given a detailed account of the use of photographic exposure meters for the measurement of luminance.

8.3 Control of luminance

In visual research, it is often necessary to vary the luminance of a stimulus. There are three basically different ways of doing this:

(1) by manipulating the intensity of the source,
(2) by varying the distance between the source and the stimulus field,
(3) by interposing an attenuator in the optical path between the source and stimulus field.

It is easy to vary the intensity of a tungsten-filament lamp by altering the voltage across the filament. This method, however, produces marked changes in the colour temperature of the emitted light, and consequently it is not the preferred method when using tungsten filament lamps. The intensity of some other sources, however, can be varied in this manner without unduly affecting the spectral quality; the intensity of fluorescent tubes and light-emitting diodes varies with the current, and the luminance of electroluminescent panels can be controlled by varying the voltage. Specially designed gas discharge tubes, known as glow modulators, have a highly linear relationship between luminous intensity and cathode current; they are mainly used in facsimile transmission equipment, but have also been used in visual research. Unfortunately, the spectral characteristics of all the sources which can be directly controlled renders them unsuited to most investigations in which colour is an important factor. In most quantitative visual investigations, the light source is a tungsten filament lamp which is energized from a stabilized d.c. supply, and the luminace is varied by one of the other methods.

An absolute method for varying the luminance employs the inverse-square law, varying the distance of the source from the stimulus field in the same manner as in the Lummer–Brodhun photometer (Section 8.2). This method gives high precision when the source approximates to a point (that is it subtends a small angle at the stimulus field), but, for extended sources, the relationship is only approximate. This places a lower limit on the distance between the source and field, and so very long distances are necessary to cover the wide range of intensities involved in visual work.

The most widely used method for varying the intensity of a stimulus in visual research is to interpose a filter between the source and the stimulus field. The filter transmits a certain proportion of the light, the remainder being absorbed or reflected. The transmittance of an optical filter is the ratio of the incident to the transmitted flux. The reciprocal of the transmittance is known as the density of the filter. Thus, as the density of a filter increases, the proportion of the light transmitted decreases. A neutral-density filter has a density which is independent of the wavelength of the incident light, that is it will add no colouration to white light. Inexpensive gelatine filters are manufactured in a wide range of densities. It is usual to express the density as a logarithm to base 10. This gives great convenience, for, when stock value filters are combined to produce some desired density, the log densities of the individual filters are merely added. For example, a filter of log density 3·0 (transmitting 1/1000 of the incident light) could be constructed by combining filters of log density 2·0 and 1·0 (transmitting 1/100 and 1/10, respectively, of the incident light). Continuous variation of density is possible by the use of a neutral-density wedge, in which the density varies along the length, but is constant across the width. Ingling (1970) reviews the properties of the various types of commony used neutral-density wedges, and gives a method of calibration. In order to obtain a uniform field, a pair of overlapping wedges are usually employed, having their density gradients in opposite directions. A crude form of variable-density filter can also be constructed by varying the angle between two sheets of polarizing filter. The neutrality of the resulting filter is far from ideal at the higher densities, but it is inexpensive, and can easily be made to give a large field of view.

An aperture control or diaphragm may be located in an optical system to give control of the luminance. If the diaphragm is evenly illuminated, then the transmitted flux will be proportional to the area of the aperture. Careful design is necessary to ensure that the final field is evenly illuminated, and therefore a diffusing plate is often included for this purpose.

Talbot's law states that the brightness of a rapidly fluctuating light depends on its average luminance. It holds only when the frequency of the fluctuations is greater than about 60 Hz. Thus, if the light is interrupted sufficiently frequently, it will have the same visual effect as interposing a neutral-density filter with a transmittance equal to the proportion of the time for which the light is not interrupted. This cyclic interruption is most conveniently achieved by the use of an episcotister. This comprises a pair of motor-driven discs, each having equal open and closed sectors. The angular relationship between the two discs can be adjusted. When they are set parallel, the transmittance is maximum, but if one disc is rotated with respect to the other, the angle of the combined closed sector is increased, thereby reducing the transmittance.

Useful reference sources for optical techniques in visual research have been written by Boynton (1966) and Riggs (1965).

8.4 Control of chrominance

It is often necessary to provide light with spectral characteristics which can be both varied and specified. As in the case of auditory stimuli, it is sufficient for some purposes that the stimuli are merely tagged with some distinctive characteristic. For example, lamp indicators may be fitted with crude colour filters to indicate the various phases of an experimental procedure. In such areas as colour-vision research, however, precise control and specification are necessary.

For quantitative work in colour vision, three basic kinds of equipment are required.

(1) a standard source of white light,

(2) a means of processing the light to select certain wavelengths,

(3) a means of measuring the energy at different wavelengths in the spectrum.

Specific wavelengths can be selected from a white-light source by using an instrument known as a monochromator. This instrument contains a prism, which disperses the light and forms a spectrum. A slit is moved to different parts of the spectrum to select light of the desired wavelength. In some instruments, the spectrum is formed by a diffraction grating, which consists of a plate ruled with a series of closely spaced lines. A colorimeter is a device which allows light to be synthesized by combining three primary monochromatic sources. Instruments of this kind are normally found only in specialist laboratories. Strictly monochromatic light is not necessary in all cases, and adequate selection can often be achieved by the use of colour filters. Dyed gelatine filters are available with a variety of fairly broad, but well specified, transmission characteristics. Simple colorimeters can be constructed using a projector, a microscope stage and a set of suitable gelatine filters (Riggs, 1964; Murch, 1972; Cavonius, 1974).

In recent years, interference filters have been developed which provide light with characteristics similar to that from a monochromator, but in a much more convenient form. An interference filter consists of two precisely separated layers which cause most of the light outside a specific wavelength to be cancelled by producing a reflection of equal amplitude, but opposite phase. Interference filters are manufactured with uniform characteristics for a single wavelength, and also in the form of an interference wedge. In this type, the wavelength of peak transmission depends on the part of the wedge to which the light is directed (Bornstein and Cox, 1974).

The quantitative specification of the stimulus requires some form of spectrophotometer. This is an instrument which combines a monochromator, for selecting a region of the spectrum, with a photometer, for measuring the radiant energy in the selected region.

The colour of a stimulus object may be specified by reference to the Munsell Color System (Newhall, Nickerson and Judd, 1943), which was developed from judgements of equal hue, brightness and saturation. *The Munsell Book of Color* contains over a thousand sample chips of colour in equal visual intervals, and these are arranged on a numerical-coordinate system.

8.5 Tachistoscopic presentation

The tachistoscope is an apparatus which allows the presentation of a stimulus pattern, usually written on a card, for a controlled period of time and with a controlled level of illumination. The instrument is usually fitted with a viewing hood which fits closely round the subject's face, thus restricting the subject's field of view to the stimulus materials (Figure 8.12).

Early instruments employed various mechanical devices for brief presentation, but modern instruments are almost all electronically controlled. It is

146

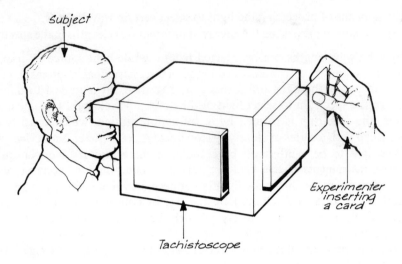

Figure 8.12. *A typical laboratory tachistoscope. Note how the viewing hood prevents the subject seeing the stimulus materials as they are handled by the experimenter.*

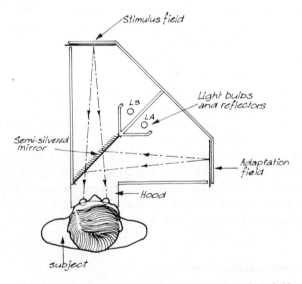

Figure 8.13. *The optical arrangement in a simple 2-field tachistoscope. Lamp LA illuminates the adaptation field, making it visible to the subject by reflection in the semi-silvered mirror. When the experimenter operates a control, lamp LA is switched off and lamp LS is switched on for a preset duration, allowing the stimulus field to be seen through the mirror. At the end of the exposure, the adaptation field is illuminated again.*

usual to have an adaptation field which is presented before and after the stimulus field (sometimes the terms fixation and exposure field are used). The adaptation field is normally a piece of card, similar to that used for the stimulus field, but marked only with a fixation cross. The pre-exposure adaptation display allows the subject's oculomotor adjustments to become steady before the stimulus is presented. A schematic diagram of a simple 2-field tachistoscope is shown in Figure 8.13. In its normal state, the tachistoscope illuminates only the adaptation field, which can be viewed by reflection in the semisilvered mirror. The mirror should be silvered on the front surface to minimize multiple reflections. The reflected image is used for the adaptation field because the left–right reversal which occurs in this field would create difficulties in preparation of the written material normally used as stimulus items. The reflected image is also more distorted by any slight curvature in the mirror than the transmitted image, and the adaptation field is normally less critical. When colour is of importance, care should be taken that the two fields match in spectral characteristics. With many semireflecting mirrors, the ratio of reflected to transmitted light varies with the wavelength of the light. Inexpensive tachistoscopes often use acrylic sheet, which is very poor in this respect. The colour match between the two fields can be improved by fitting appropriate colour filters. The geometry of the box should be square and the mirror so positioned that the two fields appear to be coincident. This is easily checked by rapidly alternating the two fields, so that dots in the corners of the two fields appear to be in the same plane. The boundaries of the two fields should also coincide, otherwise a disturbing phi phenomenon will cause the subject to attend to the boundary of the field, rather than the intended stimulus items. Thin black cards may be stuck over the edges of the fields to minimize the effect after the depths have been made coincident. Baffles should be fitted to minimize the amount of light spilling from one field to the other, and the whole interior of the box should be painted dead black. In most applications, light spilling from the adaptation field to the stimulus field is the more serious problem, because this might give the subject some information about the stimulus items. A simple worst-case test is to fit a white card with a small black patch to one field, and to check whether a pattern in the corresponding part of the dark stimulus field can be detected in normal viewing. A spot photometer (Section 8.2) can be used for quantitative measures.

By combining several optical units of this type, it is possible to construct multifield tachistoscopes. It is not possible, however, to provide direct viewing of the additional stimulus fields, and therefore the characteristics of the materials used for the mirrors are more critical in multified tachistoscopes. As more fields are added, the maximum angle of view is also reduced, and the task of aligning the fields becomes more difficult.

The most widely used means of illumination for tachistoscopes is a miniature fluorescent tube supplied with direct current. The normal method for starting these tubes and limiting the current flow (Section 8.1.3) is not suitable for use in a tachistoscope. To allow a rapid start, the fluorescent tube heaters are

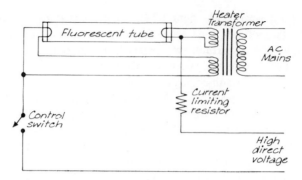

Figure 8.14. *A control circuit for a fluorescent tube, suitable for use in a tachistoscope. The tube heaters are operated from a low alternating voltage, but direct current flows through the tube.*

continually energized from separate transformer windings (Figure 8.14). The tube is driven from a direct-current supply to give illumination which is free from flicker. A high-voltage source is used with a series resistor to limit the current through the tube. The luminous intensity is adjusted by varying the value of the series resistor. When direct current is passed through a fluorescent tube, the heavy positive ions always flow in the same direction, causing deterioration of the phosphor to occur more rapidly at one end of the tube than at the other. After some use, this can cause uneven illumination of the fields. Tachistoscopes may be fitted with a switch which reverses the connections to the tubes, allowing the ageing of the ends to be equalized. Some tachistoscopes automatically reverse the connections to the tubes at every exposure. The voltages which drive the tubes are very high, and so great care should be exercised when making any internal adjustments to a working tachistoscope.

Another approach to the problem of precisely timed presentation is to fit an electromechanical shutter to a conventional slide projector. This method allows tachistoscopic presentation to groups of subjects, and is very flexible. If a number of projection tachistoscopes are directed at the same screen, a multifield tachistoscope can be constructed; by using automatic slide projectors, quite complex presentation sequences can be programmed. Some manufacturers have even incorporated slide-changer mechanisms to allow automatic sequencing of stimuli in conventional tachistoscopes, although the more usual method is to attach a specially designed card changer.

The limitations of electromechanical shutters in projection tachistoscopes may be overcome by replacing the conventional projection lamp by a more readily controlled source; unfortunately, this will generally result in a lower light level. Mylrea (1966) used glow modulator tubes in a 16-field tachistoscope which allowed exposure times from a few microseconds to 1 s per field. Xenon flash tubes may be used when a very brief exposure is adequate.

Figure 8.15. *A typical student-quality memory drum. The drum has three presentation rates: one item every 1 s, one item every 1·5 s and one item every 3 s. The drum is mounted behind an aluminium screen, and the items are displayed in a slot 2·5 in wide and 0·25 in high. The drum is shown with the long paper attachment in use (Gerbrands model M1-A).*

8.6 Memory drums

The memory drum is a device frequently used for serial presentation in verbal learning experiments. In its simplest form (Figure 8.15), it consists of a drum which is driven by a synchronous motor via an intermittent-motion pin-and-star-wheel mechanism. The list to be presented is written on a strip of paper and attached to the drum. A shield is mounted over the drum with an aperture in which the individual items are displayed. Thus, the apparatus provides a controlled serial presentation of the list, one item at a time. Various presentation rates can be selected by changing the number of pins in the drive mechanism. The amount by which the drum indexes is designed to allow lists to be typed on a standard typewriter. Short lists are simply wrapped around the drum; a weighted roller attachment is used for longer lists of up to about 50 items.

More sophisticated memory drums accept wider paper, and are often fitted with shuttered windows which allow one of several lists to be selected without changing the paper. Means may be provided for remotely stepping the drum and operating the shutters. Positive positioning of the stimulus material is ensured by use of a sprocket drive for the paper. Some drums accept fanfold paper, allowing very long lists to be presented. Mayes (1976) has described a versatile memory drum which is based on a modified kymograph drum.

In many experiments, the traditional place of the memory drum has now been taken by the automatic slide projector (Section 8.7.2) and the cathode-ray tube display (Section 8.7.4).

8.7 Image-forming systems

If a ray of light passes from a given medium to one of a greater optical density, at an angle other than the normal to the surface, it undergoes a change of direction, and is deflected towards the normal (Figure 8.16). This effect is due to the different velocities of light in the two media. The ratio of the velocity of light in a vacuum to the velocity in a medium is known as the refractive index of the medium; the amount by which the refracted ray is deflected is not

150

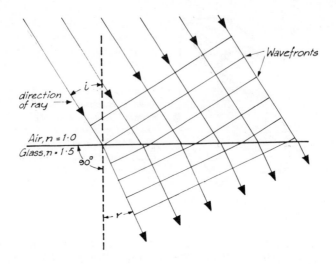

Figure 8.16. *Refraction of light at a surface between air and glass. The velocity of light is less in glass than in air.*

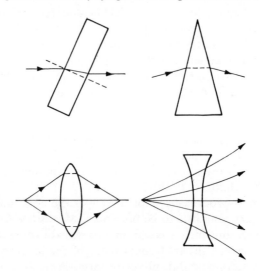

Figure 8.17. *Refraction in plane glass, a prism, a convex (convergent) lens and a concave (divergent) lens. From Riggs (1965).*

constant, but depends on the refractive indices n_a and n_g of the two media, and on the angle of incidence of the ray. The angle of refraction r is given by Snell's law:

$$n_a \sin i = n_g \sin r$$

Examples of refraction are shown in Figure 8.17.

When light passes into a less dense medium, it will be deflected away from the

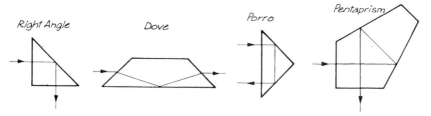

Figure 8.18. *Reflection of light by prisms of various kinds. The Dove prism allows an image to be rotated by turning the prism around its axis. The Porro prism sends the light back parallel to its original path; pairs of such prisms are used in prismatic binoculars. A pentaprism gives a reflection through a right angle with a high degree of precision; it is used in the viewfinder of a single-lens reflex camera (Section 8.7.1). From Riggs (1965).*

normal to the surface. An interesting case occurs when the angle of incidence exceeds a critical value which would make the angle of refraction equal to a right angle, that is it would cause the refracted ray to travel along the surface. At angles of incidence greater than the critical value, the refracted ray does not pass into the less dense medium, but is reflected from the surface according to the normal laws of reflection. This phenomenon is known as total internal reflection, and is exploited in optical prisms (Figure 8.18) and fibre optics (Section 8.7.5).

Refraction of light also occurs in lenses, which form an important part of many optical instruments. Figure 8.19 shows in diagrammatic form how an image is produced by a convex lens. The most important property of a lens is its focal length; this is the distance from the lens at which rays from an infinitely distant source are brought to focus. In this figure, an object PQ is at a finite distance from a lens which forms an image P′ Q′. The size and location of the image can be determined by tracing a few key rays through the lens. First, a ray from Q parallel to the axis will, after refraction in the lens, pass through a focal point. Conversely, a ray from Q which passes through a focal point before being refracted in the lens will emerge parallel to the axis, and intersect with the first ray at Q′. Last, a ray from P travelling along the axis is undeflected by the lens, because it is normal to the surface. The construction based on these

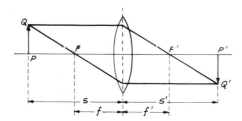

Figure 8.19. *Construction for determining the size and position of the image P′Q′ of an object PQ produced by a lens of focal length f.*

rays allows two important lens formulae to be derived. If an object is at a distance s from a lens of focal length f, then its image will be formed at a distance s', according to the formula

$$\frac{1}{s} + \frac{1}{s'} = \frac{1}{f}$$

The linear magnification produced by a lens is defined as the ratio of the size of the image h' to the size of the object h; it is equal to the ratio of the distances of image and object from the lens, that is

$$\frac{h}{h'} = \frac{s'}{s}$$

These formulae assume that the lens is thin; in the case of a thick lens, each distance is referred to the principal point for the appropriate surface of the lens. Sometimes, instead of focal length, the term power is used; a lens of short focal length is said to have more power, that is it refracts the light to a greater degree than a lens of long focal length. The unit of power is the dioptre, defined as the reciprocal of the focal length in metres.

   In any medium other than a vacuum, the velocity of light varies slightly with its wavelength, and therefore the refractive index of the medium will depend slightly on the wavelength. This variation of refractive index causes dispersion, that is light of a short wavelength (blue) undergoes more refraction than light of a long wavelength (red). Dispersion of light in a simple wedge prism produces the familiar spectrum; dispersion in atmospheric raindrops gives the rainbow. In a simple lens, this variation of refractive index causes chromatic aberration, light of various wavelengths being brought to a focus at different distances from the lens. Spherical aberration is another defect; it causes the light rays which strike the lens at various distances from the centre to come to a focus at different points. Such aberrations are considerably reduced in a well designed lens system constructed from elements of different refractive indices.

   As we discussed in Section 8.2, it is often necessary in visual research to control changes in pupil diameter. The simplest way to do this is to use an artificial pupil. This may be a small aperture cut in a thin metal plate, and positioned in front of the eye as close as possible to the cornea. As long as the diameter of the subject's pupil is not less than the diameter of the artificial pupil, the amount of light entering the eye will be unaffected by pupillary contractions. Because the artificial pupil does not lie in the plane of the real pupil, it causes some restriction in the field of view. This does not occur with the Maxwellian view; this method uses an optical system to create a very small artificial pupil within the subject's eye. Another advantage of the Maxwellian view is that very high levels of effective luminance are easily achieved. Diagrams of both systems are shown in Figure 8.20. With these arrangements, it is necessary that the eye should be accurately located, and therefore a bite board (Section 10.3.7) is usually employed.

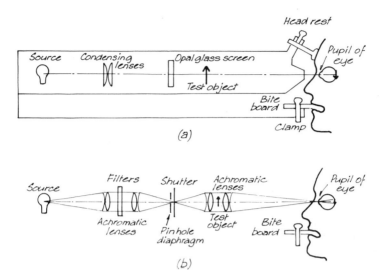

Figure 8.20. *Arrangements for eliminating the effects of pupillary contraction. The arrangement in (a) is an artificial pupil. In the Maxwellian view (b), the first pair of lenses after the source focuses the light onto the pinhole diaphragm. The second pair of lenses produces an image of the diaphragm in the subject's pupil, and, in conjunction with the lens of the eye, causes an image of the test object to be projected onto the retina.*
From Riggs (1965).

All optical elements should be attached rigidly to a solid baseplate. The most convenient method is to use an optical bench. This consists of a bar along which holders can slide and be locked into place. Various optical components can be mounted on the holders and precisely aligned. If a bite board is used, this also should be mounted on the bench.

8.7.1 *Photography and photocopying*

Photographic techniques are used not only in stimulus presentation, but also in recording responses, both directly (Section 10.1.2) and indirectly (Section 11.1.3). A camera basically consists of a lens which projects an image of an object onto a light-sensitive film. In order to produce a bright image, the lens must have a large pupil, or aperture. In a simple lens, this gives rise to various aberrations, and careful design is necessary to minimize these in a camera lens.

Under constant lighting conditions, the illuminance at the film varies with the area of the aperture. The size of aperture is controlled by a diaphragm which is normally calibrated in f numbers, or focal ratios. The f number is the focal length divided by the diameter of the aperture. A set of f numbers on a camera lens might read as follows:

154

| $f/16$ | 11 | 8 | 5·6 | 4 | 2·8 | 2 |

As the aperture diameter varies inversely with the f number, it follows that $f/16$ is a smaller diameter than $f/2$. The corresponding diameters are therefore in the approximate ratios

| 1 | $\sqrt{2}$ | 2 | $2 \times \sqrt{2}$ | 4 | $4 \times \sqrt{2}$ | 8 |

The area of an aperture varies with the square of its diameter, and so the illuminance at the film for the corresponding f numbers will be in the approximate ratios

| 1 | 2 | 4 | 8 | 16 | 32 | 64 |

Increasing the aperture not only lets in more light, but also makes focusing more critical. For a given lens-to-film distance, only those rays originating from a particular object-to-lens distance will be in focus. A certain amount of defocusing can be tolerated in the final picture; the range of near and far distances which reach this threshold value is termed the depth of field. Wide apertures reduce the depth of field, and make it difficult to achieve sharp focus for objects which are at different distances from the camera. This effect is particularly marked when taking closeups and when using long focal length lenses.

Many cameras incorporate some kind of focusing aid. In the single-lens reflex camera (Figure 8.21), the image which will be projected onto the film is viewed by reflection in a surface-silvered mirror. This also has the advantage that the viewfinder shows clearly what will be included in the picture. This type

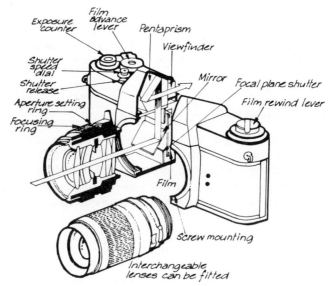

Figure 8.21. *The interior working of a typical single-lens reflex camera.*

of camera usually has an interchangeable lens so that the standard lens can be replaced by lenses of different focal lengths for specialized purposes.

The camera shutter allows the film to be exposed for a preselected period of time. If the subject is moving, or the camera is held by hand, very short exposures are necessary. In cameras with interchangeable lenses, the shutter is normally fitted just in front of the film, and is of the type known as a focal-plane shutter. Cameras with non-interchangeable lenses usually have the shutter built into the lens. Shutter speeds are typically in the range 1/500–1 s, the control usually being marked in reciprocal times, so that 100 would mean 1/100 s. Shutter controls often have two extra positions marked B and T. These allow the shutter to be opened for manually controlled times. B (brief) opens the shutter when the release is depressed and closes it again when the release returns. T (time) opens and closes the shutter for alternate operations of the release. When using long exposure times, the camera should be mounted on a stable tripod and a cable release used to reduce hand vibration.

An exposure meter is normally used to determine the exposure time. A scale on the exposure meter is set to the speed of the film in use, and a light reading is then taken. The result is presented as the exposure times corresponding to a series of f numbers, and the user chooses that combination which is suitable for the subject being photographed. Two kinds of photocells are used in exposure meters: the selenium photovoltaic cell and the cadmium sulphide (CdS) photoconductive cell (see Section 5.9.14). When a photovoltaic cell is used, the light falling on the cell generates the current which deflects the meter, and therefore no battery is needed. CdS meters usually employ a mercury button cell as the power source, and are smaller and more sensitive than meters which use a photovoltaic cell. Many modern cameras have a built-in CdS exposure meter, which may be coupled to the shutter and/or aperture controls to allow automatic or semiautomatic operation of the camera. Most exposure meters are of the reflected-light type, that is they measure the light reflected from the scene to be photographed. Another type is the incident-light meter, which measures the light falling on the subject from the direction of the camera. Incident-light meters are generally considered to give more accurate results when using reversal colour film, but are less convenient to use than reflected-light meters. For most scientific applications, the cost of film is a relatively small item; most workers take a number of additional photographs, using shorter and longer exposures than are indicated on the meter, and select the best copy after processing the film.

Photographic film has a light-sensitive layer (Figure 8.22) consisting of a suspension of small silver bromide crystals in gelatine. When the film is exposed to light, some of the silver bromide is converted to silver with the liberation of bromine; other crystals are modified in a way which is not visible, but renders them more susceptible to chemical reduction. The extent to which these processes occur depends on the intensity of the light; when an optical image is projected on a film, the pattern of illumination is recorded in the changes to the silver bromide crystals. This latent image is made visible by chemically

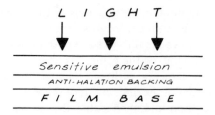

Figure 8.22. *Section through a black-and-white photographic film. The anti-halation backing reduces the amount of light reflected from the film base, which is usually cellulose acetate.*

reducing the film in a developing solution. The developed black-and-white film is fixed by dissolving away the unused silver bromide, after which the processing solutions are washed from the film. The result is a photographic negative; the highlights of the original scene are reproduced as black, and the shadows are reproduced as light. To produce a positive print, a sheet of photographic paper is placed in contact with the negative, exposed to light and processed. Because small frame sizes are commonly found on modern cameras, an enlarged print is usually required. This is made by projecting a magnified image of the negative onto the printing paper.

A simple silver bromide emulsion is not equally sensitive at all wavelengths of visible light; it is mainly sensitive to light at the blue end of the spectrum. Dyes are added to the emulsion to extend its sensitivity. Orthochromatic film has its sensitivity extended to include green light; it may be processed in light from a red safelight, but panchromatic film, which is sensitive to the whole of the visible spectrum, must be processed in total darkness.

The speed of a film is a measure of its sensitivity to light. Two scales of speed (Figure 8.23) are in common use: ASA (American Standards Association) and DIN (Deutsche Industrie Norm). The ASA scale is arithmetically based; doubling the ASA value corresponds to doubling the film speed, and only half the exposure would be required. Fast black-and-white films have speeds up to

ASA	DIN	ASA	DIN
16	13	160	23
20	14	250	25
32	16	320	26
40	17	500	28
64	19	650	29
80	20	1000	31
125	22	1250	32

Figure 8.23. *Comparison of ASA and DIN film speeds.*

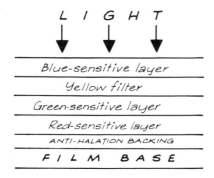

Figure 8.24. *Section through a colour film, showing the sequence of light-sensitive layers. The yellow filter prevents blue light reaching the green- and red-sensitive layers. The filter is removed by the developing process.*

about 1000 ASA, and colour films have speeds in the range 16–160 ASA. The DIN scale is logarithmically based, as with the decibel (Section 7.4); an increase of 3 in the DIN value corresponds to a doubling of the film speed.

In colour photography, each of the three primary components of the light image are recorded in separate layers of the film (Figure 8.24). When colour negative film is developed, dyes of the complementary colours are formed in each layer. The silver images are then bleached out, leaving only the dye images. Positive prints are made on paper which has been coated with a similar set of emulsions.

Reversal colour film produces positive transparencies directly. First, the film is developed to give a silver negative in all three layers. Then it is exposed to light, and the newly exposed emulsion is reprocessed using a colour developer. This produces a positive dye image. The silver is bleached out, and the film is washed and dried. The positive transparency may be either viewed directly by transmitted light or projected on a screen.

The Polaroid–Land process has the great advantage of eliminating the delay and inconvenience of the usual wet-processing stages; a finished print is obtained within seconds of making the exposure. A special camera is used with a processing compartment at the back. The film is supplied in a pack which contains both the negative and positive materials. The negative is exposed in the usual manner, and then, by pulling a tab, it is brought face to face with the positive paper. As the two sheets emerge, they pass between rollers which burst capsules of developer and disperse the chemicals over the positive–negative interface. The sheets are left in contact for a few seconds, and then separated, the positive print being retained. Both black-and-white and colour film packs are available. The advantage of having a print available so quickly is obvious, but there are some disadvantages with the process. A

158

conventional negative is not produced, making it difficult to produce high-quality enlargements, and also rapid sequences of photographs are not possible, because of the need to operate the film pack between each exposure, although recent developments in the process may remove these difficulties.

Modern photocopying machines provide a convenient means for reproducing many kinds of stimulus materials. The xerographic process is based on electrostatic principles. A drum coated with a photoconductive material is electrostatically charged in the dark. An image of the material to be copied is projected onto the drum, causing the white areas of the drum to be discharged. A fine toner powder is then dispersed over the drum by small steel and quartz balls. The toner remains in those areas which have retained a charge. This process develops a positive toner image on the drum. This image is transferred to the plain copy paper by wrapping the paper around the drum and applying a further electrostatic charge to the back of the paper. The thermoplastic toner is then fused to the paper by a final heating stage. The xerographic process produces a very sharp image, but is rather poor at reproducing large areas of uniform density. The slower, wet diffusion transfer process is better in this latter respect. The diffusion transfer process uses the reflex method, in which an intermediate negative sheet is placed in contact with the original, the pair being illuminated through the back of the negative. Light falling on the white areas of the original is reflected back to the negative, giving a greater exposure to these areas than to the dark areas. The negative is then placed in contact with a sheet of positive transfer paper, and fed through rollers into the machine, where the negative is developed and a positive image is chemically transferred to the positive sheet.

8.7.2 Still and cine projectors

The modern automatic slide projector is a convenient device for the presentation of sequences of visual material. A schematic diagram of the optical system of a slide projector is shown in Figure 8.25. The lamp emits light in all directions, and so a concave reflector is fitted to the rear of the lamp, to reflect light which would not otherwise be used back into the plane of the filament.

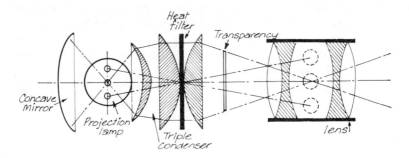

Figure 8.25. *The basic optical system of a slide projector.*

The condenser collects light over a large angle, and brings it to a focus within the projection lens, whilst providing even illumination over the whole area of the slide. Because the lamp generates a great deal of heat, a plate of heat-absorbing glass is mounted in the condenser system. Air from the cooling fan is directed over the heat filter in addition to the projection lamp and the slide.

In the traditional manually operated slide projector, the slide is inserted into a carrier which moves the slide into the optical axis. Simple projectors of this kind are used to present fixed displays, and are often used as components in experimental apparatus, for example in the simple colorimeters mentioned in Section 8.4. The most generally useful kind of projector, however, is the automatic type, in which a series of slides is inserted into a magazine from which they are presented sequentially. Such projectors are fitted with a remote-control socket, allowing the projector to be advanced by the operation of a switch contact. The duration of the contact closure is often critical; if it is too short, the projector may not advance, whereas, if it is too long, a double advance may occur.

Recently, random-access versions of automatic slide projectors have been produced (Figure 8.26) which are mainly intended for such applications as information retrieval in process-control consoles and for use in military display systems. A random-access slide projector can be instructed to move the slide tray to any desired position and display the slide, without having to display all the slides in the intervening positions. Although any sequence of slides can be displayed in this manner, the tray still has to be moved serially, and it may take up to a few seconds to access a given slide. For rapid random access of a small number of items, a projection indicator (Figure 8.27) may be suitable (see also Section 8.7.3). The main disadvantages of this device are poor resolution, small screen size and the semipermanent nature of the display material.

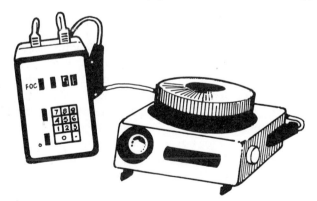

Figure 8.26. *This random-access projector is a special version of the well known Carousel projector. The required slide may be selected on the pushbutton control shown in the figure, or the projector may be interfaced to a laboratory computer or modular programming system (Kodak model S-RA2000).*

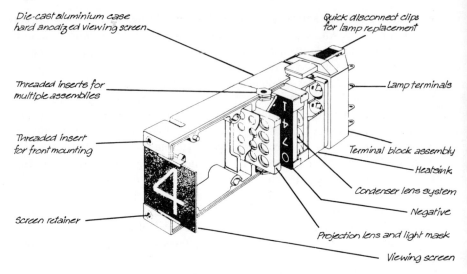

Die-cast aluminium case
hard anodized viewing screen

Quick disconnect clips
for lamp replacement

Threaded inserts for
multiple assemblies

Lamp terminals

Threaded insert
for front mounting

Terminal block assembly

Heatsink

Condenser lens system

Negative

Screen retainer

Projection lens and light mask

Viewing screen

Figure 8.27. *A sectional view of a typical projection indicator. Light from the selected bulb illuminates one of the symbols on the transparency, causing the symbol to be projected on the screen. Projection indicators in common use have 12 projection channels, and range in height from about 1 to 4 in (Counting Instruments Ltd.).*

Projection indicators are often used for the display of simple shapes in animal discrimination-learning experiments.

The filmstrip projector is similar to the slide projector, but the transparencies are kept in the original strip form. It is mainly used to project material which has been duplicated, and it has recently undergone a great deal of development, which is primarily aimed at producing a convenient audiovisual sales and teaching aid. The unit usually has an integral rear-projection screen. Modern instruments incorporate a tape player which allows synchronized operation of the filmstrip projector. The synchronizing pulses are either recorded on a separate track from the commentary, or consist of low-frequency tones which are filtered out from the audio signal on playback. The traditional film size for filmstrip is 35 mm, but recently a number of audiovisual systems have used 16 mm and even Super-8 cine film. Some of these devices have a very fast frame-changing mechanism which can be operated at up to 18 frame/s, allowing the inclusion of motion sequences.

When selecting a projector for use in an experiment, some thought should be given to the arrangement of the projector and screen. It is often convenient to use a rear-projection screen, as this allows the equipment to be housed behind the display and away from the subject. It also eliminates the problem of the subject's head interrupting the optical path from the projector. Traditionally, rear-projection screens were made from sheets of ground glass. This material has the disadvantage that the luminance of the image decreases rapidly as the viewing angle deviates from the normal to a screen surface, so that, at average viewing distances, the edge of the screen appears quite dim. The central area of

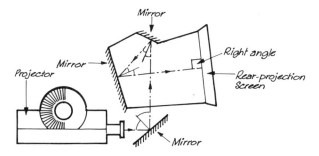

Figure 8.28. *A typical folded optical path which may be used to reduce the projector-to-screen distance. The mirrors should be surface-silvered in order to prevent the formation of multiple images on the screen. From Cleary, Mayes and Packham (1976).*

the screen, however, has a so-called hot spot which moves with the position of the observer's head. The problem can be overcome by using modern materials, such as Lenscreen, manufactured by Polacoat, Inc. This material gives an image of high resolution, and permits a very wide viewing angle, thereby eliminating the hot spot. It is available on a wide variety of base materials, such as glass, rigid acrylic and flexible vinyl plastics, making it useful for the construction of various types of rear-projection stimulus-response keys (Section 10.1). When projecting, the lens-to-screen distance s depends on the required linear magnification m and on the focal length f of the projection lens, according to the approximate formula

$$s = m \times f$$

Space can often be saved by using a folded optical path (Figure 8.28), or by using projectors which will accept wide-angle lenses with a very short focal length; the Kodak Carousel SAV-2000, which has been specially designed for audiovisual work, is one such projector.

Cine projectors can be used for the presentation of continuous motion stimuli. Additionally, many projectors have a stop-frame facility, but it is not usually possible to step reliably from frame to frame under remote control as in a filmstrip projector. Exceptions are a few specialized models known as analyst projectors. Such projectors are designed to allow the frame-by-frame study of cine film, and are often used in time-and-motion studies, traffic-flow analysis and athletics training. Film to be analysed in this way is often made using a time lapse between the frames (Section 10.1.1) instead of being taken at normal cine speeds.

There are three commonly used gauges or widths of cine film. The widest is 35 mm film, which is almost entirely restricted to the professional cinema. The middle size is 16 mm, which is the standard gauge in education and training. Most amateur film is 8 mm wide. There are various standards of sprocket holes and cartridges, but the overwhelming majority of modern amateur equipment uses Super-8 film. Some of the better Super-8 equipment approaches professional standards, and is used for such purposes as television news reporting.

The cine camera is basically an instrument for taking a large number of photographs in rapid succession. The internal workings of a simple cine camera are shown in Figure 8.29. Most modern cameras are driven by an electric motor. The feed spool carries the unexposed film, which is unwound by the sprocket wheel and moved along the film gate. In Super-8 cameras, a film cartridge is loaded into the camera, and no threading is necessary. A pressure plate keeps the film flat as it moves past the film gate. After being exposed, the film is advanced one frame by the feeding claw. This movement occurs intermit-

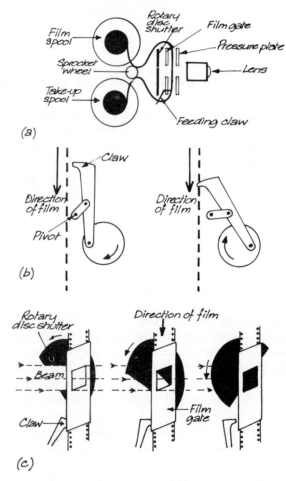

Figure 8.29. *A simple cine camera is shown in (a). The film is advanced intermittently by the claw mechanism detailed in (b). The rotating shutter shown in (c) ensures that the film is only exposed when it is stationary.*

tently, but the sprocket rotates continuously, and the film path includes small tension relieving loops. While the film is being advanced by the feeding claw, the disc shutter covers the film to prevent the image being blurred. The feeding claw and the shutter are, therefore, mechanically coupled.

The standard speeds in cine photography are 18 frame/s for silent films and 24 frame/s for sound films. Soundtracks run along the edge of the film, and can be either a magnetic stripe or optical, that is recorded photographically. Optical soundtracks are only used for films which are to be printed in quantity.

A cine projector (Figure 8.30) works in much the same way as a camera; but, whereas, in a cine camera, an image of the subject is projected onto the film, in the projector, the photographic image in the film is projected by the lens onto the screen. As in the camera, the film gate must be obscured while the film is in motion. A simple shutter arrangement would produce flicker at 18 or 24 Hz, which is below the critical flicker-fusion frequency. This problem is solved by using a multiple shutter which also obscures the light while the film is stationary, thereby raising the flicker frequency. In Figure 8.30b, a double shutter is shown for simplicity, but many projectors have a triple shutter. In analyst projectors, the shutter is kept in motion at the normal rate, even when a

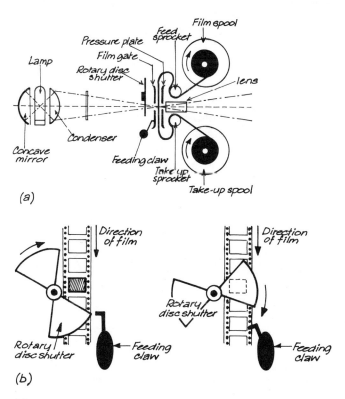

Figure 8.30. *The mechanism of a simple cine projector (a). The operation of the rotary disc shutter is shown in (b).*

frame is held. Thus, on any occasion when a frame change takes place, whether by manual selection or under slow-speed continuous operation, it must be at one of the times at which frame change would occur during full-speed projection, and so the projection speed is not infinitely variable.

8.7.3 *Alphanumeric displays*

The mass production of integrated circuits, and the consequent reduction in the cost of digital equipment, such as pocket calculators and electronic watches, has brought about the fairly widespread use of alphanumeric displays in recent years. Most alphanumeric displays for industrial and scientific use are manufactured in modular form, each module being designed to display one character of the message. A number of similar modules are mounted together by the user to allow the required maximum length of message to be displayed.

The methods employed to form characters in alphanumeric displays may be classified as follows:

(1) selection of a discrete fully formed character from a set stored during manufacture,
(2) selection from a set of dots in a grid or matrix,
(3) selection from a set of bars or segments.

We have already described one form of discrete character display—the projection indicator (Section 8.7.1). This device is sometimes used as a numerical indicator by fitting a transparency which contains the symbols 0 to 9 and possibly $+$ and $-$. The most commonly used device in this class, however, is the Nixie tube, in which the numbers are formed as shaped metal cathodes, stacked one behind the other in a glass bulb filled with neon and mercury vapour (Figure 8.31). The bulb also contains a fine metal mesh which serves as the anode. When a voltage is applied between the anode and one of the cathodes, the gas in the immediate vicinity of the selected cathode glows,

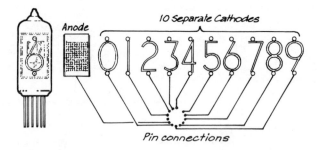

Figure 8.31. *A schematic diagram of a typical glow-discharge numeric-indicator tube. The arrangement of electrodes shown here is for side viewing; in tubes which are designed to be viewed from the top, the electrodes are arranged normally to the axis, and the tube has a flat top.*

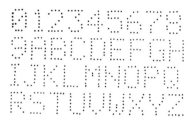

Figure 8.32. *These characters are formed on a 7 × 5 grid of the type used in many dot-matrix displays.*

resulting in the display of an orange-coloured number. Nixie tubes have been widely used because they are reliable and have a fairly long working life. Their main disadvantage is that they need high voltages, which makes them awkward to drive from integrated circuits. Another disadvantage, when considering stimulus displays, is that the plane of each character is slightly different. The same problem arises with another form of stacked display containing a series of acrylic plates, each engraved with a symbol and capable of being edge lit by a small incandescent lamp. The light from each lamp is kept within the corresponding plate by total internal reflection, except at the discontinuities of the engraved characters. Because the most distant characters are viewed through the nearer characters, stacked displays can only be used for small character sets, and are not normally used for the full alphabet.

A very versatile display can be formed from a matrix of dots, each of which can be illuminated as required. Such displays can generate a wide variety of characters. The quality of the resulting image depends on the number of elements in the matrix, but, of course, the complexity of the logic needed to generate the character increases with the number of elements. Most commercial devices use a 7 × 5 matrix (Figure 8.32). Some dot-matrix displays are intended only for generating numbers, and have less than the full matrix. Although any light source could be used to drive this class of display, the majority of commercially available devices use light-emitting diodes (Section 8.1.4), the small diode chips being laid out on a single slice of semiconductor material. Because semiconductor materials are expensive, LED displays are normally kept fairly small, less than 1 in in height. Their compatability with integrated circuits, however, does make the driving circuits simple; some manufacturers even include the logic for generating the characters within the display package. A particularly convenient display, evaluated by Nealis, Engelke and Massaro (1973), accepts the input in ASCII code (Section 11.2.3), and is therefore easily driven by minicomputers and related equipment (Chapter 12). A more recent development is the plasma panel, which comprises two flat sheets of glass with sets of parallel conductors mounted at right angles. The space between the glass is filled with neon. The application of a voltage between the appropriate pairs of conductors allows a glow discharge to be established at a

166

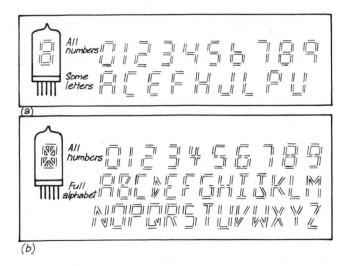

(a)

(b)

Figure 8.33. *Characters formed by two kinds of segment displays.*
The range of characters formed by the commonly used 7-segment
display is shown in (a). For the full upper-case alphabet, a 14-seg-
ment display (b) is needed. Most segment displays give the
characters a slight slope to improve legibility.

selected point. Plasma panels are currently being manufactured in small
quantities, and have been used in the student terminals of the PLATO IV
computer-assisted instruction system at the University of Illinois (Bitzer and
Skaperdas, 1973).

Currently, the most widely used numeric displays are the 7-segment or bar
displays (Figure 8.33a) which allow all the numbers and a few letters to be
formed. The complete set of numbers and upper-case letters can be formed by
a 14-segment display (Figure 8.33b). A wide variety of light sources is used for
displays in this class, including incandescent filaments, glow discharge, electroluminescent panels and rows of LEDs. Liquid-crystal displays are sometimes
used in digital watches and other applications where a low power consumption
is necessary. These displays do not switch light sources, but operate by changing
the surface reflectance of part of the display. Although at present they are
only used in specialized applications, this area is currently the subject of very
intensive development work.

The various types of numeric display are reviewed by Sobel (1973).

8.7.4 *CRT displays*

The cathode-ray tube (CRT) is the most widely used and versatile electronic
display device. It consists of a vacuum tube containing a heated cathode which
emits electrons (Figure 8.34). These electrons are formed into a beam by a
positively charged cylindrical anode and produce a spot of light when they

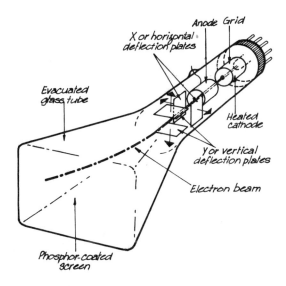

Figure 8.34. Electrostatic deflection and focusing
in the cathode-ray tube.

strike a phosphor-coated screen at the other end of the tube. The electron beam
may be deflected in the X and Y directions by applying voltages to pairs of
deflection plates. The cathode-ray tubes normally found in television receivers
employ electromagnetic deflection.

The light emitted by the phosphors has a fairly complex frequency spectrum,
and so cathode-ray tube displays are not suitable for use in experiments which
require close control of chrominance. Two other characteristics of phosphors
are important when they are used to display stimuli. One, called fluorescence,
is the light emitted during bombardment by electrons. The other, called
phosphorescence, is the light emitted subsequent to the bombardment, and
may continue for many seconds. The characteristics of some standard phosphors are summarized in Figure 8.35. The figure quoted for persistence is the
time taken for the luminous intensity to fall to 10% of the initial value. Tubes
with a long persistence are often used to display slowly changing physiological
signals.

The greater the number of electrons striking the screen per second, the

Type	Fluorescence	Phosphorescence	Persistence	Use
P1	yellow-green	yellow-green	24 ms	oscilloscopes
P4	white	white	60 μs	television
P33	orange	orange	2·2 s	oscilloscopes
P34	blue-green	yellow-green	100 ms	oscilloscopes

Figure 8.35. Characteristics of some common phosphors.

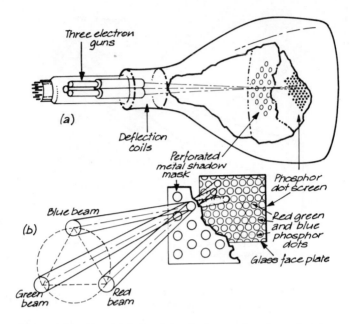

Figure 8.36. *The principle of the shadow-mask colour-television tube. The general arrangement of the three electron guns and the shadow mask are shown in (a), and details of the selection of electron beams by the shadow mask are shown in (b).*

brighter will be the spot of light. By altering the potential difference between the cathode and the grid (Figure 8.34), the intensity of the beam, and hence the brightness of the display, can be controlled. Varying the beam current in this manner is often termed Z modulation, because it provides a third dimension which may be used in the display.

The colour television tube (Figure 8.36) contains three electron guns, each producing a separate beam, one for each primary colour. The screen contains one set of uniformally distributed dots of phosphor for each of the three primary colours. The electron beams scan over the screen simultaneously, but the shadow-mask ensures that only those electrons which originated from the appropriate gun strike each dot of phosphor. Some colour tubes have the phosphors arranged in stripes rather than clusters of dots, because this design has been found to give a brighter picture.

Long persistence phosphors were at one time often used in oscilloscopes for the display of transient phenomena, but this problem is better solved today by the storage oscilloscope. One type of storage tube has a specially constructed phosphor screen, which produces a positively charged image when it is struck by the high-energy beam from the image-forming electron gun. The stored image is displayed by flooding the screen with low-energy electrons from a separate gun, and it is erased by discharging the screen. The tube can also be used in the non-store mode. The main disadvantages of storage tubes are a lower resolution than conventional cathode-ray tubes, and a long erasure time of about 1 s. Erasure is also accompanied by a flash of light over the whole screen face.

In order to present a display on a cathode-ray tube, the electron beam must be moved around the tube face. Further, unless a storage tube is used, the process must be repeated for the duration of the display. Storage tubes may be suitable for the presentation of stationary displays if the erasure time and the accompanying flash of light on the screen can be tolerated; but, for most stimulus display applications, a conventional CRT and a means of refreshing the display are required. There are basically two methods of refreshing a CRT display. One method is to move the electron beam over that part of the screen for which a bright point is required. This method requires the coordinates of each point in the picture to be stored and used to generate repeatedly the series of X and Y coordinates. This is the method employed in many computer graphic displays. The second method is to sweep the electron beam systematically over the screen, and to vary the beam current, and hence the brightness of the spot, according to the picture content at the current coordinates. This is the method used in television.

The simplest way to generate a display from a computer is by point plotting. The picture is formed by a series of discrete points. The computer generates the X and Y coordinates for each point, and loads the values into a pair of of digital–analogue converters (Section 12.1.2). The analogue voltages are fed to the X and Y deflection amplifiers of the display monitor. After allowing a few microseconds for the amplifier to settle, the computer sends a pulse to the Z-modulation input of the monitor, which causes the beam in the monitor to be switched on for a brief period. This process is generally referred to as brightup. Point-plot displays are the type generally found on laboratory computers. Alphanumeric characters are constructed in a dot-matrix format (Section 8.7.3). Sperling (1971) discusses the use of point-plot displays for stimulus presentation, and includes advice on the selection of suitable phosphors. More sophisticated displays have hardware which can draw lines on the display. The computer sets coordinates for the ends of the line vector, and control circuits in the display generate voltages which move the beam steadily between the two points. The computer is able to signal whether the vector is to be drawn with the beam on or off, and so the beam can be moved to a new point without drawing a line. Curves are drawn by making a series of short lines. Vector displays are also available with storage tubes.

A simple television camera of the type used in closed-circuit television systems is shown in Figure 8.37. The lens forms an image of the scene to be transmitted on a light-sensitive target. The material in the target is photoconductive, and the resistance of each point is measured by scanning the target with a constant-current electron beam. If the area of the target sampled by the beam is dark, the voltage at the target will be higher than if a light area is sampled.

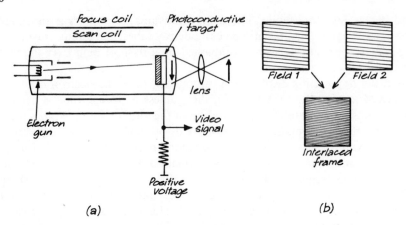

Figure 8.37. *The vidicon television camera (a) and the interlaced scanning process (b). In the UK television system, two fields of 312·5 lines interlace to give a complete frame of 625 lines every 1/25 s.*

In the standard UK television system, the complete picture is scanned 25 times per second. In order to reduce flicker, this process takes place in the form of two interlaced scans, giving a total of 625 lines. The scanning pattern is called a raster, and the electrical signal containing the picture information is called a video signal. When a television receiver reproduces a picture, the cathode-ray tube must be scanned synchronously with the television camera which is generating the picture, the beam current being varied according to the level of the video signal. Synchronizing pulses are transmitted for this purpose along with the picture information (Figure 8.38).

Because video signals range in frequency up to a few megahertz, video tape recorders need a much higher tape speed than audio tape recorders. This is achieved by scanning the head over the moving tape. Recorded television displays are useful when a fixed sequence of visual stimuli are to be presented in an experiment, but video tape recorders are not suitable for regular presentation of a single still frame. Video disc recorders are available which will repeatedly replay single frames or selected sequences of frames, but at present they are very expensive items, and are normally only available in broadcasting studios.

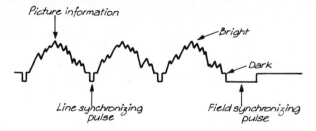

Figure 8.38. *A simplified representation of a television video signal.*

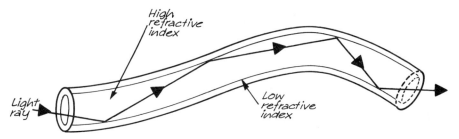

Figure 8.39. *In a fibre-optics bundle, each fibre contains a core with a high refractive index surrounded by an outer coating of a low refractive index. Light rays entering one end of the fibre at an angle nearly parallel to the axes will repeatedly undergo total internal reflection and be transmitted to the other end of the fibre.*

8.7.5 *Fibre optics*

When a fibre of glass having a high refractive index is surrounded by a sheath of glass with a lower refractive index, total internal reflection (Section 8.7) can occur at the boundary between the two glasses. If light is directed into the end of such a fibre in a direction nearly parallel to its axis, repeated total internal reflection will take place, allowing the fibre to transmit the light from one end of the fibre to the other with very little attenuation (Figure 8.39). Bundles of such fibres enclosed within an opaque black plastic sheath are commercially available, and are useful for transmitting light over difficult paths. In addition to glass fibres, plastic and quartz fibres are sometimes used. Plastic fibres are cheaper, but introduce slightly more colouration into the transmitted light than glass fibres. Quartz fibres transmit ultraviolet light.

In the simplest kind of fibre bundle, the arrangement of the fibres is random or incoherent, and the bundle acts merely as a flexible light guide. A common use for light guides is to provide light without the accompanying heat of the source. Thus, a bundle can transmit cool light into areas of the body or other sensitive regions, as for example in photoplethysmography (Section 10.3.2). Light guides are simple to use; they can be run from one room to another, making it as easy to conduct light to a distant location as to conduct electricity.

Fibre-optic bundles can also be made which preserve the arrangement of fibres at the two ends; an image projected onto one end will be transmitted to the other end. Coherent-fibres optics are much more expensive than light guides, but are often used when it is necessary to transmit an image over a variable geometry path, as in the mobile eye recording system described in Section 10.3.7. Blocks of tapered fibres can be made into optical magnifiers and reducers. They have also been used in oscilloscope recorders to transmit light from the tube face to the photosensitive paper with greater efficiency than a conventional lens.

8.8 Summary

For quantitative visual work, very close control over the intensity and spectral quality of the light is required. The source is usually a tungsten lamp, and treatment of the light is provided by components mounted on an optical bench, or some similar rigid base. In other areas of psychology, the interest is more in the spatial or temporal aspects of the stimulus. Fluorescent tubes operated from d.c. supply provide a convenient easily switched light source, and are used in many tachistoscopes. The memory drum is a traditional means for serial presentation of fixed lists of items, but, in many modern experiments, it has been replaced by the automatic slide projector and video tape recorder. Computer CRT displays are particularly useful when the items in the sequence are often changed.

CHAPTER 9

Presentation of Reinforcers

9.1 Material reinforcers

The most commonly used reinforcer for animals is food. It is normal practice to control the effectiveness of the reinforcer by keeping each animal on a diet which maintains its body weight at a fixed proportion of its free-feeding or ad lib. body weight.

For rats, the standard reinforcer is a small pellet of food weighing a few milligrams. Suitable pellet dispensers are available from most manufacturers of operant conditioning equipment. They usually work on the principle illustrated in Figure 9.1. The dispensing mechanism is operated by a solenoid which advances a disc having a series of holes near its periphery. Each step of the disc brings a new hole over the end of a tube, allowing a pellet to fall into a cup in the experimental box. The disc also forms the bottom of the food magazine, and therefore, as each empty hole leaves the delivery point, it passes under the pellet load, and a fresh pellet falls into the empty hole; this pellet will in turn be dispensed when it reaches the delivery point. When using this kind of dispenser, it is possible to arrange partial reinforcement schedules without conventional programming equipment; a special disc is fitted which has fewer holes than indexed positions. Thus, if a dispenser which indexes in 15° steps is fitted with a disc which has holes every 90°, a reinforcer will be dispensed every six responses (FR6). This produces conditions which are slightly different from a conventionally programmed schedule, for, when the special disc is used, the secondary reinforcement noises of the feeder are still present for those responses which are not reinforced with pellets.

Particular care is necessary when solid-state modules are used in the same experiment as inductive loads, such as relays and solenoids. When current flows through a coil, energy is stored in the magnetic field (Section 5.5). When the supply is switched off, the current suddenly drops to zero, and the stored magnetic energy causes a high-voltage spike to be generated across the coil. This is the principle on which the ignition coil of a car works. The voltage spike can damage transistors in the driving circuit or cause the relay switching contacts

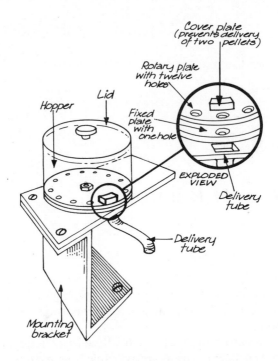

Figure 9.1. *The mechanism of typical pellet dispenser.*

to weld together. The radio frequency interference caused by the spikes can also cause spurious operation of associated solid-state logic. If the coil is operated by direct current, the spike can be suppressed by connecting a silicon diode across the coil in such a direction that it does not conduct when the coil is energized. When the supply to the coil is switched off, the energy stored in the magnetic field is dissipated in the form of an electric current which flows through the coil. In the case of coils operated by alternating current, suppressor circuits can be included in the leads between the switch and the inductive load, or specially designed electronic switching can be employed which connects and disconnects the load only when the alternating voltage is near zero. Spelman and Pagano (1969) give details of techniques suitable for use in the laboratory.

The standard reinforcer for pigeons is a tray of grain which is made accessible for a short time, usually about 3 s. The tray is so positioned that it can only be reached by the bird when the tray has been raised by a solenoid. The bird eats from the tray through a small aperture in the cage panel which is just large enough to allow the entrance of its beak. The tray is filled from a hopper at the rear; every time the tray drops down, grain is shaken to the front, allowing more grain to drop from the hopper. A ring of soft rubber is usually fitted at the front end of the tray to cushion its impact on the feeding aperture and to prevent

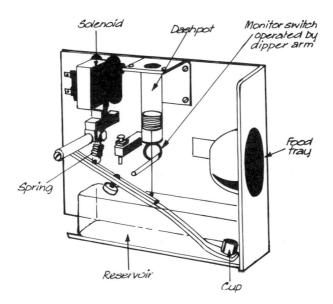

Figure 9.2. *The dipper feeder uses a solenoid-operated cup to deliver discrete amounts of liquid reinforcer to small animals. The dipper arm is pivoted, and one end dips into the reservoir. The solenoid is coupled to the dipper arm through a spring, so that, when the solenoid is energized, the spring becomes extended. The rate at which the dipper cup is lifted into the food tray is regulated by the dashpot, giving a smooth operation, and minimizing the spillage of liquid from the cup (Gerbrands model B-LH).*

spillage when the bird is feeding. During presentation, the feeding aperture is usually illuminated by a small lamp mounted in the food magazine.

Liquid reinforcements are most commonly delivered by a dipper feeder (Figure 9.2). This consists of a cup mounted on a pivoted arm. The cup is normally immersed in a reservoir, but can be raised by a solenoid to the drinking position for brief periods. Cup volumes are around 0·1 ml for rats and around 1 ml for primates. Sometimes liquid reinforcement is delivered under gravity from an elevated storage tank, the flow of liquid to the cup in the experimental box being controlled by a solenoid valve. The quantity delivered for each operation of the dispenser is regulated by adjusting the length of time for which the valve is opened and the height of the tank. A more precise system for delivering liquids is the liquid pump, which is based on a hypodermic syringe (Figure 9.3). The plunger of the syringe is driven by a stepper motor which advances one step for each contact closure on the input terminals. The step size can be varied, and syringes of various sizes can be fitted, enabling the amount of liquid dispensed per operation to be varied over the range 0·001–0·5 ml. Because liquid pumps deliver into a fixed cup, there is no danger of the mechanism catching the animal's tongue, as can happen when a dipper feeder

176

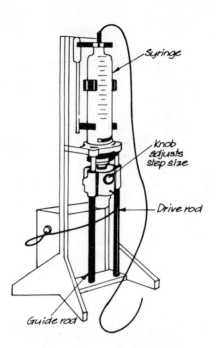

Figure 9.3. *This liquid-pump dispenser uses a standard hypodermic syringe. A preset amount of liquid is delivered each time it is operated (Davis Scientific Instruments).*

is used. On the other hand, dipper feeders have the advantage of restricting the time for which liquid is available.

Material reinforcers used with children include tokens, candy, trinkets etc. Some pellet dispensers can be fitted with discs which allow them to deliver small sweets, and special dispensers are available for delivering coins or tokens. Other small objects can be delivered by universal feeders (Figure 9.4). Such feeders may also be used to deliver a variety of reinforcers, such as brine shrimps, pieces of meat, fruit etc. to laboratory animals.

The Wisconsin General Test Apparatus (WGTA), originally described by Harlow and Bromer (1938), is a standard apparatus for primate discrimination-learning experiments. Objects are presented on a tray, a food reward having been placed by the experimenter under the correct alternative. In contrast to apparatus which employs projected visual stimuli, the WGTA permits the use of 3-dimensional stimuli. A semiautomatic form of WGTA is shown in Figure 9.5. This version is described by Davenport, Chamove and Harlow (1970), and has the following features:

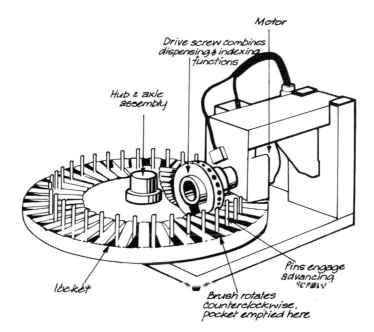

Figure 9.4. *This universal feeder can be used to deliver a wide variety of irregularly shaped objects which are difficult to handle by other means. A motor-driven brush wipes through one pocket every cycle, brushing the contents over the edge of the magazine. The brush is mounted on a large screw, which advances the magazine ready for the next operation while delivery is taking place (Davis Scientific Instruments).*

(1) a tray for presentation of the stimuli, with a food reward placed by the experimenter under the correct alternative,

(2) the option of permitting or denying the subject the opportunity of seeing this replacement,

(3) an observation interval during which the subject can see objects, but is prevented from displacing them,

(4) a subsequent response interval during which the subject has access to the objects and food reward,

(5) a 1-way screen through which the experimenter can observe the subject's behaviour.

Motorized screens give control over the observation and response intervals, and the 1-way screen can be raised between trials to allow the experimenter to arrange the stimuli and rewards. The subject's responses can be detected by microswitches mounted below the stimuli, allowing the response latencies to be recorded automatically.

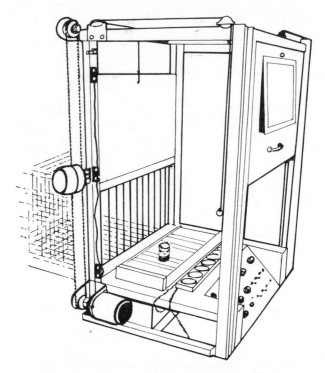

Figure 9.5. *The semiautomatic WGTA. From Davenport, Chamove and Harlow (1970).*

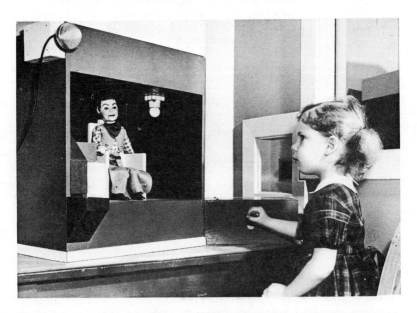

Figure 9.6. *An animated talking puppet for studies of social reinforcement with young children. From Baer (1962).*

9.2 Non-material reinforcers

Because it is not possible to use deprivation to enhance the effectiveness of materials reinforcement with human subjects, attempts have been made to find non-material reinforcers which do not result in rapid satiation. Reinforcement for adults and older children often takes the form of a confirmatory signal, usually a tone or illuminated lamp indicator, which shows that a correct response has been made. The meaning of the signal is explained to the subject when he is instructed at the start of the session. Such methods are hardly suitable for young or severely subnormal children, and, for these subjects, the most durable reinforcers contain some element of novelty. Devices which have been used include mechanized toys, articulated puppets (see Figure 9.6) and a movie cartoon which is terminated in the absence of the required response. Bijou and Baer (1966) have written a useful review of the reinforcers suitable for use with children.

9.3 Aversive stimuli

The most commonly used aversive stimulus is electric shock. With unrestrained subjects, it is usually delivered to the subject through rods forming the floor of the experimental box. If the shock voltage is applied between fixed pairs of bars, the animal will soon learn to avoid the shock by standing on bars of similar polarity. To overcome this problem, a shock scrambler (Skinner and Campbell, 1947) is used. In its simplest form, this is a device which ensures that any two pairs of electrodes are opposite in polarity for at least part of the shock period. A uniform distribution of shock density over the electrodes can be achieved by arranging that each electrode is set opposite in polarity to all the other electrodes for an equal proportion of the cycle. Masterson and Campbell (1972) have written a useful review of techniques for electric shock motivation.

With prolonged exposure to shock, many animals develop techniques for dealing even with scrambled shock; they may lie on their backs so that their fur provides electrical insulation from the grid or balance on a single bar. A remedy for such undesirable escape responses is to attach the electrodes to the subject. Rats may be fitted with subdermal electrodes or shocked at the tail. Sometimes a saddle is fitted over the body. Pigeons are usually shocked from electrodes fitted to the base of the wings. Primates are usually restrained in a specially constructed chair and shocked from electrodes attached to the foot or the base of the tail. With human subjects, electric shock is used in conditioned avoidance procedures for behaviour therapy. In such cases, the electrode placement should be such as to minimize the current flowing through the heart. This can be achieved by placing the pair of electrodes a few centimetres apart on the same limb.

The aversiveness of an electric shock is mainly determined by the value of the current flowing through the subject. Because the electrical resistance of the path through the subject may vary in value during the course of the experiment from about 1 MΩ down to as little as about 10 kΩ, a simple constant-voltage source would allow current variations over a ratio of about 100:1. Such variations can be considerably reduced by including a high resistance in series with the subject and using a high-voltage source. A series resistance of 1 MΩ would reduce the current variation to about 2:1. This method is used in unregulated shockers. An electronic feedback system which maintains a constant current is used in regulated shockers. Both types of shocker produce a.c., usually derived from the mains supply. Because such low frequencies present a safety hazard (Geddes, Baker, Moore and Coulter, 1969) to both the subject and the experimenter, a high-frequency source is to be preferred. For human subjects, a high-frequency shock source should always be used. Weiss (1973) has described a 1 kHz constant-current circuit which can be operated from rechargeable batteries, thereby giving complete isolation from the mains supply.

Much conditioned avoidance work employs the shuttle box (Warner, 1932). This apparatus has two compartments, and a response is defined as the animal moving from one compartment to the other. The animal is shocked if it remains in the compartment which it occupied when the conditioned stimulus was presented, but it avoids the shock if it goes to the other compartment. A shuttle box for fish (Figure 9.7) has been described by Horner, Longo and Bitterman (1961). An elongated tank is divided into two compartments by a hurdle. The distance between the top of the hurdle and the ceiling is sufficient to allow the fish to cross, but is small enough to discourage it from remaining in the region of the hurdle. This ensures that for nearly all the time the animal is in

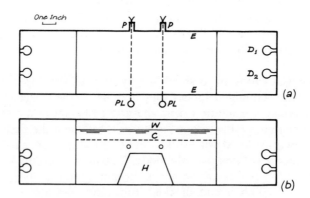

Figure 9.7. *Top view (a) and side view (b) of a shuttle box for fish. P is a photocell, and PL is its associated lamp. E is a shock electrode. D_1 and D_2 are coloured lamps which serve for presentation of the conditioned stimulus. H is the hurdle which separates the two compartments. C is the ceiling of the animal's chamber, and W is the water level. From Bitterman (1966).*

either one compartment or the other. The position of the animal is monitored by photocells which operate programming equipment so that, when a trial is scheduled, the lamps in the same compartment as the animal are used for presentation of the conditioned stimulus. A response is defined as breaking the light beam to the photocell in the other compartment. Shock is administered through electrodes on the sides of the tank. Because continuous shock would immobilize the fish, it is delivered in the form of a series of brief pulses at 2 s intervals.

Aggressive behaviour is often elicited by aversive stimulation, and therefore subjects should be handled with care. Gloves should be worn for small animals and transfer cages employed with larger animals. Aggression is also often directed at objects in the experimental cage, and therefore all objects, particularly those liable to injure the subject, which are not essential to the conduct of the experiment should be removed from the cage.

9.4 Summary

The most commonly used reinforcers for animals are food and water. A pellet dispenser is used with rats and a grain hopper with pigeons. Water is usually dispensed by a dipper feeder, but sometimes a liquid pump is used. The most widely used aversive stimulus is electric shock, but there are considerable problems of delivery and safety. For human subjects, the available reinforcers are fairly weak. The usual reinforcer is confirmatory signal, delivered as a visual or auditory stimulus. Electric shock is sometimes used in behaviour therapy; care should be taken in the placement of electrodes to minimize the current flowing through the heart.

CHAPTER 10

Detection of Responses

10.1 Motor responses

10.1.1 *Discrete events*

In any experiment involving automated control, the subject's responses must be converted into electrical signals. This is normally done by incorporating some form of switch into the response device.

The response device in operant work is usually referred to as the manipulandum, and the form taken depends upon the species. For rats, the standard manipulandum is a bar which operates a switch when pressed (Figure 10.1). The plastic pigeon key (Figure 10.2) operates a switch when it is pecked. Variations of such systems are used for other laboratory animals. The plastic key has the advantage that a visual stimulus display can be mounted behind it (Figure 10.3). Early manipulanda used snap-action microswitches, but, in order to minimize contact bounce (Section 4.2.10), most commercial manipulanda now use magnetically actuated reed switches.

Various electronic methods for detecting when a subject touches a display have been devised (Cleary, Mayes and Packham, 1976). For work with children or animals, the advantages are that such systems will not become jammed with debris, and that the operation of the manipulandum itself does not provide a potentially confounding source of reinforcement. It is also possible to derive signals giving the coordinates of the subject's response from such devices (see Section 10.1.2). Detection of electrical contact has been used for many years in the study of consummatory behaviour. The drinkometer (Hill and Stellar, 1951) is such a system. The gramophone pickup has also been used to detect the vibrations associated with the consummatory responses of small animals (Pert and Bitterman, 1969; Eisman, 1969) and the startle response of rats (Galvani, 1970). Bitterman (1966) used a gramophone pickup to detect responses in fish. A submerged paddle was connected by a lightweight lever to the stylus of a crystal pickup (Section 7.2.1). The discrete responses detected by a pickup are amplified, usually by a conventional audio amplifier, and then standardized by a monostable (Sections 4.2.7 and 5.11.4).

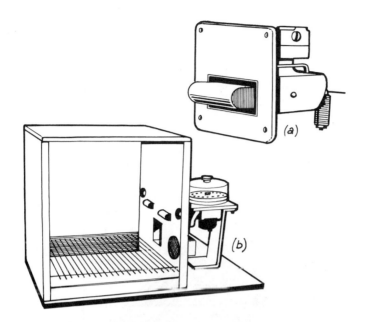

Figure 10.1. *A typical lever for use in operant condition-ing experiments with rats (a). The lever is made from stainless steel, and is 2 in wide and 1/2 in thick. An adjustable weight is mounted at the rear, allowing the operating force to be set as required. Special bearings are fitted to dampen oscillations when the lever is released. Electrical contact is made by the microswitch mounted above the lever. The experimental chamber (b) has two of the levers fitted, together with a pellet dispen-ser, stimulus lamps and a loudspeaker ((a) Gerbrands model G6312 and (b) GenRad model 1111-P).*

For human subjects, telegraph keys, lever switches and pushbuttons have been used. Such switches often produce an unacceptable amount of contact bounce when used with semiconductor circuits, and the special switches design-ed for electronic keyboards are to be preferred. A similar problem can arise when it is necessary to use a very sensitive or rapidly acting device which is able to resolve the subject's tremor at the beginning and end of a response. Unless such signals are specially processed, parts of the tremor may be treated by an automated system as separate responses. Figure 10.4a shows a common method of signal conditioning for signals from switch contacts. Response switch SW_1 shorts out a positive voltage source fed through a low-value resistor R_1. The intermittent pulses at the beginning and end of the response are smoothed out by the resistor–capacitor filter R_2 and C_1, producing the waveforms shown in Figure 10.4b. R_2 has a higher value than R_1, and therefore the time constant (Section 5.6) has approximately the same value $R_2 \times C_1$ for charging and

Figure 10.2. *A typical pigeon key. It is usual to illuminate the translucent disc only when responses are required. Most panels have lamps which allow the key to be illuminated in any one of three colours. It is good practice to have a pair of lamps wired in parallel for each colour, so that the key will still be illuminated if any one lamp burns out during the session. Also shown are the aperture allowing access to the tray of grain which is used as a reinforcer, and the grille of a loudspeaker which may be used to present white noise to mask the sounds of associated electromechanical control gear.*

discharging. The component values are such that the time constant is greater than the maximum expected duration of contact bounce. The Schmitt trigger is a voltage-level detector which is widely used to derive defined logic levels from varying signals. When the input voltage is increased from an initial value of zero, the output voltage switches to logic 1 as the input passes a defined trigger level, and will then not change even though the input signal makes small variations. The output will not switch back to logic 0 until the input signal falls below another defined trigger level which may be 1 V or so below the upper trigger level. This difference between the two trigger levels is termed

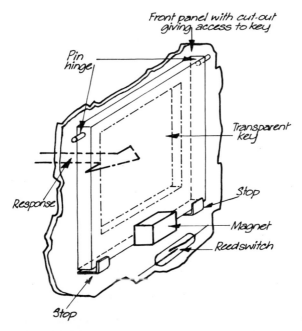

Figure 10.3. *A typical stimulus-response key. A miniature projection indicator, or even a random-access slide projector, may be mounted behind the transparent key. When the key is moved away from the panel, the magnet moves closer to the reed switch, and causes the contacts to close. If the key is mounted in a vertical position, the weight of the magnet provides a restoring force; otherwise a spring may be required.*

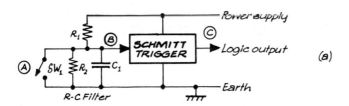

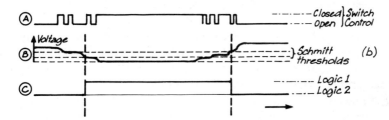

Figure 10.4. *The use of a resistor–capacitor filter and a Schmitt trigger to eliminate contact bounce (a). Typical waveforms are shown in (b).*

186

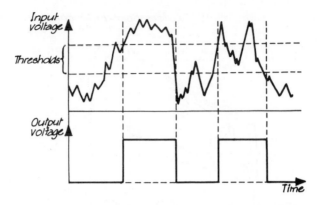

Figure 10.5. *The action of a Schmitt trigger on a noisy signal.*

hysteresis, and it is this characteristic which is useful for countering the effects of noise (Figure 10.5).

When subjects are required to make multichoice responses or to indicate ratings, and it is not necessary to record response latency, the usual method of recording the data is pencil and paper. If many subjects are involved, and a computer centre with a document reader is available, then mark sense forms may be used. This method of collecting data is especially valuable if computer analysis is intended.

In many cases, the behaviour of interest is difficult to instrument, and direct observation is employed. A 1-way screen is often used to minimize the effects of an observer's presence. The effectiveness of such a screen depends on maintaining a lower level of illumination in the observation room than in the experimental room. This difference is usually achieved by using a semireflecting mirror for the screen, which transmits only a small amount of light into the otherwise dimly lit observation room. Any other lighting for the observation room should be by means of artificial lights directed away from the screen. When viewed from the experimental room, the screen looks like a normal mirror, with the reflection of objects in the experimental room masking any view of the observation room. Some care is necessary when using a 1-way screen, because even a well designed system will reveal white clothes or reflecting jewellery if observers stand too close to the screen. Sound attenuation between the two rooms is improved by double-glazing the screen and carefully sealing the glass edges. If it is necessary to listen to the experimental room, an electronic sound system should be installed. A useful guide to the specification and design of observation rooms is given in Horowitz (1969).

If the reflecting surface of the 1-way screen is very conspicuous, it is likely that some subjects, particularly children, will attend more to the mirror than to the experimental task. In such cases, special screens without a reflecting surface (Lott and Woll, 1966; Passman, 1974) or closed-circuit television may be used. Video tape recording and photography may be used to record behaviour for later analysis. Time-lapse photography allows behaviour to be sampled at regular intervals over an extended period; the single-shot release on a cine camera is actuated by a timer and solenoid. Such records are most conveniently studied on an analyst projector (Section 8.7.2). If the behaviour is intermittent, its occurrence may be used to trigger the camera release. For example, in field studies of animals, a light beam directed across the entrance of a burrow onto a photocell can be used as an activity detector. The photographic record will allow subsequent identification of the triggering event. Times can be recorded by including a clock in the field of view.

10.1.2 *Continuous events*

Continuous measures of motor responses in humans often involve some kind of tracking behaviour. At its simplest, the apparatus may be a paper pull (Poulton, 1962; 1964). The target course is marked on a paper roll which is pulled past a slot, thereby presenting a view of the target to the subject, whose task is to keep a pencil on the target. After the trial, the paper roll contains a record of the subject's responses alongside the target course. A somewhat similar device which permits automatic scoring is the pursuit rotor (Figure 10.6). This instrument is often based on a gramophone turntable, revolving at a speed which may be set within the range of about 20–80 rev/min. The subject's task is to keep a hinged stylus in contact with a target set in the turntable near to its edge. Contact with the target is detected electrically, allowing the automatic scoring of cumulative on and off target times.

A potentiometer (Figure 10.7) is perhaps the simplest and most commonly used device for converting the setting of an adjustable control to an electrical

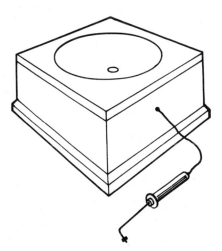

Figure 10.6. *A typical pursuit rotor.*

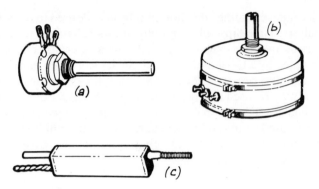

Figure 10.7. *Various types of potentiometer: (a) is a type used for front panel controls, (b) is a precision rotary potentiometer, and (c) is a linear-displacement potentiometer.*

representation. Potentiometers are available in rotary and linear form in a wide range of values and qualities. The potentiometers used for front panel controls in electronic equipment normally have the resistance element constructed from carbon. Potentiometers are available with two kinds of law relating the voltage at the wiper to movement of the control: linear law and logarithmic law. The latter are mainly used as audio volume controls to give approximately the same perceived change in loudness for a given amount of movement of the front panel control. For low values of resistance or high power ratings, potentiometers are also wound from resistance wire. When smooth movement and fine resolution are required, potentiometers which have been designed for use as position transducers in automatic control systems should be used. These often employ a plastic-film resistance element, and are considerably more expensive.

The potentiometer principle can be used to monitor a position response in two dimensions. Bauer, Woods and Held (1969) describe a system for digital recording of the end position of a pointing response in two dimensions. The system uses a sheet of Teledeltos paper. This is metallized paper with a uniform electrical resistance in all directions across its surface. Figure 10.8 shows the electrical connections to the paper. When the bias voltage is as shown in the figure, current will flow across the paper only in the horizontal direction through the diodes on the vertical edges. The diodes along the horizontal edges are reverse-biased, and offer a very high resistance. Thus, a stylus applied to the paper behaves as the slider of a horizontal potentiometer, and the voltage at the slider represents the X coordinate of the response position. If the potential of the bias voltage is reversed, the current flow switches to the other sets of diodes, and the stylus behaves like the wiper of a vertical potentiometer. With either polarity of bias voltage, the current flow across the paper is substantially uniform, because of the frequent spacing of the diodes. The voltage on the

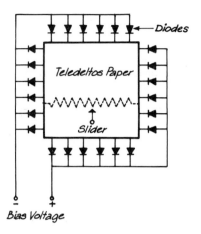

Figure 10.8. *Teledeltos paper response board. The diodes are connected in different directions for the X and Y coordinates. From Bauer, Woods and Held (1969).*

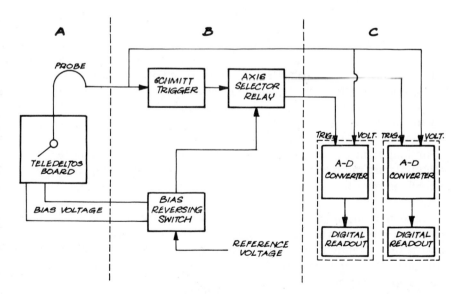

Figure 10.9. *2-dimensional digital measurement and display system. Section A is the transducer, B the control unit, and C the analogue–digital converter and display. From Bauer, Woods and Held (1969).*

190

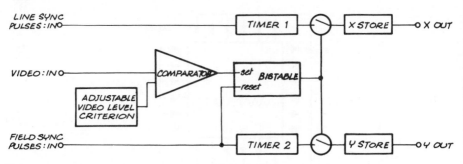

Figure 10.10. *Simplified block diagram of the teletracker system. For simplicity, the forbidden-zone logic and pulse generators for labelling the video output are not shown in the diagram.*

stylus is switched to a pair of analogue–digital converters and digital displays (Figure 10.9) for presentation to the experimenter.

A system for deriving X and Y coordinates for the position of a single light or dark element in a television display has been used by Downing (1972; 1976) to monitor the behaviour of a freely moving animal. The teletracker, as the device is termed, takes as its input the video signal (Section 8.7.4) from a standard television system. It produces two output signals proportional to the X and Y coordinates of the target object, referred to an origin at the top left-hand corner of the picture. A television video signal includes line and field synchronizing pulses along with the picture-brightness information. These synchronizing pulses are used in the teletracker to reset and start the line and field timers (Figure 10.10). When the video signal exceeds a criterion value of brightness for the first time in a field, the values of the X and Y coordinates are transferred to a pair of stores, where the values are held until they are updated in the next field. The teletracker also has a facility for defining forbidden zones in the picture within which triggering will not occur. A video output is provided which shows the forbidden zones and labels the object which is currently being tracked (Figure 10.11). It is generated by adding a positive-going pulse into a copy of the video input whenever the bistable changes state.

For long-term tracking of animals, some investigators have tagged them with miniature radio transmitters (Jackman and Cowgill, 1970). This method of tracking may be combined with the telemetry of physiological functions (Mackay, 1970).

A common means for measuring the presumed emotional reactivity of laboratory rats is provided by the open-field test. At its simplest, the apparatus consists of a brightly illuminated enclosure, the floor of which is marked off into squares of equal area. The animal's activity is recorded by counting the number of units entered during a given time. It is also usual to record the amount of defecation and the latency of moving from the starting square. Various automatic recording methods have been used with the open-field apparatus, such as electrical contact grids in the floor of the apparatus, radio

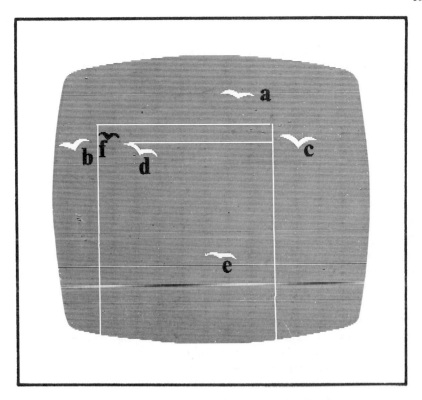

Figure 10.11. *A typical television picture from the video output of the teletracker. The television input to the teletracker is of several birds, most of which are brighter than the background. The position of bird d is to be recorded. Birds a, b, and c appear before it in the scan, but bird f is ignored because it does not meet the brightness criterion. Forbidden zone positions shown in the display as bright lines inhibit detection of birds b, a and c. Thus bird d is the first object to trigger the detector, indicated on the display by the superimposed horizontal bright line.*

frequency coils which register a change of resonant frequency and the reflection of ultrasonic energy. Cohen and Denenberg (1973) describe a system based on infrared light-emitting diodes arranged in a grid. The apparatus gives the position of the animal in the form of X and Y coordinate values which may be fed to a chart recorder or processed by a minicomputer.

Two common devices for measuring the general activity of small animals are the stabilimeter cage and the activity wheel. The stabilimeter cage is supported by springs, and therefore movements of the animal also cause the cage to move. The movement of the cage is detected by a mechanical transducer, which may be merely a microswitch operating an electromechanical counter every time contact is made. The counter is read at regular intervals to give a record of activity over time. The activity wheel or treadmill gives a measure of running activity by counting the rotations of the wheel. The rotations may be counted directly by a mechanical cyclometer, or by operating an electromechanical counter from a microswitch actuated by a cam mounted on the axle of the wheel. If a printout counter (Section 11.2.2) is used, it can be arranged to print the contents of the counter at regular intervals. Finger (1972) has reviewed techniques for the measurement of behavioural activity.

10.2 Verbal responses

A tape recorder (Section 7.5) is frequently used for the routine recording of verbal responses. Playback of the material allows careful analysis of the recorded material, and also facilitates the use of independent judges for scoring responses. Automatic analysis of verbal content is not yet possible, and progress in the field of speech recognition is not encouraging.

When verbal-reaction times are required, a voice key may be used. Early instruments relied on electrical contacts fitted to the subject's lips or actuated by the vibrations produced in a membrane-covered drum, but modern voice keys use a microphone and amplifier to drive a trigger circuit. The main difficulty with voice keys is their inability to discriminate between a subject's grunts and mumbles and his intentional responses. Electronic voice keys usually have various controls for adjusting such parameters as the gain and frequency response of the amplifier and the duration of sustained input signal necessary to operate the trigger circuit, but even the most careful adjustments will not entirely eliminate some triggering from spurious signals. If the nature of the experiment is such that detection of the subject's verbal responses is not essential during the experimental session, then it is preferable to record the responses and to analyse the record for latencies during replay. If auditory stimuli are being presented, these can be recorded on one track of a stereo tape recorder, the subject's responses being recorded on the second track. On replay, two voice keys would be used, one with the stimulus as input starting a timer/counter, and the other with the responses as input stopping the timer/counter. If a non-auditory stimulus is in use, the time of presentation could be indicated on the stimulus track of the tape recorder by switching a brief audio tone to the input of the recorder simultaneously with the presentation of the stimulus, and then using the same procedure for analysis. The posibility of repeated playback allows the voice-key controls to be adjusted for best results. If spurious sounds still cause difficulties, they may be carefully erased, or the audio signals may be transferred to a polygraph, preferably after being rectified (Section 5.9.6), for visual analysis.

10.3 Physiological responses

The terms physiological psychology and psychophysiology are generally used to describe two different traditions in the study of the relationship between brain and behaviour. The approach in physiological psychology is invasive, and often involves irreversible manipulation of a physiological system, followed by measurement of the resulting behavioural change. It may also involve surgical intervention for the purpose of sampling body fluids or tissue, or for the direct recording of physiological variables. Because such techniques cannot generally be used with human subjects, experimentation in physiological psychology is largely confined to work with animals. Psychophysiological investigations, on the other hand, are characterized by non-invasive techniques, and therefore normally use human subjects. Psychophysiology is mainly concerned with the study of physiological variables in an attempt to devise objective measures of the more elusive psychological concepts such as emotion, although many psychophysiological techniques are also used in animal studies.

Perhaps the most characteristic piece of apparatus found in a physiological psychology laboratory is the stereotaxic instrument (Figure 10.12) invented by Horsley and Clarke (1908). This is used to place an electrode, cannula or some other kind of probe at a preselected point in the brain of an experimental animal. The stereotaxic instrument holds the head in a fixed position, and allows the electrode to be inserted at a location which has a known relation to well defined features of the skull. Anaesthetics are used, and the animal's head is held rigidly in position by bars inserted in the external auditory canals and by a bar upon which the incisor teeth are located. The electrode carrier can be

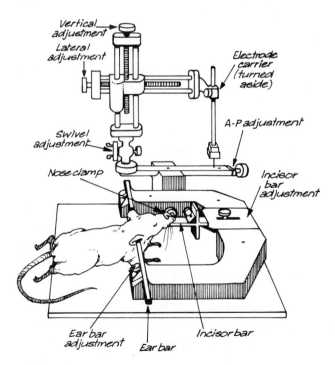

Figure 10.12. *A stereotaxic instrument with a rat properly positioned. From Hart (1976).*

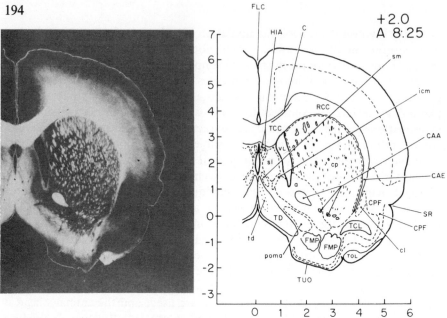

Figure 10.13. *A page from a stereotaxic atlas. The numbers are coordinates referred to the standard points on the skull. From Skinner (1971).*

moved to the required position by means of calibrated controls. To use such an instrument effectively, it is necessary to know the location of the brain structures to be investigated relative to the landmarks by which the skull is located. Brain atlases (Figure 10.13) have been prepared for the common laboratory animals. Lesions are normally made by radio frequency heating or by d.c. electrolysis. Microelectrodes are used both for stimulation and for recording. Cannulation allows the introduction of small amounts of chemical substances to particular areas of the brain. Although neurophysiological studies can be made on the brain of an anaesthetized acute animal preparation, for many purposes, it is necessary that the animal should be conscious and able to move fairly freely. Chronic implantation is now a well established technique. Typically, electrodes are inserted into the appropriate region of the brain, and fastened to a connector which is fixed to the skull. The animal is then plugged into the apparatus when the experiments are to be run. Special cable arrangements are necessary to allow the animal freedom of movement, and mercury sliprings (Figure 10.14) are commonly employed. Some investigators have even used miniature radio receivers for brain stimulation of unrestrained animals (Delgado, 1967).

It is not feasible in a general book of this kind to give a comprehensive treatment of all the specialized techniques employed in physiological psychology. Introductory laboratory manuals, such as those writen by Hart (1969) and Skinner (1971), are available. More advanced treatment of physiological techniques will be found in the books edited by Bradley (1975), Bureŝ, Petráñ and Zacher (1967) and Myers (1971; 1972).

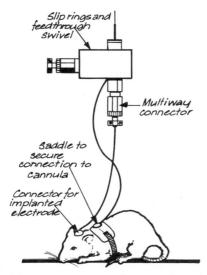

Figure 10.14. *A rat with a cannula and electrodes implanted chronically. A miniature connector is mounted on the skull allowing the recording leads to be connected and disconnected for the experimental sessions. Sliprings and swivelling cannular feedthrough allow the leads to turn freely as the animal moves around the cage.*

When recording a particular bioelectric signal, it is important to try to minimize the inclusion of signals from other physiological systems. This is particularly the case when the subject is required to make motor responses. When an electrocardiogram is being recorded for diagnostic purposes in a hospital, unwanted muscle potentials can be minimized by asking the patient to relax on a couch and to hold his breath. Under such conditions, a good electrocardiogram can be obtained from electrodes connected to the limbs. If a subject is engaged in active physical exercise, however, it may be necessary to attach the electrodes to the chest, in order to maximize the wanted signal from the heart and to minimize the unwanted skeletal muscle potentials. In some cases, the frequency spectra of the wanted and unwanted signals differ greatly, and it is possible to discriminate in favour of the wanted signal by the use of an appropriate filter (Section 7.6.3). Physiological amplifiers often have high- and low-frequency controls which allow the passband of the amplifier to be adjusted. On some amplifiers, the low-frequency control is designated the time constant, and the high-frequency control may be designated the risetime. These terms refer respectively to the settling time and transient response of the amplifier. To convert these times to the half-power or 3 dB points, use the formula

$$\text{frequency} = \frac{1}{2\pi \times \text{time}}$$

Unwanted signals picked up from items of electrical equipment constitute another form of inteference. Electrical power wiring radiates with a frequency of 50 or 60 Hz, and presents the most serious problem. Motors and transformers should be kept well clear of the area in which low-level signals are present. In some cases, it is necessary to place the subject within an electrically screened cage containing only battery-powered equipment. This is used to amplify the signals before they are brought out of the cage to the mains-operated recording equipment. Leads carrying low-level signals are usually screened by an earthed copper braid or formed into a twisted pair of the leads for each signal circuit. Nevertheless, however much care is taken, the subject and leads will still pick up some interfering signals, but the effects of this interference can be considerably reduced by using a physiological amplifier. This is a special kind of amplifier with two input lines, neither of which is at earth potential, but each of which affects the output signal in an equal and opposite manner. Such amplifiers are called differential amplifiers, and are designed to amplify only the difference in voltage between the input lines. In practice, differential amplifiers are still affected to some extent by voltage differences between the inputs and earth, but this common-mode voltage is amplified very much less than the differential input. Because the intefering signals tend to produce similar potentials over the body surface with respect to earth, and the electrodes are usually sited to maximize the potential difference of the wanted signal, differential amplifiers discriminate greatly in favour of the wanted signal. The ratio of differential-mode to common-mode amplification is termed the common-mode rejection, and this ratio should be high for a physiological amplifier, at least 10^4. Some noise is generated within the electrodes and also within the amplifier itself (Section 7.6.1). This noise provides a physical limit to the size of signal which can be reliably detected.

The classical recording device for physiological variables was the kymograph drum. This has now been largely superseded by the multipen chart recorder and instrumentation tape recorder (Section 11.1). Special versions of chart recorders known as polygraphs (Figure 10.15) are used in psychophysiology. These incorporate physiological amplifiers and couplers for various transducers. They are often modular in design, so that they can be configured to suit the needs of a particular experiment.

When surface electrodes are used, the contact to the skin must be very good to give a low resistance at this point. This is usually achieved by abrading the skin with sandpaper or a dental burr to remove the horny outer layer, and by the use of electrolyte jelly between the electrode and skin surface. The resistance between the electrodes R_e should be very much less than the input resistance of the physiological amplifier R_a, because the signal input to the amplifier from a bioelectric event V will be reduced on the basis of Ohm's law to $V \times R_a/(R_e + R_a)$. An even more serious effect is that the input to the amplifier will vary if the electrode resistance varies during the experiment. Each metal–electrolyte interface acts as half a voltaic cell. If the two interfaces are identical, they will cancel out, otherwise some voltage, varying with the

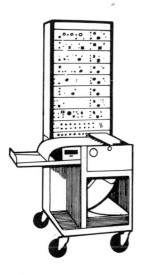

Figure 10.15. *A typical polygraph used for psychophysiological recording. It is fitted with a multichannel pen recorder and uses fanfold paper. Above the recorder is a rack which can house various physiological amplifiers and couplers (Grass Instruments model 7B).*

nature of the interface, will result. This is not normally a problem when recording high-level a.c. phenomena such as the electrocardiogram, but it can present serious difficulties for low-level d.c. recording of such- phenomena as the electrooculogram. In any recording circuit, some current must flow through the electrodes, and therefore electrolysis will occur. The byproducts of this electrolysis modify the metal–electrolyte interface, a process known as polarization, thus causing a change in the half-cell potential. Various electrode materials have been used in an attempt to reduce these effects, but the silver/silver chloride electrode is most widely used for low-level or d.c. recording. Chloriding of silver disc electrodes is accomplished by immersing them in saline solution and making them positive with respect to a silver plate for a few minutes. Geddes and Baker (1975) is a good general work on biomedical instrumentation, and includes a chapter reviewing various electrode techniques. Standard reference works on psychophysiological methods have been edited by Brown (1967), Venables and Martin (1967b) and Greenfield and Sternbach (1972).

Recently, there has been much interest in biofeedback, a technique which aims to give a subject improved control over one of his physiological systems by giving him a display of its state. It is, in effect, an attempt to extend the well established finding that knowledge of results facilitates learning, from the voluntary nervous system, within which feedback is readily available, to the visceral system, for which instrumentation is needed to close the control loop. Biofeedback apparatus is manufactured for clinical and personal use, the main interest being in control of EEG, skin resistance level, skin temperature, EMG, heart rate and blood pressure. Biofeedback instrumentation has been reviewed by Paskewitz (1975).

10.3.1 *Skin resistance and skin potential*

The discovery that the resistance offered to a small electric current passed

198

through the body between two points on the skin decreases when the subject is stimulated is generally attributed to Féré (1888). Soon afterwards, Tarchanoff (1890) discovered that the potential difference between two points on the body surface also varied when the subject was stimulated. After further work, Veraguth (1909) introduced the term psychogalvanic reflex (PGR). The other commonly used term, glavanic skin reflex (GSR), was introduced by Gildermeister and Ellinghaus (1923).

The continued use of these terms to cover a variety of measurements has caused much confusion in the literature. Venables and Martin (1967a) advocated general use of the following explicit nomenclature, which will be adopted in this section:

SRR   skin resistance response
SRL   skin resistance level
SCR   skin conductance response
SCL   skin conductance level
SPR   skin potential response
SPL   skin potential level.

Conductance is the reciprocal of resistance, and is, in essence, just another way of expressing the same electrical measurement.

SRL and SPL refer to basal levels of resistance and potential, whereas SRR and SPR refer to the changes in these levels which occur with characteristic waveforms as a result of stimulation (Figure 10.16).

Before discussing the methodology, we will briefly review the evidence for the mechanisms underlying skin resistance and skin potential. Both phenomena are thought to be due to the activity of the eccrine sweat glands, the parts of the body having the highest concentration of sweat glands (e.g. palms and soles) showing lowest SRL and most frequent SRR.

The SRR was at one time thought to be due to the emergence of sweat causing

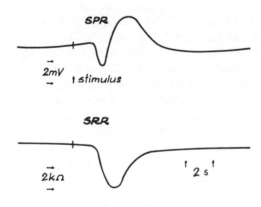

Figure 10.16. *Characteristic skin resistance and skin potential responses. From Venables and Martin (1967a).*

a moistening of the skin, but it has been shown that the response occurs before the emergence of the sweat, and depends rather on the presecretory activity of the semipermeable membrane in the sweat glands.

The terms exosomatic and endosomatic are sometimes used to describe the measurement of skin resistance and skin potential, respectively. The terms derive from the locus of the electromotive force for the measurement, which is outside the subject's body for resistance measurement, and within it for potential measurement.

SRL for the palms of human subjects is in the range of a few kilohms to several thousand kilohms. SRR takes the form of sudden drop in resistance, typically having a magnitude of a few ohms to several kilohms, and has a latency of around 2 s.

The resistance of the skin may be thought of as due to the effect of a number of resistors (sweat glands) in parallel, the number of resistors involved being proportional to the area of the skin through which current is passed. For a given electrode area, the electrical conductance of the skin will be proportional to the number of such hypothetical sweat glands which are conducting. Edelberg, Greiner and Burch (1960) showed that the relationship between the current and the voltage across the skin is linear up to a current density of 11 μA cm^{-2}. Edelberg (1967) found that the current–voltage relationship is also linear for low voltages. This suggests that higher current densities may affect the functioning of the sweat glands.

Two types of approach may be used for the measurement of resistance using Ohm's law:

(1) constant current, in which the current is kept constant, and the voltage across the unknown resistor is measured,
(2) constant voltage, in which the voltage is kept constant, and the current flow is measured.

Both methods have been used for measurement of skin resistance. With the constant current method, the current density must be kept above a minimum level, or the voltage generated will be of the same order as the skin potential, thus giving rise to artefacts. On the other hand, it must not be raised high enough to effect the functioning of the sweat glands. The usual compromise is to aim for a figure of 8 μA cm^{-2}. Venables and Christie (1973) recommend the use of constant-voltage measurement of skin conductance using bipolar recording.

Bipolar (two active electrodes) and unipolar (one active and one inactive electrode) recording may be used (Figure 10.17). Bipolar recording has the advantage that skin potentials at the two sites will tend to cancel each other. Figure 10.18 shows the recommended placements for electrodes. If it should be necessary, for some special reason, to fit the two electrodes on different limbs, very great care must be taken that the equipment is safe, and that a large current is not passed through the subject's heart. The inactive site is prepared to minimize resistance between the electrode and the body fluids.

200

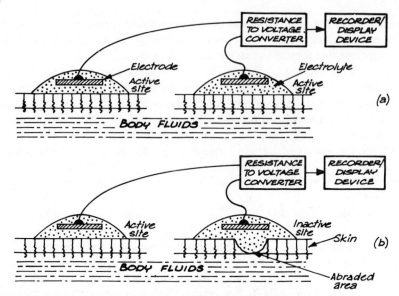

Figure 10.17. *Bipolar (a) and unipolar (b) recording of skin resistance responses.*

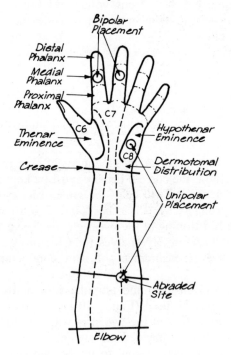

Figure 10.18. *Recommended placement of electrodes for electrodermal measurements. For skin potential, only unipolar recording is used. From Venables and Christie (1973).*

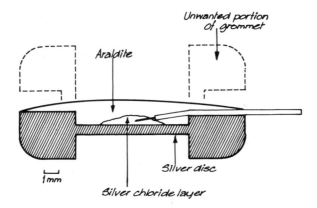

Figure 10.19. *Construction of a silver/silver chloride electrode. From Venables and Martin (1967a).*

The material from which the electrode is made should minimize polarization. This is usually achieved by coating a metal with one of its soluble salts, the usual choice being the silver/silver chloride electrode (Figure 10.19). The preparation of suitable electrodes is detailed in Venables and Martin (1967a). For the constant-current method, polarization may be reduced by an annular arrangement in which the electrode which supplies the current is separate from that which is used for measurement of the voltage (Lykken, 1959). If alternating current is used to eliminate the effects of polarization, the frequencies used should be low, to avoid artefacts from the capacitance of the skin.

For stable recordings, the electrode should be kept at a constant moisture level by the use of a viscose electrolyte in jelly form, and the electrode should be sealed to prevent the electrolyte from drying. Care should also be taken to keep the electrolyte localized, or this will alter the effective area of the electrode. The palmar regions are the usual site for the active electrode, but cuts and abrasions should be avoided, because these act as short circuits across the sweat glands, and greatly reduce the measured values of skin resistance. The inactive electrode site is usually the forearm of the same limb as the active site. It should be prepared by gentle abrasion with sandpaper or a dental burr.

The classical method of measuring resistance is by means of a bridge circuit (Figure 10.20) in which one arm is a calibrated variable resistor, the value of

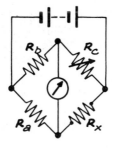

Figure 10.20. *The Wheatstone bridge. The bridge is balanced by adjusting R_c for zero deflection of the meter. The value of R_x is then given bn $R_c \times R_a/R_b$.*

which is adjusted for zero current through the galvanometer. Variants of this circuit have been used for measurement of skin resistance, the traditional place for the galvanometer in the circuit of Figure 10.20 providing a voltage which indicates the variation of resistance around the balance point of the bridge. This voltage is amplified and the output recorded in much the same way as for skin potential. Venables and Christie (1973) give constructional details of a constant voltage circuit for skin conductance measurement.

When measuring skin potential, unipolar recording is necessary, otherwise the two skin potentials would tend to cancel out. The basal potential between active palmar and inactive forearm sites is about 60 mV, and the response is diphasic in character (Figure 10.16). The electrodes employed are usually silver/silver chloride, and the inactive site is abraded to reduce the skin resistance and to short circuit the skin potential.

The electronic equipment required for skin potential recording is the same as for much physiological work. The electrodes are connected to a physiological amplifier for amplification and signal conditioning. The output of the amplifier may be recorded by any suitable analogue recorder (Section 11.1) or laboratory computer. If SPL is to be recorded, a d.c. amplifier must be used.

Skin temperature has been found to affect skin resistance and skin potential measurements. Therefore the room temperature should be kept constant, and it is also good practice to monitor the skin temperature by using a thermistor or thermocouple.

10.3.2 *Heart rate*

In psychophysiology, two fundamentally different methods are used for the detection of heart beats:

(1) electrocardiography (EKG or ECG), in which the electrical signals accompanying cardiac activity are amplified and used directly,
(2) pulse plethysmography, in which transducers are used to detect the changes in peripheral vascular volume which accompany each heart beat.

Plethysmography allows the size of each pulse volume to be monitored. This is of interest in psychophysiology, because the arterioles and capillaries are constricted by sympathetic innervation, causing a reduction in the amplitude of the pulse plethysmogram.

When EKG is used, the heart rate is usually obtained by counting the large spikes which are associated with ventricular contraction. Typical EKG records are shown in Figure 10.21, which also gives details of the more commonly used lead configurations in clinical EKG. The exact placement is not critical for psychophysiological purposes, but the lead II configuration usually gives the largest spike, and makes the detection of individual beats easier. EKG electrodes are normally made of silver or stainless steel (Figure 10.22). They are about 10 cm^2 in area, and are curved to allow good contact with the limbs.

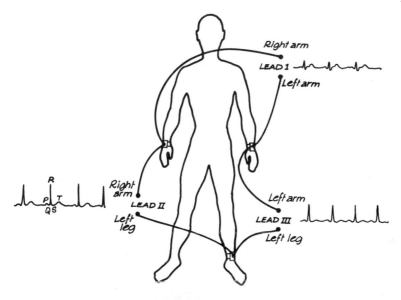

Figure 10.21. *Typical EKG records from three standard lead configurations.*

The skin should be abraded and the electrodes spread with a thin film of electrode jelly before they are applied to the subject. Commercial electrodes are normally secured by rubber straps. These should be adjusted to hold the electrodes firmly in place, but not fitted so tightly that muscle tremor results.

EKG signals are about 2 mV in amplitude, and most general-purpose physiological recording equipment can be used to make direct recordings of EKG. A ratemeter may be used to convert the EKG signal into a voltage proportional to heart rate. When any automatic analysis of EKG is to be performed, great care must be taken to minimize the amount of spurious muscle-

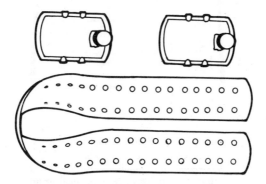

Figure 10.22. *Typical EKG electrodes. The hooks on the electrode allow the elastic strap to be adjusted to suit different sizes of limb.*

204

potential signals in the recording. These are particularly troublesome when the subject is required to make motor responses. In such cases, the electrodes should be connected to limbs which will not be moved. Filtering the signal to leave only a band of frequencies around 8 Hz is recommended by Brenner (1967) for the best signal-to-noise ratio.

Plethysmography is a term derived from the Greek *plethysmos*, meaning an enlargement. In physiology, the term refers to a technique for the measurement of blood flow based on venous occlusion and measurement of the resulting change in volume of the limb or organ. Pulse plethysmography, on the other hand, is used in patient monitoring and psychophysiology for the detection of small changes in volume which occur as the blood is forced through the vascular system at each heart beat. Such changes in volume may be detected by means of a strain gauge or photoelectrically.

The usual form of strain gauge for plethysmography is a narrow elastic

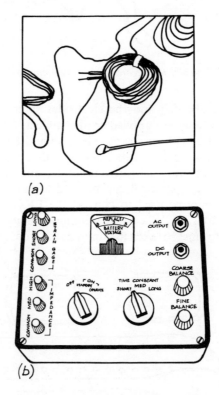

(a)

(b)

Figure 10.23. *Typical mercury strain gauges (a) and an instrument (b) for converting the gauge resistance to a voltage signal. This particular instrument also has facilities for impedance plethysmography (Section 10.3.4) (Parks Electronics Laboratory model 270).*

silicone rubber tube containing mercury, with metallic electrodes sealing each end (Figure 10.23). The gauge is wrapped around the fleshy part of a finger or toe. When the digit changes volume, corresponding changes occur in its circumference, and therefore also in the length of the mercury column. Because the volume of the mercury is constant, the cross-sectional area of the mercury column changes in inverse ratio to the length. If ρ is the specific resistance of a conductor, its resistance is given by

$$R = \frac{\rho l}{a}$$

where l is the length of the conductor and a is the cross-sectional area. Thus, the resistance of the strain gauge will increase with the volume of the digit. Strain gauges used in engineering are of somewhat different design. They are usually made from thin metal foil, and are intended to be cemented to the component under investigation.

The main disadvantage of mercury strain gauges is their susceptibility to chemical deterioration. In time, the mercury attacks the copper electrodes, and causes a break in the continuity of the gauge. If latex rubber tubing is used, it also reacts with the mercury.

The photoplethysmograph (Figure 10.24) uses a miniature light source to illuminate the skin, and detects the changes in transmitted or backscattered light by means of a photoconductive cell. Weinman (1967) discusses the application of the technique to psychophysiology, and Fine and Weinman (1973) give a more recent account of the use of photoconductive cells in photoplethysmography. With photoelectric detectors, stray light sometimes produces artefacts in the recordings, and therefore adequate shielding should be provided. Commercial photoplethysmographs are often housed in black fabric, which is wrapped around a finger to secure the transducer and make a light seal. When pulse volume is being monitored, an important consideration is the amount of heat produced by the light source. Heat causes dilation of the blood vessels and therefore alters the pulse volume. Fibre-optic light guides can be used to provide a cool light source (Section 8.7.5).

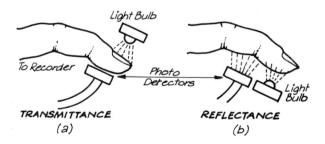

Figure 10.24. *Two types of photoplethysmograph, using (a) transmitted and (b) backscattered light. From Geddes and Baker (1975).*

206

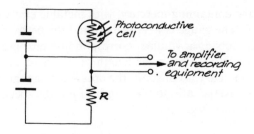

Figure 10.25. Simple circuit for generating a voltage signal from the photoconductive cell in a photoplethysmograph. Resistor R should be of similar value to the resistance of the photo-conductive cell under working conditions.

Both kinds of plethysmograph convert the physiological events to a change of resistance. As with skin resistance, it must be converted to a voltage to allow signal conditioning and recording to take place. The resistance of a mercury strain gauge is typically of the order of 1 Ω, and so a special low-impedance bridge circuit is usually employed. The resistance of the cadmium selenide photoconductive cells, which are normally used in photoplethysmographs, is around 100 kΩ. As they are quite sensitive devices, a simple circuit of the type shown in Figure 10.25 is adequate.

10.3.3 *Blood pressure*

Blood is circulated by discrete ejections from the heart during each cardiac cycle. Because of the elasticity of the arterial system, some of the energy is stored, thereby maintaining a certain minimum pressure with superimposed cyclic variations (Figure 10.26).

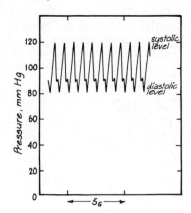

Figure 10.26. Typical recording of blood pressure by the direct method. From Greatorex (1971).

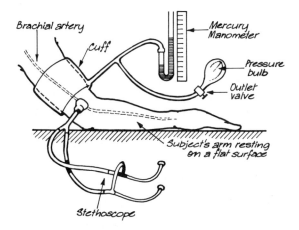

Figure 10.27. *Method of using a sphygmomanometer
for the indirect measurement of blood pressure.*

Blood pressure may be measured either directly or indirectly, but, because
the direct method involves insertion of a cannula into an artery, the indirect
method is usually employed in psychophysiological investigations. The classical
instrument for indirect measurement is the sphygmomanometer, which is
used routinely in medical practice. It consists of an inflatable cloth-covered
rubber cuff connected by a flexible tube to a mercury manometer calibrated to
read the pressure in millimetres of mercury (Figure 10.27). The cuff is wrapped
around the subject's upper arm and inflated by squeezing the rubber bulb
until the blood flow through the brachial artery is occluded. A stethoscope is
then applied to the brachial artery on the inside of the elbow, and the cuff
pressure slowly reduced by means of a valve on the bulb until sounds heard in
the stethoscope (Korotkoff sounds) indicate that the peak of the systolic pressure
is just in excess of the cuff pressure. The manometer reading at this point is
taken as the systolic pressure, the blood pressure during ventricular contraction.
The reduction of pressure is then resumed until the sound becomes muffled
and is suddenly reduced in intensity. The manometer reading at this point
is taken as the diastolic pressure, corresponding to the relaxation of the
ventricles.

Automatic methods for monitoring blood pressure generally use a cyclical
procedure in which the cuff is radidly inflated and steadily deflated, the Korotkoff sounds being detected by a contact microphone, usually of the piezoelectric
type (Section 7.2.1). If the cuff pressure and Korotkoff sounds are recorded
on separate channels of a polygraph, the systolic and diastolic pressures can be
obtained by manual analysis. Sophisticated processing of the two signals allows
quasicontinuous measures of systolic and diastolic pressure to be derived.
Indirect methods of monitoring blood pressure are reviewed in Greatorex
(1971). Tursky, Shapiro and Schwartz (1972) describe a system which auto-

matically adjusts the cuff pressure for detection of 50% of the Korotkoff sounds at the systolic and diastolic points.

10.3.4 *Respiration*

The traditional instrument used in physiological studies of respiration is the spirometer (Figure 10.28). This is only used in behavioural investigations when precise volumetric measures are essential. For most purposes, indirect methods are preferred, because they do not interfere with speech, and cause less discomfort to the subject.

Information about respiration may be derived either from changes in the volume of the body or from the variations in temperature which occur in the air flowing over a miniature bead thermistor (Section 5.9.15) mounted by the nose. This latter method is very easy to use, and couplers for thermistors are available for use with many physiological recorders. The main disadvantage is that the method is obviously subject to error if the subject breathes through the mouth.

The classical method for detecting changes in body volume during respiration is the pneumograph. This consists of a bellows-shapped rubber hose which is

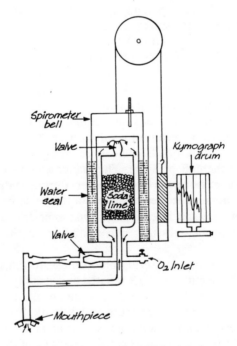

Figure 10.28. *Schematic diagram of the Benedict–Roth closed-circuit spirometer. As the subject breathes the air in a spirometer, oxygen is converted into carbon dioxide. In this form of spirometer, the carbon dioxide is removed by the soda lime and fresh oxygen allowed to replace it. A stylus attached to the cord traces the spirogram on a kymograph drum.*

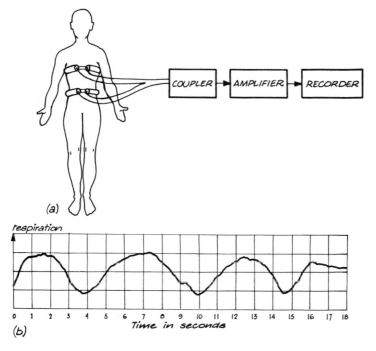

(a)

respiration

(b) Time in seconds

Figure 10.29. *Two mercury strain gauges connected in series for measurement of respiration (a). One gauge is fitted around the chest at about the level of the mammillae and the other around the abdomen at about the level of the umbilicus. A typical recording is shown in (b).*

strapped around the chest. The changes in air pressure in the hose which result from expansion and contraction of the chest are transmitted pneumatically to a stylus which traces a record on a kymograph drum. A modern version of the device replaces the pneumatic system by a linear transducer, such as a mercury strain gauge (Section 10.3.1). Because both the abdominal and intercostal muscles are involved in respiration, it is good practice to sum the signals from the chest and the abdomen (Ax, Singer, Zachery, Gudobba and Gottlieb, 1964). When mercury strain gauges are used, they may be simply connected in series (Figure 10.29).

The ventilation of the lungs causes changes in the electrical impedance of the chest. Impedance plethysmography allows the detection of changes in volume in any part of the body, although it is perhaps most commonly used on the chest. The method consists of attaching electrodes to the chest, and using an a.c. bridge circuit to monitor the impedance continuously. Frequencies of around 50 kHz are used, because the effects of electrical current on biological tissue decrease with frequency (Geddes, Baker, Moore and Coulter, 1969). A review of biomedical applications of impedance measurements is given in Baker (1971), and a detailed account of its application to pneumography is given in Valentinuzzi, Geddes and Baker (1971). Technical details of a circuit which provides measures of tidal volume and the volume of flow per minute by impedance plethysmography are given by Barker and Brown (1973).

Respiration measures used in psychophysiology include those common in physiological investigations, such as tidal volume and volume per minute, as well as measures which reflect short-term changes in respiration pattern, such as the ratio of inspiration to expiration time and the respiration rate. Many commercial ratemeters have ranges suitable for both respiration and heart rate.

10.3.5 *Electroencephalography*

Fluctuations of electrical potential on the surface of the brain were first reported by Caton (1875; 1877). This discovery was made possible at that time by the availability of very sensitive galvanometers. During the following 50 years, several other workers carried out similar investigations, but the topic only achieved prominance after Berger (1929) had made recordings of the scalp electroencephalogram (EEG) in man. Adrian and Matthews (1934a; 1934b) developed more sensitive recording apparatus and replicated Berger's work. They demonstrated that the recordings could not be attributed merely to such other processes as muscle activity or pulsations in the circulatory system, and made an attempt to classify the patterns associated with pathological conditions, age, level of activity etc.

The electroencephalogram recorded at the scalp is, of course, only a gross measure of the activity of large numbers of cortical, and to some extent subcortical, neurons. Even a needle electrode inserted into the brain of an experimental animal records the activity of millions of cells. It might be expected that the combined activity of so many cells would be merely random in character. To some extent, this is the case, but several frequency patterns may also be distinguished in the electroencephalogram. These have been of some clinical value, particularly in the diagnosis of epilepsy.

Waves which occur in the normal electroencephalogram include

delta rhythm	1–4 Hz
theta rhythm	4–8 Hz
alpha rhythm	8–12 Hz
beta rhythm	13–20 Hz

It is important to realize that these bands of frequencies are used purely for convenience in describing electroencephalograms, and do not necessarily represent distinct and separate phenomena. One fairly reliable phenomenon, however, is the occurrence of a pronounced alpha rhythm when the subject closes his eyes and relaxes. When the subject opens his eyes and becomes alert, the signal becomes desynchronized. One of the main research applications of the electroencephalogram is in the study of arousal and sleep (Figure 10.30).

EEG signals have amplitudes around 50 μV, and therefore require considerable amplification. Surface electrodes are usually silver discs or platinum

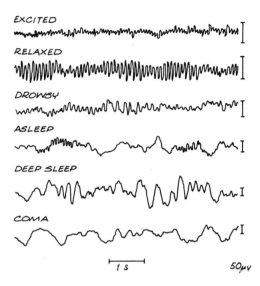

Figure 10.30. *Typical EEG records from normal subjects in different states of arousal and from a comatose subject.*

needles inserted tangentially just under the scalp. For clinical purposes, about 20 electrodes are applied, usually sited according to the ten–twenty system (Jasper, 1958) recommended by the International Federation of EEG Societies (Figure 10.31). Fewer electrodes are usually employed for such applications as sleep research and evoked potentials. Recordings may be either unipolar or bipolar between pairs of scalp electrodes. Unipolar recordings are made between a scalp electrode and either a reference electrode, which is usually placed on the ear lobe, or an average reference point, generated by connecting resistors from each electrode to a common point. Guidance on practice with human subjects will be found in Margerison, St. John-Loe and Binnie (1967) and Marshall (1967). Cooper (1971) gives a detailed account of techniques for depth electroencephalography.

Automatic analysis of EEG records is uaually based on some form of frequency analysis, and, in recent years, much effort has been directed towards the compressed graphical presentation of the results of such analyses (Figure 10.32). Attempts have also been made to devise toposcopic or spatiotemporal displays which provide a picture of the potential field on the subject's head, for example Estrin and Uzgalis (1969). Vo-Ngoc, Poussart and Langlois (1971) describe a system for automatic recognition of sleep spindles in computer-stored EEG data. For biofeedback with EEG, the signal is filtered into the commonly used rhythm bands. Thorsheim, Anderson and Schultz (1974) describe a circuit for generation of beta, alpha, theta and delta biofeedback signals.

212

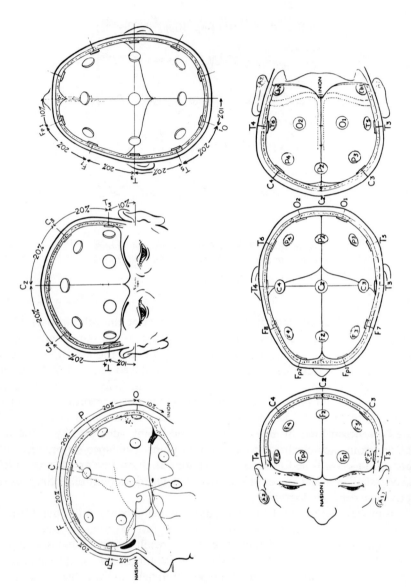

Figure 10.31. *The ten–twenty system for EEG electrode placement. From Jasper (1958).*

213

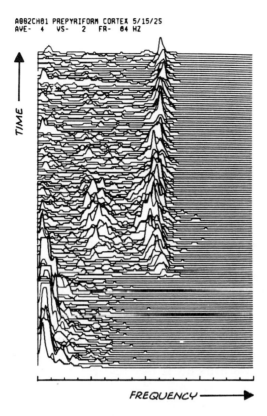

A882CH81 PREPYRIFORM CORTEX 5/15/2S
AVE- 4 VS- 2 FR- 84 HZ

TIME

FREQUENCY ⟶

Figure 10.32. *Compressed spectrum display of
EEG data. The hidden line suppression technique
used in this computer-generated display gives a
quasi-3-dimensional plot of the power spectra.
Changes in the amplitude of the various frequencies can be easily detected.*

Sensory evoked potentials (Shagass, 1972) are difficult to detect in the
noisy background of an EEG signal, and therefore online statistical techniques
such as signal averaging (Section 12.1.1) are commonly used.

10.3.6 *Electromyography*

Electromyography, or EMG, is the recording of electrical activity associated
with muscle contraction. The voluntary muscles are composed of many
separate parallel fibres, often running the whole length of the muscle. Motor
nerves carry impulses from the central nervous system to individual fibres,
each neuron dividing to innervate a number of muscle fibres (the motor unit).
A potential difference of about 75 mV exists across the muscle cell membrane,
the inside being negative with respect to the outside. When a nerve impulse

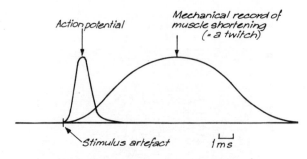

Figure 10.33. *Unipolar recording of an action potential and the mechanical contraction from a whole muscle. From Lippold (1967).*

from a motor nerve reaches a muscle fibre, an action potential occurs with a temporary reversal of the membrane potential to about 30 mV positive on the inside. This action potential lasts for about 1 ms, and precedes the contraction of the fibre, which lasts about 10 ms (Figure 10.33).

In clinical electromyography, unipolar recordings are usually made from needle electrodes inserted into the muscle tissue, giving an electromyogram which is almost entirely the result of the action potentials from a single motor unit. For psychophysiological recording, surface electrodes are used, and the electromyogram which results is therefore generated by many motor units discharging at various frequencies. A comprehensive review of psychophysiological EMG has been written by Lippold (1967). The electromyogram is not a direct measure of muscular contraction or tension, because the action potential and contraction are different events. A high correlation can, however, exist between these electrical and mechanical events under certain well defined conditions (Lippold, 1952).

The amount of muscular activity in the body as a whole is influenced by emotional and motivational factors. Measures of activity in individual muscles or muscle groups can be of value in the study of tracking behaviour and other skilled tasks. Muscle termor, small-amplitude rhythmic variations in muscle activity, is of considerable theoretical interest in the investigation of the control of motor behaviour.

In the intact human subject, bipolar recording of the muscle-action potential by surface electrodes is the normal method employed in electromyography. Figure 10.34 shows diagramatically how a diphasic waveform is produced at two electrodes located along the length of a muscle fibre. In the case of a complete muscle, the waveform is much more complicated (Figure 10.35), consisting of many such diphasic responses, and it typically has an amplitude of around 100 μV for moderate muscle tensions.

When preparing the subject for electromyography, the horny surface layer of skin should be removed and electrode jelly applied in the usual manner (Section 10.3). Since the signals are of reasonable amplitude, and only require a.c.

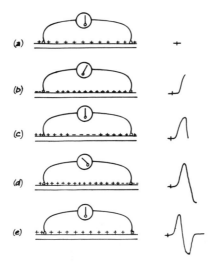

Figure 10.34. *The generation of a diphasic waveform in bipolar recording. In (a), the music is at rest, and so the potential is equal on both sides of the galvanometer, which therefore reads zero. At (b), the action potential has reached the left-hand electrode, causing a deflection of the galvanometer. At (c), the action potential is between the electrodes, and so the galvanometer reads zero again. By (d), the action potential has reached the right-hand electrode, and the galvanometer swings in the opposite direction until (e), when the action potential has passed beyond the two electrodes and the galvanometer is back to zero. From Lippold (1967).*

amplification, the choice of electrode material is not critical. Disposable self-adhesive electrodes (Figure 10.36) are very convenient, and seal the jelly, thereby reducing evaporation.

The frequencies of interest are normally in the range 10–1000 Hz. The usual measure taken is the integrated value of the rectified signal over some specified time interval (Figure 10.37). Early investigators devised special circuits for this purpose, but now, commercial instruments, such as continuous averaging devices and laboratory computers, are used. Where such sophisticated equipment is not available, and a meter display of EMG activity will suffice, the output of the physiological amplifier may be displayed on a high-impedance voltmeter (Section 6.2) using an appropriate a.c. range. Although the meter scale will be calibrated in r.m.s. volts, most meters of this type actually measure the average value. Figure 10.38 shows the results from such an experiment.

Where EMG is to be used as a quantitative measure, the muscular contrac-

216

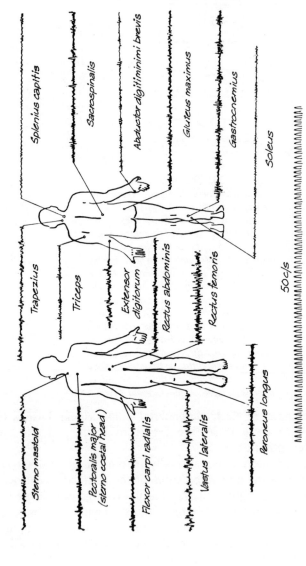

Figure 10.35. *Typical EMG recording from bipolar surface electrodes. From Lippold (1967).*

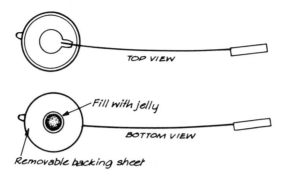

Figure 10.36. *Self-adhesive electrodes suitable for EMG recording.*

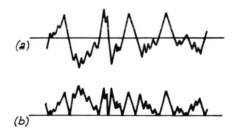

Figure 10.37. *To make measurements from an electromyogram, the signal (a) is first rectified (b), and then integrated by measuring the area under the curve for specified short periods of time.*

tion must be isometric (at the same length during measurements), and fatigue should be minimized. Artefacts which can affect EMG include

(1) the effects of lead movement (tape the leads to the subject),
(2) EKG signals,
(3) EOG signals from sites near the eyes.

The latter two artefacts may be reduced by filtering out frequencies below 30 Hz.

10.3.7 *Eye movements*

The main reason for recording eye movements in psychology is to monitor the subject's point of fixation. Most methods only give information on the eye position relative to the head, and therefore it is necessary either to locate the head rigidly, usually by a bite board (Figure 10.39), or to monitor simultaneously the position of the subject's head.

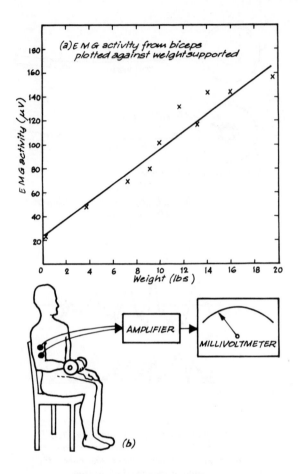

Figure 10.38. *(a) A plot showing the highly linear relationship which can be obtained between EMG activity and tension under isometric conditions. These records were obtained from surface electrodes on the biceps muscle. The simple arrangement of subject, physiological amplifier and a.c. millivoltmeter is shown in (b).*

Subjective methods are easy to use, but do not provide a continuous record. Methods which have been used include the placing of an afterimage at the centre of the field of view and asking a subject to report its subsequent position. It is also possible to use entoptic phenomena, such as the subject's perception of his own macula using suitably filtered light (Alpern, 1962).

An early objective method (Dodge and Cline, 1901) is based on recording the reflection of a small light source from the corneal bulge. Infrared light is preferred, as it does not distract the subject. The ophthalmograph is an instrument which has been used for the study of eye movements during reading. It

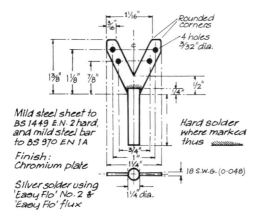

Figure 10.39. *Constructional details of a bite board. Two lumps of thermosetting dental wax are softened in hot water and moulded onto the arms of the board. The subject then sinks his canine and adjacent teeth into the wax, which is allowed to harden. From Shackel (1967).*

uses corneal reflection to record eye movements on a moving strip of film. The instrument usually has provision for recording only the horizontal movements, but the optical system can be adapted to resolve the movement of the spot, sometimes referred to as the fixation marker, into both the horizontal and vertical vectors. Mackworth and Mackworth (1958) have modified the method using television techniques to superimpose the fixation marker on a picture of the stimulus material. A further development (Mackworth and Thomas, 1962) allowed the subject mobility by mounting the television camera on the subject's head. Figure 10.40 shows a commercial version of this system which considerably reduces the weight of equipment to be carried on the head by transmitting the images from the optical unit through a pair of fibre-optic cables to a camera slung by a strap from the subject's shoulder. In this instrument, the fixation marker and field of view are optically combined, allowing the choice of either a cine camera, giving full mobility, or a television camera, for immediate viewing. The recording accuracy of the system is claimed to be $\pm 1°$. The laboratory version uses a bite board, and gives about twice this recording accuracy. The television signal may be processed to give the X and Y coordinates of the fixation marker in a similar manner to that employed in the teletracker system described in Section 10.1.2.

Some workers have used reflection from a small plane mirror attached to the eye by a contact lens or sucker, but, because of slippage and the discomfort caused to the subject, such methods have not gained great popularity.

The photoelectric method is based on changes in the amount of infrared light reflected from a spot focused on the junction of the dark iris and the light sclera. The light is directed to a photocell. When the eye moves, more or less

220

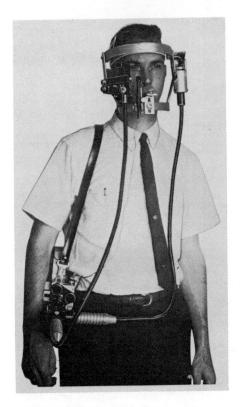

Figure 10.40. *Mobile eye-movement recorder. This instrument records the corneal reflection fixation marker superimposed on an image of the area viewed by the subject. The optical unit weighs only 2 lb, and is secured on the subject's head by a bite board and head band. Binocular vision is only slightly obscured, and the subject has mobility and freedom of head movement. Such equipment is widely used in human-factors research (Polymetric Company model V-0165).*

light is reflected, causing the output of the photocell to vary. The method is fairly straightforward for horizontal movements, but vertical movements are not so easily detected, because the upper and lower boundaries of the iris are obscured by the eyelids. Craske and Smith (1974) have devised a system using four spots in a rectangular arrangement 10 mm wide and 6 mm high. Sums and differences of the photocell outputs are computed by operational amplifiers to give horizontal and vertical vectors.

The electrical method is known as electrooculography (EOG), and is based on

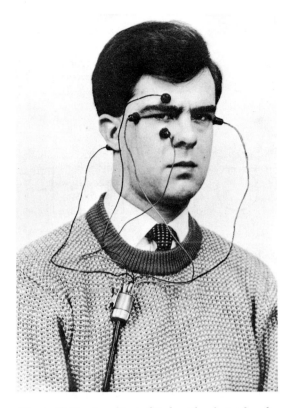

Figure 10.41. *A subject fitted with electrodes for electrooculography. The horizontal EOG is normally recorded binocularly.*

the fact that a fairly constant potential difference of several millivolts exists between the front and back of the eye. This potential difference moves when the eye rotates, and therefore appropriately placed electrode pairs (Figure 10.41) will resolve the potentials into vertical and horizontal vectors (Figure 10.42). Because electrooculography involves recording d.c. signals of around 100 μV, great care is necessary during the preparation of the skin and electrodes. The electrodes normally employed are silver/silver chloride, and they should be stored in saline solution with the leads of the electrode pairs shorted together to allow the electrodes to stabilize. Before fitting the electrodes, the horny layer of the skin is drilled with a dental burr to reduce skin potential artefacts. Shackel (1967) gives a detailed account of the method. When modern semiconductor amplifiers are used, the problems of drift encountered with valve amplifiers at that time are largely eliminated. In recent years, impedance plethysmography has also been used for eye-movement measurement (Geddes and Baker, 1975).

All methods require some calibration procedure. Typically, the subject is asked to fixate successively on a series of targets, comprising a central point and equal positive and negative X and Y displacements. A comprehensive survey of

222

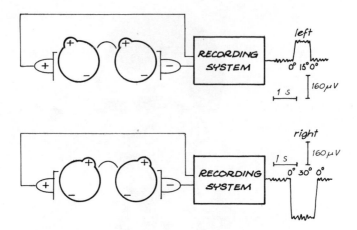

Figure 10.42. *The basis of electrooculography shown diagrammatically for the horizontal binocular EOG. The eyeball may be considered to be a miniature battery. As it rotates, the poles of the battery come nearer to the electrodes, causing a change in the steady potential across the electrodes. From Shackel (1967).*

eye-movement recording methods is given in a paper by Young and Sheena (1975). Monty and Senders (1976) have edited the proceedings of a symposium on eye movements which also includes papers on the physiology of eye movements and applications of eye-movement recording in psychology.

10.4 Summary

In most automated experiments, responses are detected by a transducer which converts the response into an electrical signal. For discrete motor responses, a switch is used. Pushbuttons of the kind used in professional electronic equipment are suitable for human subjects, but, for animal subjects, special manipulanda have been devised.

When studying continuous motor behaviour, the responses are usually recorded on a chart recorder or some other type of anologue recorder which preserves the time course of the movements. For human tracking behaviour, the target course is often recorded alongside the responses.

Verbal responses cannot be analysed easily for content by any automatic procedure, but utterances can be timed with the aid of a voice key.

Physiological responses involve a wide range of specialized techniques. Psychophysiological techniques are non-invasive in character, and allow a range of responses in human subjects to be recorded with safety.

CHAPTER 11

Data Recording

11.1 Analogue recording

Data recorders are instruments which provide a permanent record of experimental data. The first basic consideration in selecting a suitable data recorder is the nature of the data, that is whether it is analogue or digital. With the widespread use of high-speed digital techniques, this decision is not quite as straightforward as it might seem, for there are cases when it is desirable to perform an analogue–digital conversion to enable analogue data to be recorded in digital form. The second consideration is whether the data should be recorded in a visible form for manual analysis or in a machine-readable form to allow automatic analysis. Machine-readable recordings can gave much time and trouble, and eliminate the possibility of human error, if the data values are to be used for subsequent computation. If both kinds of recording are required, a visible recording can be produced automatically from a machine-readable recording, but it is only possible to read a visible recording automatically by the use of very specialized equipment. The two most frequently used kinds of analogue recorder are pen recorders, which are used for visible recordings, and instrumentation tape recorders, on which data can be recorded and replayed. A minor, but sometimes useful, additional technique for making a visible recording of analogue signals is oscilloscope photography.

An important procedure when using any recording system is the calibration of the system. If possible, the complete system should be calibrated by replacing the signal to be recorded by a series of known signals which extend over the entire range of values to be recorded. For example, if skin resistance level is to be recorded, the system could be calibrated by replacing the subject in turn by resistors of values of, say, 50, 150, 200 and 250 kΩ and noting the recorded levels. The use of more than two calibration levels allows a check on the linearity of the complete system over the range of interest. If responses are of interest rather than absolute levels and the recording system in use only has an a.c. response, the calibration can be effected by briefly adding in a known amount to the signal being recorded. Thus, for skin resistance response, an additional

224

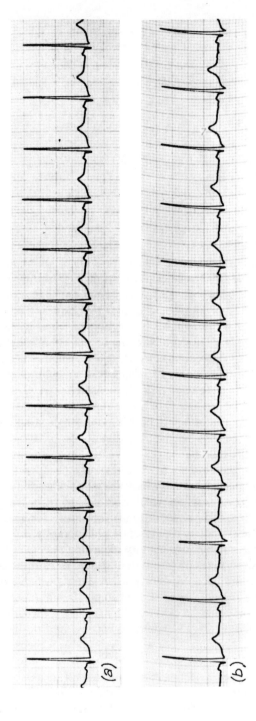

Figure 11.1. Examples of (a) rectilinear and (b) curvilinear recordings of EKG signals.

known resistance is switched in series with the subject, and commercial ECG recorders have a calibration pushbutton which adds a 1 mV step to the input signal before amplification. It is good practice to include a calibration run before and after each recording. Sometimes it is not possible to carry out this routine calibration using the physical quantity which is under investigation. For example, if the movements of a baby's head are being monitored by a position transducer which converts head position to a voltage signal, the routine calibrations of the recording system with the subject present will probably use voltage signals which replace the transducer output. The transducer would be calibrated between trials with the subject absent.

11.1.1 *Pen recorders*

Almost all analogue chart recorders employ some kind of galvanometer coupled to a pen in order to produce a record on a moving strip of paper of changes in a signal over time. Ink-writing pens are most frequently used, the ink being fed to the pen by capillary or syphon action. With a simple galvanometer and pen system, such as is often found on a physiological polygraph (Figure 10.15), the pen moves in an arc and produces curvilinear recording (Figure 11.1). Care is necessary when interpreting curvilinear recordings, especially when relating events on different channels. Special recording paper is used as an aid, printed with a curvilinear grid. Sometimes pens can be fitted which have a linkage mechanism designed to give rectilinear recording, but the attendent friction causes some loss of high-frequency response. Thermal writing (Figure 11.2) gives rectilinear recording without causing loss of high frequencies, but has the disadvantage of requiring a more expensive paper. The stylus is electrically heated and melts the white opaque surface of the special paper, revealing the black backing. The stylus makes contact with the paper

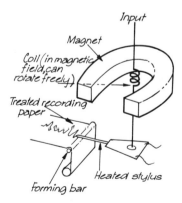

Figure 11.2. *Method of producing rectilinear recording using a headed stylus and forming bar.*

226

only where it passes over a forming bar and produces the rectilinear conversion. Thermal recording is particularly convenient for portable equipment.

Galvanometer pen recorders of the kind fitted to polygraphs are in the medium frequency range, covering from d.c. to about 100 Hz. Recording of frequencies from d.c. to about 1 kHz is possible using methods which do not involve mechanical contact between a moving pen and the paper. The ultra-violet recorder uses a mirror galvanometer to reflect ultraviolet light onto a special photographic paper which is insensitive to normal ambient lighting. The paper does not require chemical processing unless the recordings are needed for long-term storage. Because the lever is of an optical form and not mechanical, the excursion of each trace may be over the entire width of the paper; it is even possible for one trace to cross over another. Paper costs are high, and these recorders are normally only used for short recordings of high-frequency phenomena. A high-frequency recorder which uses ordinary paper is the ink-jet recorder, in which a fine jet of ink is deflected by the galvano-meter. The ink is pumped to a high pressure and the flow of ink regulated in accordance with the writing speed. Unfortunately, the fine jet makes the ink system rather sensitive, and the cost of the equipment is fairly high.

At the low-frequency end of the range are strip-chart recorders with a frequency response from d.c. to about 5 Hz. These instruments usually employ a servomotor to drive the pen and give rectilinear recording. They also have a pointer which displays the value of the parameter under observation on a calibrated scale, rather like a moving-coil meter. They are commonly used in laboratories for recording temperature and other slowly changing quantities. A special version of this type of recorder is the $X-Y$ recorder (Figure 11.3), which plots the relationship between two variables. In its simplest form, it consists of a pair of servomotors driving a pen in two axes over a fixed sheet of paper. There is usually a facility of remotely raising and lowering the pen.

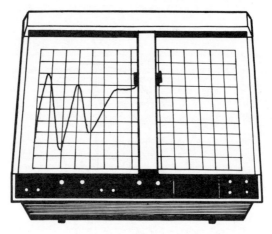

Figure 11.3. *A typical X–Y recorder (Hewlett–Packard model 7044A).*

More sophisticated devices, known as graph plotters, use a drum which drives the paper bidirectionally for one of the axes, but these are normally only used for graphical output from computers.

11.1.2 *Instrumentation tape recorders*

There are basically two methods for recording analogue data on magnetic tape:

(1) direct recording,
(2) frequency-modulated recording.

Direct recording is the method used in audio tape recorders, and is described in Section 7.5. Its main disadvantage for general recording of analogue signals is that d.c. and low frequencies cannot be recorded, the frequency response of a typical high-quality audio tape recorder being from about 50 Hz to 15 kHz. Frequency modulation overcomes the problem by using the input signal to alter the frequency of a high-frequency carrier signal which is then recorded on the tape. When the tape is replayed, the high-frequency signal is demodulated to produce an output which is proportional to the original input signal.

Many instrumentation recorders use a modular form of construction which allows direct-recording and frequency-modulation channels to be mixed as desired. At a given tape speed, direct recording gives a higher frequency response than frequency modulation, and it is also useful for recording a voice commentary during the course of an experiment. Instrumentation tape recorders usually have a wide range of speeds, and, by recording and replaying at different speeds, time can be compressed or expanded. Thus, an event containing frequencies of interest up to, say, 2 kHz could be recorded on tape at 60 inches per second and replayed at $1\frac{7}{8}$ inches per second. On replay, the highest frequencies of interest would be 62·5 Hz, allowing a visible recording to be made on an ordinary polygraph. By recording at a low speed, and then replaying the tape at a high speed with the outputs displayed on an oscilloscope, long periods of data may be scanned very rapidly.

The US Inter-Range Instrumentation Group (IRIG) have originated standards for instrumentation tape recorders, which, amongst other things, specify the position of the channels on the magnetic tape. Thus, tape recordings made on IRIG-compatible machines are interchangeable, although IRIG-non-compatible machines may be available at lower cost.

11.1.3 *Oscilloscope photography*

A display on a cathode-ray oscilloscope may be photographed as a permanent recording, often for use in a report or publication. Mounting brackets are available which allow recording cameras to be fitted to most of the common laboratory oscilloscopes. Often the bracket incorporates a hinge which allows the camera to be swung away from the tube face for direct viewing, and then to be quickly moved back into place when it is desired to record the display. Polaroid film is a popular medium, because it provides an immediate check that the recording has been successful, and also eliminates the need for darkroom processing. When recording single transient events, the camera shutter is opened, and the oscilloscope is set to suppress the trace until the event occurs. When a steady display is possible, as with repetitive events or with a refreshed computer CRT display, it is normal to use the camera shutter to give a timed exposure. An introduction to photographic principles is given in Section 8.7.1. For automatic recording, motorized cameras may be used which advance the film after each exposure.

At one time, it was quite common to make continuous recordings from an oscilloscope by switching off the timebase and running film through a camera at a steady speed. This provides a record of events over time in much the same manner as a pen recorder, but with the advantage of the fast response time of the cathode-ray tube. To allow accurate measurements to be made from the film, it is optically projected, one section at a time. This recording technique has been largely superseded by ultraviolet and instrumentation tape recorders.

11.2 Digital recording

There has been a great increase in the variety of digital recording devices in recent years, mainly because of the rapid developments in the field of digital computing. In this section, however, we will concentrate primarily on digital recorders, which can be used without computers, although the increasing availability of low-cost microcomputers does mean that the distinction between computers and other digital systems is likely to become rather less clear in the future.

11.2.1 *Event recorder and cumulative recorder*

The event recorder is basically a strip-chart recorder in which each pen can take only one of two positions. The pen is spring-biased to a resting position, but can be deflected to the other position by operating a miniature solenoid. Most polygraphs have a single event channel along the edge of the paper chart. This channel is often operated remotely by the experimenter to indicate a particular phase in the experiment, but it may also be operated automatically to indicate, for example, when a stimulus is being presented.

Event recorders usually have from four to ten channels. Because they employ a much simpler pen mechanism than analogue recorders, they cost much less. They are often used in industry for dedicated applications, such as monitoring the operation of machines, and, accordingly, they are often manufactured with a single chart speed which can only be changed by replacing the motor or a gear train. Because they are normally used for the long-term monitoring of slow events, most units are fitted with a low-speed drive.

The basic event-recorder mechanism usually has an a.c. motor for the chart

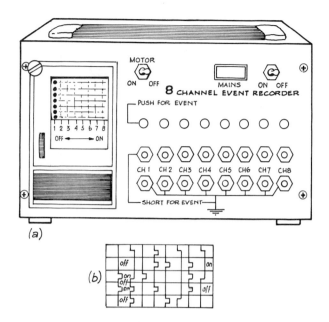

Figure 11.4. *(a) An 8-channel event recorder. Each channel can be operated either by local pushbutton or by remote contact closure; (b) a sample record (BRD (Electronics) Ltd.).*

drive and requires a low direct voltage to operate the pen solenoids. For dedicated applications, the unit is normally built into the monitoring equipment, but, for student use and other short-term applications, it is more convenient to use an instrument of the form shown in Figure 11.4, in which the basic mechanism has been built into an instrument case together with a power supply. This allows the event channels to be operated by pushbutton or remote contact closure. Because there is no requirement for analogue fidelity, simple writing methods may be used. The instrument shown in Figure 11.4 uses a robust pressure-sensitive system in which a pointed stylus cuts through the white coating on specially prepared paper, so that the trace is formed by the black backing. Ink-writing event recorders are also manufactured which use lower-cost paper but require more maintenance.

The cumulative recorder (Figure 11.5) is an instrument which plots total responses as a function of time, and is widely used for recording data in operant conditioning experiments. The cumulative record is produced by stepping the recording pen across the paper by a fixed increment for each response, whilst the paper is driven at a steady speed. Thus, the slope of the record is steeper when responses are emitted at a faster rate, and the changes in slope provide a detailed picture of the changes in response rate over time. Just before the pen reaches the top of the paper, a switch is tripped, causing the pen to be rapidly reset to the zero position. It may also be reset remotely to facilitate comparisons of different phases within an experimental session. The pen is also some-

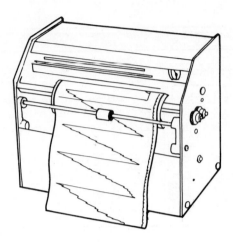

Figure 11.5. *A typical cumulative recorder with a sample recording (Gerbrands model C-3).*

times reset at a regular rate, so that the positions reached by the pen give a measure of the number of responses made during each interval. Most instruments have provision for introducing a temporary displacement of the stepped pen. This is often used to place a pip on the cumulative record indicating presentation of reinforcement or changes in the stimulus conditions. A second pen is often fitted below the zero point of the cumulative record to give a conventional event recorder channel. This is also useful for indicating the occurrence of key events during the session. In addition, the undeflected trace of the second pen is often used as a baseline from which to measure the slope of the cumulative record.

11.2.2 *Printout counter*

The printout counter (Figure 11.6) is basically an electromechanical counter fitted with a means by which the value accumulated in the counter can be printed as required onto a paper roll. The current value of the counter is displayed in a window on the front of the instrument. The counter mechanism is operated in the same way as a simple electromechanical counter, the pulsed operation of a solenoid incrementing the least significant decade by one count with carries incrementing the more significant decades. The counter may be reset to zero by operating another solenoid. Some of the more sophisticated types of counter have separate incrementing solenoids for each decade, with electrical contacts being used to generate the carry pluses. This allows the user to split the register for the counting of various events.

Printout counters are widely used for recording responses in animal work. As well as recording cumulative events, they can also record low resolution response latencies by resetting the counter to zero, pulsing it at, say, 10 Hz and

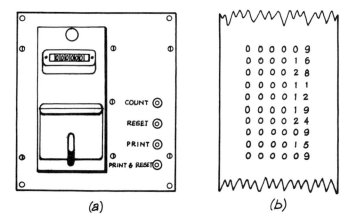

Figure 11.6. *A typical printout counter (a) and a sample of output (b). When analysing the data, it should be remembered that the first output is printed at the bottom of the paper roll (Campden Instruments model 262).*

operating the printer when a response is made. The mechanical nature of the counter mechanism means that it cannot be used reliably at much higher frequencies than this. If it is possible to split the counting register, one decade may be used to label the printout according to some feature of the response, such as position or whether reinforcement was given. For simple binary information, this is done by resetting the decade after each print operation and then incrementing or not incrementing the decade when the response is made, so that the next printout will contain a 1 or 0 in the label column. Clearly more extensive coding is possible by generating a series of up to nine pulses to label different events, but the control circuits become rather complex, and, as printout counters usually have many decades, it is simpler to add extra binary labels if more information is required.

11.2.3 *Tape punch*

Experiments which are not conducted under computer control may still generate a large quantity of data requiring analysis on a computer. In such cases, it is desirable to collect the data initially in a machine-readable form. This removes the possibility of introducing errors during manual keypunching operations, and can greatly reduce the time delay before the results of the analysis are available.

Before starting to collect the data, it is important to check what forms of data input are available on the computer system which is to be used for the analysis. If a central computing facility is to be used, the management probably has well defined and inflexible rules regarding the media which may be used and the format in which the data should be recorded. If, on the other hand, a mini-computer is to be used, the situation is rather different, for it would be perfectly

232

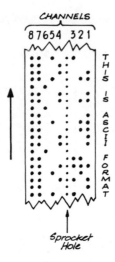

Figure 11.7. *A sample of ASCII-coded punched-paper tape. The tape is divided into channels, which run along the length of the tape, and into columns, which extend across the width of the tape. In ASCII code, each character occupies one column.*

feasible to add another peripheral to allow some particularly attractive recording medium to be used.

The most common input medium for large data-processing installations is the punched card. Unfortunately, card punches are very expensive devices, and it is usually quite impractical to collect data in this form. The commonest medium for automatic data collection is probably punched paper tape. This is the main input medium for minicomputers, and most central computing facilities will also accept input in the form of paper tape. Standard paper tape is 1 in wide, and has an 8-hole format (Figure 11.7). It is possible to punch data onto paper tape in an arbitrary binary format, for example each column could represent an 8 bit value of reaction time in 10 ms units giving a maximum of 2550 ms. It is, however, usually preferable to use a standard code such as ASCII (Figure 11.8), the American Standard Code for Information Interchange. This is not as efficient in packing data on the tape as an arbitrary binary code; the 8 bit reaction time would need at least three characters if punched in ASCII-coded decimal. In addition, the group of ASCII numeric characters would probably also be followed by a terminating character, such as carriage return. The resulting tape, however, would be acceptable to many more computer systems, and the tape could also be edited and listed on a teletypewriter in local mode (i.e. without a computer being connected). The channel 8 bit in the ASCII code can be used as a parity check bit. This gives a simple method of checking received characters for the occurrence of certain types of transmission errors. A convention is adopted that the sum of the binary 1s in any single character will always be either an odd number (odd parity) or an even number (even parity). Both conventions are in common use. In the case of odd parity, the 7 information bits would be summed before transmission and the parity bit set to a 1 only if the sum were even. At the receiver, each character would have all 8 bits summed, and would signal an error if an even number were found.

233

Figure 11.8. *ASCII code. Channel 8 is sometimes used for parity. In this figure, it is shown always punched.*

A single error occurring in any bit will be detected, but errors occurring simultaneously in an even number of bits will remain undetected. If the error rate is low, and the probability of error in each channel of the tape is independent, then the rate of such multiple errors will be very low.

Paper-tape punches are available which operate at speeds within the range of about 10–100 character/s. The higher-speed punches are considerably more expensive than the lower-speed units, and also make considerably more noise. In order to operate a tape punch, it is usually necessary to provide driving circuits for the solenoids which set up the bits of the character to be punched, and then to operate a further solenoid which engages a clutch connecting an electric motor to the punching mechanism for the duration of the

234

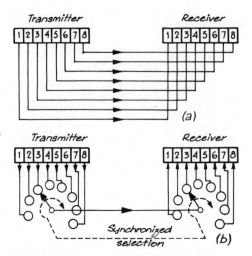

Figure 11.9. *In parallel data transmission (a), each element of the code has its own communication channel, whereas, in serial data transmission (b), each element of the code is transmitted in turn along the same channel. From Cleary, Mayes and Packham (1976).*

Figure 11.10. *A typical teletypewriter (a). The model shown here is fitted with a paper-tape reader and punch and is described as an ASR (automatic send/receive) version. A model without paper-tape facilities is termed a KSR (keyboard send/receive) version. The keyboard layout is shown in (b).*

punch sequence. Most interfaces for punches are of the parallel type, in which a separate circuit is provided for each of the data bits, which are transmitted simultaneously. Serial interfaces will often be found on equipment which has been designed primarily for data communications applications. In serial transmission, each element of the coded character is sent in turn along a single communication channel (Figure 11.9). This has obvious advantages for communication over long distances, and the adoption of serial interfaces for some fairly standard pieces of equipment means that they are now frequently used for entirely local applications. There are two basic methods for the serial transmission of data: synchronous and asynchronous. Synchronous transmission is usually restricted to high-speed communications for such applications as links between computer installations. Asynchronous transmission is the method used for computer terminals, such as the teletypewriter (Figure 11.10), and it is particularly suited to the transmission of small quantities of intermittent data. Each character transmitted has three parts:

(1) a bit to define the start of the character,
(2) the 8 data bits,
(3) a stop bit.

11.2.4 *Digital tape recorder*

Because paper-tape punches are mechanical devices, they make rather a lot of noise, which makes them unacceptable in some experiments. When silent recording is necessary, digital tape recorders may be used, but the many varieties of magnetic media and recording formats mean that problems of compatibility are more likely to arise when transferring data to a computer than when paper tape is used.

A wide range of digital tape equipment is available. The simplest is the digital cassette or cartridge unit, often used on minicomputers as a replacement for paper tape equipment, and operating at similar data rates. Such recorders are fairly inexpensive, and are suited to many data-recording applications, but compatible equipment is, unfortunately, not likely to be available in a computer centre. Such installations normally use what are termed industry standard or IBM-compatible tape units. These use open-reel 1/2 in wide tapes which can store large quantities of data. Tapes can be searched at speed and the data transferred at very high rates. Drives for these tapes are expensive, and are only rarely found on minicomputer systems. It is difficult to use similar drives for recording laboratory data unless some form of buffer storage is employed, because characters cannot be written onto the tape singly; they must be written in groups while the tape is moving. Special incremental drives, however, are available for recording intermittent data. Again it is important to check carefully on the format requirements of the computer centre before specifying a tape drive for data recording. Even so-called industry standard tape drives may use different bit densities and methods of recording.

11.3 Summary

There are basically two classes of recording instruments: analogue and digital. Pen recorders, such as physiological polygraphs, give a visible record of the changes in analogue signals over time. When one variable is to be plotted as a function of another, an $X-Y$ recorder can be used. Similar recordings can be made using an oscilloscope and a photographic camera. It is often preferable to record analogue signals first on an instrumentation tape recorder, even when a visible record is finally required. A tape recording allows selected passages to be replayed for detailed analysis.

Digital recorders are widely used in animal laboratories. Traditional instruments are the printout counter and cumulative recorder. When a large amount of data is to be collected, it is often better to record it in a machine-readable form. The most frequently used recorders of this kind are the tape punch and digital tape recorder.

CHAPTER 12

Computer Control of Experiments

12.1 Computers in the laboratory

The main reasons for using a laboratory computer are to control the timing and sequencing of operations in an experiment and to record the values of experimental variables. A laboratory computer can also be used to carry out the data analysis. If very extensive analyses are required, it may be necessary to transfer the data to a computer centre for processing.

Most readers have probably used computer terminals on a time-shared computer system. Although the response of such systems to typed input may seem fairly fast, it is not reliably fast enough for running an experiment. For laboratory applications, a minicomputer is normally used, because it can be completely dedicated to running the experiment. The connection of various items of laboratory equipment to a minicomputer is also much easier and cheaper than it would be if a big machine were used.

From the viewpoint of an experimenter, a typical laboratory computer system (Figure 12.1) is like a set of modular programming and data-recording equipment which can be controlled from a teletypewriter. When the experiment is completed, the minicomputer can double as a sophisticated desk calculator. Great operational convenience in the use of the minicomputer is gained by having a large-capacity backing store, preferably in the form of a magnetic disc. This gives rapid access to any point on its surface, allowing programs and data to be edited and saved without the tedium of dealing with paper tape every time a new program is to be run or some data are to be analysed. In fact, unless the minicomputer is to be used for only one regular application and can be left from day to day with the same program loaded, it is probably not worth buying a machine without a backing store.

It is only possible to give a very basic introduction to the use of laboratory computers in a single chapter. If more than an introduction is required, it is really necessary to acquire some practical experience, and the reading in preparation for this will be specific to the particular system. Manufacturers' handbooks should be studied to gain familiarity with the basic principles of the hardware,

238

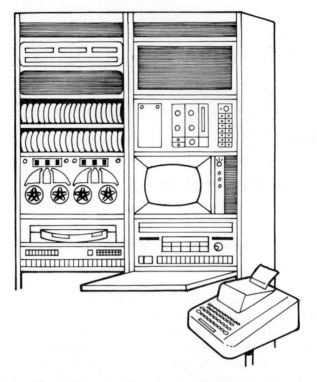

Figure 12.1. *A typical laboratory computer system. The system includes a teletypewriter, laboratory interface, disc and tape storage (DEC LAB-8/E).*

standard software and operating system. If a particular system is to be used regularly, it is worth joining the appropriate user group. The manufacturer will be able to supply the address. Two useful texts for further reading have been edited by Apter and Westby (1973) and Uttal (1968). Weiss (1973) has also edited a collection of papers on specialist applications, and Korn (1973) has written a basic introductory text on minicomputers. It is also worth consulting back issues of the journal *Behavior Research Methods and Instrumentation* published by the Psychonomic Society.

12.1.1 *When to use computers*

A laboratory computer system with a reasonable range of input and output facilities and suitable programming languages can be used to run most instrumented experiments, and would probably be the preferred method for an experimenter who is proficient in the use of the system. Unless expert assistance is available, it may be necessary to make a considerable investment of time and effort to reach the point when it seems easier to use a computer system than to interconnect programming modules, or more convenient to keep data in computer files than in notebooks. It may take up to a year's experience to reach this stage. If much highly instrumented experimentation is envisaged, and a working laboratory computer systme is available, preferably with someone knowledgeable to give guidance in the initial stages, then it will certainly be worth the investment of time and effort to become proficient in its use. If a working system is not available, much more investment would be necessary to set up a system and become competent without any resident guidance. If the system is to be shared by a number of users, it will probably also involve someone in the halftime task of managing the installation, maintaining the basic documentation and programs, and getting applications software working for the special laboratory interfaces.

Although, once a system is available, most laboratory work can benefit from its use, there are some areas in which the use of computers is specially indicated.

The generation of complex stimulus displays is one such case. Julesz (1971) has produced a wide variety of random dot patterns for the investigation of binocular depth perception (Figure 12.2), and Mathews (1969) working in the field of psychoacoustics has developed a computer program MUSIC V which allows specification and generation of very complex multiple-voice acoustic stimuli.

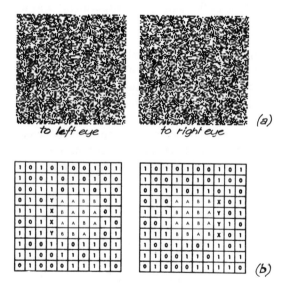

Figure 12.2. *Julesz random dot patterns. (a) When the stimuli are inspected separately, they appear uniformly random, yet when they are stereoscopically fused, a centre square is seen in depth above the surround. (b) A small array used to illustrate the way in which (a) was generated. The material in the centre is shifted to the left or right to simulate binocular disparity. From Julesz (1971).*

If large quantities of data are to be collected, whether interresponse times of simple key presses or complex analogue signals, they can be converted into digital form and stored in a computer system. In many cases, the cost of a flexible laboratory computer system will be no more than the cost of traditional recording systems. Each computer word is typically 12 or 16 bits long, and can be used to store data of any type. In fact, the memory of most computers does not make any distinction at all, even between the storage of program and data. The distinction arises merely in the way the program works when it is started from some specific location in the memory. If a backing store and an operating system are being used, fine details of the organization of the hardware are not apparent to the user.

Once data have been collected, simple statistical analyses can be easily programmed. They may actually be appended to the experimental control program, so that a summary analysis is printed out on the teletypewriter at the end of each session. If the experiment involves a number of sessions or subjects, the individual sets of data can be written into files on the backing store. When the experiment is completed, the files can then be accessed by an analysis program written in a high-level language, such as FORTRAN or BASIC. As we shall see in Section 12.2.2, it is possible in many cases to use the same programming language for both running the experiment and analysing the data. The main advantage of this is that the experimenter will become particularly fluent in the use of the language.

In some cases, analysis of data is carried out during the experiment, and is used to make decisions about the course of the experiment. Taylor and Creelman (1967) devised a psychophysical procedure called PEST (Point Estimation by Sequential Testing), which used contingent programming to determine the stimulus intensity and also the point at which the experiment should be terminated. The procedure also ensured economy of effort by concentrating data points around the critical stimulus values. A more commonly used technique which relies on computation during the course of the experiment is signal averaging. This is a technique for improving the signal-to-noise ratio of analogue signals in situations where repeated measurements are possible. Signal averaging is operated online, and allows the experimenter to see results as the experiment progresses, the redundancy in each repetition of the signal being used to reduce the noise in the display. Perhaps the most important constraint is that the signal which is sought must have a fixed latency with respect to the stimulus which is used to trigger the averaging process. A typical application of signal averaging is the detection of evoked potentials in EEG (Section 10.3.5). Figure 12.3 shows photic stimulation and the recording of evoked potentials from the scalp in the region of the occipital cortex. The first time a stimulus is presented, the sampling process is triggered; a digitized representation of the EEG is sampled for a predetermined period and stored in the computer. Because so much other EEG activity is included, it is not possible to see the evoked potential at this stage. The second occasion the stimulus is presented, the process is repeated, but, in addition, the values of the signals at the corresponding

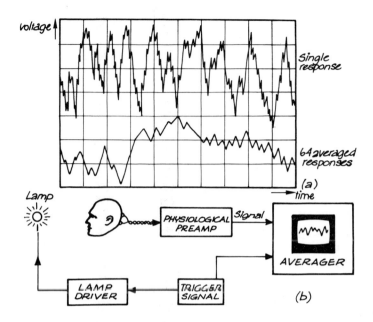

Figure 12.3. *Signal averaging helps to reveal the evoked potential from an EEG signal even when the raw data seems to contain no useful information. (a) A single response and an averaged display after 64 repetitions. (b) The experimental arrangement. A synchronizing signal triggers the averaging process when the photic stimulus is presented. The computer samples the ADC input at regular intervals, and stores the values of the samples in memory. It then computes the average value for the corresponding samples over all repetitions. The noise portion of the signal gradually dies out with successive repetitions, because its randomness ensures that both negative and positive contributions are made to corresponding samples.*

sampling times in the first and second signals are summed, and the averages displayed on the computer CRT. On each subsequent triggering, the new signal is added to the previous signals and a new average displayed. The averaging process gives an improvement in signal-to-noise ratio of $\sqrt{m}$, where m is the number of repetitions. Thus, four repetitions will halve the noise. Averaging is just as effective in reducing systematic interference, such as interfering mains frequencies, as it is with random noise. As long as the stimulus presentation is not time-locked to the mains frequency, each successive presentation is equally likely to contain either positive or negative disturbances in the signal. In a practical signal-averaging program, it is not necessary to store the complete history of responses in order to compute a new average. The same result can be obtained by combining the old average value a_{n-1} and the new sample value s_n for each point in repetition n, to give the new average a_n:

$$a_n = \frac{(n-1) \times a_{n-1} + s_n}{n}$$

Although minicomputers are widely used for signal averaging and similar online statistical signal processing (see, for example, Donchin and Heffley (1975)), special-purpose computers are also used for such applications.

12.1.2 *Interfacing to experiments*

The organization of a minicomputer system with backing store is shown in Figure 12.4. Computer core is usually specified in units of kilowords, one kiloword (1K) actually being 2^{10} or 1024 words. The minimum amount of core normally supplied with a minicomputer is 4K, and most machines can be expanded up to at least 32K. The minicomputer manufacturer's operating system and utility programs are usually held on a backing store from which they are loaded into core, as and when required. This storage facility often saves the user a great deal of programming effort in handling experimental data when only limited amounts of core are available.

Some care is necessary in the choice of a suitable operating system for laboratory work. Many operating systems are described as real-time, which means that they respond to events occurring at peripherals by running the appropriate task. Such operating systems are usually designed to maximize the throughput of a multiple-job data-processing system, and are not strict-time in the sense that they will respond reliably within, say, 1 ms to an input at a laboratory interface. This kind of performance is usually only possible on a system which is dedicated to running a single job, or has been designed to give overriding priority to a specified single job.

The teletypewriter may incorporate a low-speed paper-tape reader and punch. If they are not fitted, a separate reader and punch will probably be needed, because paper tape is a fairly universal medium for the exchange of data and programs. It is also frequently used for the collection of laboratory data for subsequent computer analysis.

In order to turn a minicomputer system into a laboratory computer system, some additional peripherals are required (Figure 12.5). Perhaps the most fundamental addition is a real-time clock. This allows the measurement of elapsed times, or the presentation of stimuli for a predetermined interval of time. The simplest kind of clock is one which sends a signal to the computer at regular intervals, typically every 10 ms. This causes the computer to briefly

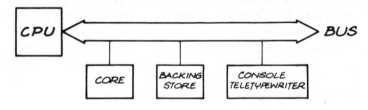

Figure 12.4. *A basic minicomputer system. The bus is the signal channel through which the processor and peripheral devices communicate.*

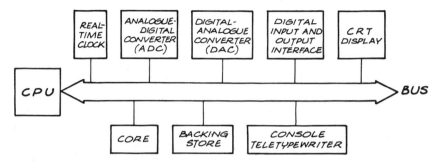

Figure 12.5. *A typical laboratory computer system. The central processing unit (CPU) performs the arithmetic operations and controls the bus, which communicates with the core memory and peripherals.*

stop execution of the main program and to enter an interrupt service routine in which the clock interrupts are counted. Simple clocks of this kind are often used in real-time data-processing systems, and are adequate for laboratory applications involving only low data rates, such as operant conditioning experiments. For experiments involving high data rates, or applications in which time resolution must be better than 10 ms, a more sophisticated type of clock is needed. Usually this takes the form of a programmable real-time clock, which is able to count the timing signals without interrupting the computer, and can be read, preset and reset to zero under computer control. It can also be made to interrupt the computer when a preset time interval has elapsed. Some clocks also have programmed control of their oscillator frequency so that they can be used with equal facility for timing events with microsecond or second resolution.

Input and output signals from the computer are needed to be able to present stimuli and detect responses. For some experiments, the console teletypewriter will suffice, but, in most cases, special purpose displays and response-detection devices are required. Two types of input and output are possible: digital and analogue. Laboratory computers which are sold as complete systems usually emphasize analogue input and output, because they are mainly intended for use in the physical and biomedical sciences. For behavioural applications, digital input and output are just as important, because they are used in the control of external equipment, such as Skinner boxes and tachistoscopes. The usual method for digital output is to have a set of bistables (termed a register) which can be loaded with a binary value under program control. Because bistables are used, the value set in the register is retained while the program carries out other tasks, and an output instruction is only needed when the value in the register is to be changed. The number of bits in the register is often made equal to the length of the computer word so that data can be transferred directly from memory to the register. The way in which individual bits of the output register are used in an experiment is entirely under the control of the experimenter. In many cases, the individual bits of the output register will be used to switch on and off separate stimuli via external relays. A simple case might be the measurement of reaction time to auditory, visual or combined auditory and visual stimuli. Let us assume we have a pair of 12 bit registers, one for input and the other for output. For purposes of identification, we will label the 12 bits of a register, starting at the least significant bit, by the numbers 0 to 11 corresponding to the powers of 2 relating to the binary weight of each bit. We might choose to let bit 11 of the output register control the presentation of the visual stimulus, and bit 10 control the presentation of the auditory stimulus. In both cases, a value of 1 in the appropriate bit of the register will be used to start presentation of the stimulus, and a value of 0 in the same bit will be used to terminate the stimulus. Thus, at the start of the experiment, the output register would be loaded with 000000000000. In order to present a visual stimulus, the register would be loaded with 100000000000, and, to stop the presentation, it would be cleared (loaded with 000000000000). To present an auditory stimulus, the word 010000000000 would be output, and the register cleared to terminate the stimulus. To present both stimuli, the register would be loaded with 110000000000. Even with only 2 bits, more complicated sequences are possible. For example, the sequence shown in Figure 12.6 might be used to present two 100 ms duration stimuli, one of them being delayed by 10 ms.

Commercial electronic instruments with facilities for remote control often use binary-coded decimal (Section 1.4). A programmable audio oscillator might have three decades for the control of frequency, and another three decades for

Step	Program	Register
1	load register	100000000000
2	wait 10 mS	unchanged
3	load register	110000000000
4	wait 90 mS	unchanged
5	load register	010000000000
6	wait 10 mS	unchanged
7	load register	000000000000

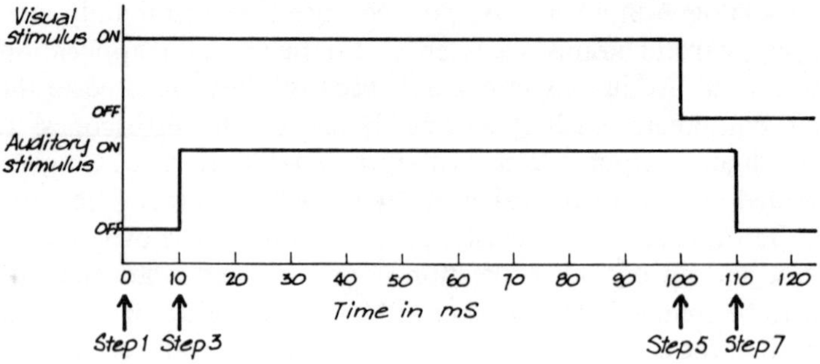

Figure 12.6. *A sequence of steps which will present two stimuli of 100 ms duration, with one stimulus delayed by 10 ms. Bit 11 controls the visual stimulus and bit 10 controls the auditory stimulus.*

	most significant decade	middle decade	least significant decade
b.c.d. weights	8 4 2 1	8 4 2 1	8 4 2 1
bit numbers	11 10 9 8	7 6 5 4	3 2 1 0

Figure 12.7. *Allocation of bits in a 12 bit register which is used for three decades of b.c.d. (binary-coded decimal).*

the control of amplitude. Each decade would require 4 bits, and therefore one 12 bit output register could be used for frequency and another for amplitude. The bits of each register might be allocated as shown in Figure 12.7. In order to set the oscillator frequency control to the value 496, the output register would be loaded with the value 0100 1001 0110. Because computer arithmetic is carried out in pure binary, a conversion routine would be executed to convert the binary equivalent of 496_{10} to binary-coded decimal before loading the output register. In order to use a programmable oscillator completely under remote control, another output register would be needed to operate the range and waveform controls and to switch the audio output on and off.

Digital input to a computer is usually accomplished by reading in a complete word from an input register. As with an output register, individual bits can be treated separately for simple key-press responses, or the whole word may represent a value in pure binary or b.c.d. from a commercial instrument. In the case of input in b.c.d. form, a conversion routine is needed to change the bit pattern to pure binary-number form before any arithmetic processing of the data can take place.

The signals at the digital registers are usually TTL levels (Section 5.9.13). For many purposes, operating speed is not crucial, and so the computer circuits can be isolated from the experimental apparatus by relays on the input and output registers (Figure 12.8). Conventional miniature relays take about 10 ms and reed relays about 1 ms to operate. This electrical isolation protects the computer circuits from transient interference generated by the heavy current electromechanical derives which are often used in animal laboratories. It also protects the computer from possible damage if the interface is inadvertently connected to a high-voltage source.

Because analogue signals cannot be directly represented inside a digital computer, input of an analogue signal takes place through an analogue–digital converter, and output of an analogue signal takes place through a digital–analogue converter. The digital–analogue converter (DAC) works by summing voltages which are proportional to the weight of the bits in the binary number (Section 1.4). Most digital–analogue converters used in laboratory computers have a resolution of 10 or 12 bits, and give outputs of about 10 V. For simplicity, we will consider the case of a 3 bit DAC which gives an output in the range

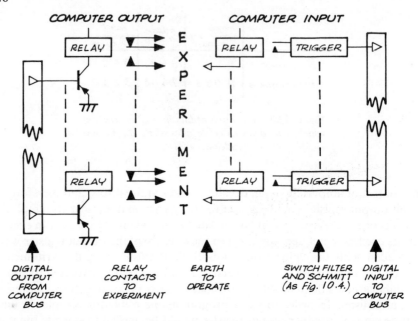

Figure 12.8. *Relays on the input and output registers slow down operation, but give a high degree of protection. Electronically unsophisticated users are able to connect their own apparatus to this kind of interface, making it easier for a few users to share the same computer system.*

0–7 V (Figure 12.9). The digital value to be converted is first staticized by loading it into a digital output register. Bit 0 of the output register is the least significant bit, and controls the switching of 2^0 or 1 V into the summing circuit. Bit 1 controls 2^1 or 2 V, and bit 2 controls 2^2 or 4 V. Thus, a digital output of value 6 or binary 110 would generate an analogue output of

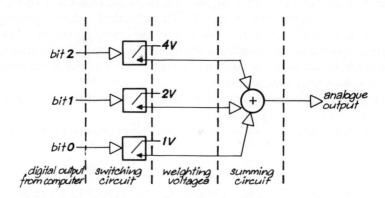

Figure 12.9. *A simplified representation of a 3 bit DAC.*

$$1 \times 2^2 + 1 \times 2^1 + 0 \times 2^0$$
$$= 1 \times 4 \ + 1 \times 2 \ + 0 \times 1$$
$$= 6 \text{ V}$$

More switching circuits and weighting voltages are added to give greater precision. DACs with fast switching circuits are used to generate the X and Y signals for computer CRT displays.

An analogue–digital converter (ADC) works by comparing the incoming analogue signal with an approximate digital representation. This approximation is modified until an acceptable match is found. An ADC therefore includes a DAC to generate the analogue version of the digital approximation. Because the conversion process takes longer (typically 20 μs) than the normal time for executing a computer instruction (typically less than 2 μs), the interfacing of ADCs is somewhat more complex than the other peripherals we have discussed. It is necessary for the computer to be able to initiate a conversion when it is desired to sample an analogue signal, but the computer should not actually read the value until the ADC has signalled that the conversion is complete. All peripherals which involve operations which cannot be carried out synchronously with the timing pulses used to operate the computer logic have means to signal to the computer that the process is complete. They may do this by causing an interrupt, as in the case of the real-time clock. An ADC is often fitted with a multiplexer which allows any one of a number of input channels, usually 8 or 16, to be switched to the converter under program control.

It is very convenient when developing experimental-control programs to have lamps which indicate the status of each bit of the digital output register, and also to have a switch register for controlling the value of bits in the digital input register. Similarly analogue input signals may be derived from a stabilized power supply and multiturn potentiometers, and the analogue output signals may be displayed on a meter or an oscilloscope. The controls and displays should be mounted so that they can be used easily when sitting at the console teletypewriter.

12.2 Programming for experimental control

A digital computer can be made to carry out an action by means of a program consisting of a sequence of binary-coded instructions. Each instruction usually occupies one computer word and is composed of two portions:

(1) an operation code which defines the basic action of the instruction, such as add or make an input/output transfer,
(2) an operand which may be the memory address referred to by the operation code or some defined subset of the operation code.

The program is stored in the memory of the computer, and, when it is executed, individual instructions are passed to the control portion of the computer. Instructions are executed sequentially unless an instruction specifically transfers control to a different location. Programming is the process of creating a list of instructions which will carry out some desired action. At its most primitive, this may be done by using the front panel controls of the computer to select addresses in the memory, and to load them with binary numbers set up on a switch register. Many minicomputers have lights and switch registers which allow locations in the memory to be examined or altered and the computer to be started at a selected location. On some modern machines, there are no physical front panel controls, but similar facilities are provided through a virtual front panel, which is programmed to use the console teletype-writer. It is very tedious to load any but the shortest of programs from the front panel controls. This means of loading programs is normally used only for starting up a system or during maintenance.

The next stage of sophistication is to load a program by use of the console teletypewriter. This may be done with the aid of a short utility program which is loaded from the switches into a reserved part of the memory. When using the teletypewriter, the address and contents of a location are normally expressed in octal form (Section 1.4). The PDP8 is a widely used minicomputer with a simple and easily understood instruction set. We will use the instruction of this machine to give examples of simple experimental-control programs. The description of the instruction set given here is not complete, and the manufacturer's manuals should be consulted by anyone intending to write programs for use on an actual machine. Readers with access to a PDP8 should also note that the front panel of the machine has the bits of the accumulator labelled in the reverse order to the binary weight convention used in this chapter. The PDP8 has a word length of 12 bits, and numbers of this length are represented in octal by a 4-digit number. The most significant octal digit defines the operation code:

0xxx: logically AND each bit of memory location xxx with the corresponding bit in the accumulator.

1xxx: add the contents of location xxx to the accumulator.

2xxx: increment the contents of memory location xxx (and skip the next instruction if the result is zero).

3xxx: deposit the contents of the accumulator in memory location xxx and clear the accumulator.

4xxx: jump to a subroutine at location xxx. A mechanism is provided which allows the subroutine to transfer control back to the main program.

5xxx: jump unconditionally to memory location xxx.

6aab: perform an input/output operation on device allocated code aa. Digit b defines one of up to eight possible functions which may be carried out by the device.

7xxx: operate class instructions. These enable various logical operations to be carried out, and do not refer to memory locations or input/output devices. Examples are:

7200: clear the accumulator

7640: skip next instruction if accumulator zero, then clear the accumulator

7650: skip next instruction if accumulator non-zero, then clear the accumulator

7001: increment the accumulator

7040: complement the accumulator

Let us assume we have a system with the following laboratory peripherals:

(1) a real-time clock with device code 13

6131: skip next instruction if clock flag set

6132: start clock oscillator (1 kHz) and clear flag

6133: stop clock oscillator

6134: load clock counter and clear accumulator

6135: read clock counter into accumulator

(2) digital input/output registers with device code 50

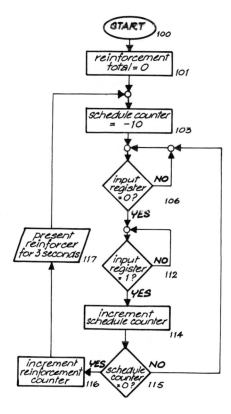

Figure 12.10. *Flowchart for FR10 schedule of reinforcement. The numbers against the boxes are the corresponding addresses in the computer program.*

6504:   read input register into accumulator
6507:   load output register and clear accumulator

The following program would control a fixed ratio reinforcement schedule in a similar manner to the modular programming equipment shown in Figure 4.18. We will use bit 0 of the input register to detect responses and bit 0 of the output register for presentation of reinforcers. In this case, the reinforcer is presented for 3 s, as might be required for a grain hopper when the subject is a pigeon. A flowchart of this program is given in Figure 12.10.

ADDRESS CONTENTS   REMARKS

PROGRAM

0100	7200	clear accumulator
0101	3133	zero reinforcement counter
0102	1130	get − 10 decimal
0103	3134	and set up schedule counter
0104	6504	ensure input register is zero
0105	0131	AND with 0001 for response bit
0106	7640	skip if accumulator zero then clear
0107	5104	wait until zero
0110	6504	look for non-zero input
0111	0131	AND with 0001
0112	7650	skip if accumulator non-zero then clear
0113	5110	keep waiting for response
0114	2134	found one, increment schedule counter
0115	5104	no reinforcement if here
0116	2133	reinforcement, so increment counter
0117	7001	set accumulator to 0001
0120	6507	load output register for reinforcement
0121	1132	get − 3000 decimal
0122	6134	load clock counter
0123	6132	start clock
0124	6131	test clock flag
0125	5124	wait for clock flag
0126	6507	reinforcement off after 3000 ms
0127	5102	start another count of 10

CONSTANTS

0130	7766	− 10 decimal
0131	0001	mask for bit 0
0132	7014	− 3000 decimal

VARIABLES

| 0133 | 0000 | reinforcement counter |
| 0134 | 0000 | schedule counter |

Programs written in octal notation are referred to as being in machine code. It is difficult and time-consuming to use machine code, and therefore the normal method of programming is to use special computer programs to translate the programmer's requirements into machine instructions. In general terms, there are two levels of programming languages:

(1) assemblers which are sophisticated aids to machine-code programming, and are therefore written for use on a particular machine,
(2) high-level languages or compilers which are fairly machine-independent.

12.2.1 *Assembler language*

As an example of an assembler, we will take PAL8, which runs on the PDP8 computer under the operating system OS/8 (DEC, 1974). The first point of convenience in using an assembler is that instructions are referred to by mnemonics rather than by the octal codes:

CODE   MNEMONIC

0xxx	AND xxx
1xxx	TAD xxx (twos complement add)
2xxx	ISZ xxx (increment and skip if zero)
3xxx	DCA xxx (deposit and clear accumulator)
4xxx	JMS xxx (jump to a subroutine)
5xxx	JMP xxx (jump)
6aab	specific to particular operation, e.g.
	6046 KRB (read keyboard)
	6031 TSF (skip if teletypewriter flags is set)
7xxx	specific to operation, for example:

7200 CLA (clear accumulator)
7440 SZA (skip if accumulator is zero)
7450 SNA (skip if accumulator is non-zero)
7001 IAC (increment accumulator)
7040 CMA (complement accumulator)
Many operate instructions can be combined and programmed as a single instruction.

A second point is that symbolic addresses can be used for the operands of memory reference instructions, which saves the programmer the labour of having to precalculate where in the program he should put his variables and constants. At the time of writing an instruction, we may not know the absolute address for the operand, so we just use a symbolic name for the address and then label the line in the program corresponding to that address with the same name, for example RFCNT in the following program. Assemblers also help with the calculation of constants. In PAL8, an operand preceded by a bracket causes the assembler to create a constant in a spare location. In PAL8, the fixed ratio schedule might be programmed as follows:

```
/FR10 SCHEDULE
/ANYTHING TYPED AFTER A / ON A LINE IS IGNORED BY THE
/ASSEMBLER. COMMENTS ARE NORMALLY ADDED HERE TO DOCUMENT
/THE PROGRAM AS AN AID TO LATER REVISION.
/DOT (.) IS EVALUATED BY PAL8 AS THE ADDRESS OF THE
/CURRENT LOCATION.  SO THE INSTRUCTION JMP .-1 IN THIS
/PROGRAM MEANS JUMP TO THE PREVIOUS LOCATION.

/DEFINE SPECIAL INPUT-OUTPUT SYMBOLS
         INPUT=6504     /DIGITAL INPUT REGISTER
         OUTPUT=6507
         CLFLAG=6131    /CLOCK FLAG CLEAR
         CLSTRT=6132    /CLOCK START OSCILLATOR
         CLLOAD=6134    /CLOCK LOAD COUNTER, AND CLEAR ACC.

         *100           /SET ORIGIN OF PROGRAM

         DECIMAL        /EVALUATE NUMBERS AS DECIMAL

/LABELS INSTRUCTIONS      COMMENTS

  START,  CLA           /CLEAR ACCUMULATOR
          DCA RFCNT     /ZERO REINFORCEMENT COUNTER
  LOOP,   TAD (-10      /GET -10 DECIMAL
          DCA SKDCNT    /AND SET UP SCHEDULE COUNTER
  WAIT0,  INPUT         /ENSURE INPUT REGISTER IS ZERO
          AND (1        /AND WITH 0001 FOR RESPONSE BIT
          SZA CLA       /SKIP IF ACCUMULATOR ZERO THEN CLEAR
          JMP WAIT0     /WAIT UNTIL ZERO
  WAIT1,  INPUT         /LOOK FOR NON-ZERO INPUT
          AND (1        /AND WITH 0001
          SNA CLA       /SKIP IF ACC. NON-ZERO THEN CLEAR
          JMP WAIT1     /KEEP WAITING FOR RESPONSE
          ISZ SKDCNT    /FOUND ONE, INCREMENT SCHEDULE COUNTER
          JMP WAIT0     /NO REINFORCEMENT IF HERE
          ISZ RFCNT     /REINFORCEMENT, SO INCREMENT COUNTER
          IAC           /SET ACCUMULATOR TO 0001
          OUTPUT        /LOAD OUTPUT REG. FOR REINFORCEMENT
          TAD (-3000    /GET -3000 DECIMAL
          CLLOAD        /LOAD CLOCK COUNTER
          CLSTRT        /START CLOCK
          CLFLAG        /TEST CLOCK FLAG
          JMP .-1       /WAIT FOR CLOCK FLAG
          OUTPUT        /REINFORCEMENT OFF AFTER 3000 MS
          JMP LOOP      /START ANOTHER COUNT OF 10

  RFCNT,  0
  SKDCNT, 0
          $             /END OF PROGRAM
```

Because symbols for the clock and digital input/output instructions are not included in the PAL8 permanent symbol table, they must be explicitly defined in the program. The permanent symbol table contains mnemonics for the more commonly used peripherals, such as the teletypewriter. Programs for assemblers and compilers are usually created with the help of a text editor. This is a utility program which allows the user to create files on a backing store and makes it easy to delete and insert text at selected points. Text editors which use a CRT display are particularly convenient.

When PAL8 assembles a program, it first looks through the text and constructs a symbol table for the labels and definitions used in the program. This process is termed the first pass. On the second pass, the code of the program is generated and written into a file. If a listing of the program is requested, a third pass is required. In a listing, the original source file is printed, together with the absolute addresses and the octal code generated by the assembler against the appropriate line. Listings are normally used for program development and revision. Before a newly written program is used for production work, it is important to test it thoroughly in order to ensure that it performs as intended and to remove any errors. This process is known as debugging, and usually forms a large portion of the total time involved in writing a program.

The use of assemblers is normally restricted to the production of efficient programs which will be used fairly often, and are unlikely to require frequent revision. Accordingly, systems programs such as editors and compilers are written in assembly language. Users of laboratory computers may find it necessary to use assembly language for experimental control programs in which timing is critical, or for carrying out modifications to a high-level language to enable it to operate a laboratory peripheral (Section 12.2.2). Analysis of data is nearly always performed by programs written in one of the standard scientific languages such as FORTRAN or BASIC.

12.2.2 *Modifying existing high-level languages*

When computer manufacturers are designing compilers for the standard high-level languages, they often include a facility which allows users to operate their own laboratory peripherals or to write specialized routines in assembly language which can then be called from programs written in a high-level language, such as BASIC.

BASIC was devised at Dartmouth College, and is now the most commonly used programming language for elementary applications. An introduction to BASIC has been written by Kemeny and Kurtz (1971). In this section, we will give a summary of elementary BASIC, together with examples of the way in which it may be extended to control laboratory experiments.

Each line of a BASIC program consists of a line number followed by a BASIC language statement. The following program would convert inches to centimetres:

```
100 INPUT X
120 LET Y=X*2.54
140 PRINT X;"INCHES ARE EQUAL TO";Y;"CENTIMETRES"
150 END
```

```
RUN

?12
   12 INCHES ARE EQUAL TO 30.48 CENTIMETERS

DONE
```

At line 100, the program prints a ? on the teletypewriter and waits for the user to type a numerical value terminated by the return key. This value is assigned to the variable X. At line 120 of the program, the value X in is converted to Y cm, and the result is printed out at line 140.

The following is a summary of elementary BASIC which should be sufficient to allow the reader to follow the examples in this section. There are minor variations between different versions of programming languages, particularly in respect of the more advanced features, and therefore it is wise to consult the manufacturer's handbook when using any particular system.

STATEMENTS

INPUT: read data from the teletypewriter.

PRINT: type values or text on the teletypewriter.

LET $v = f$: assign the value of expression f to the variable v. The word LET is optional.

GOTO n: transfer control to line n.

IF f_1 rel f_2 THEN n: if the relationship rel between expressions f_1 and f_2 is true, then transfer control to line n; if it is not true, then execute the next line number.

FOR $v = f_1$ TO f_2 STEP f_3: used in conjunction with NEXT to implement program loops. The variable v is set initially to value f_1, and the cycle through to the NEXT v statement is executed. Subsequently v is incremented by f_3, and the loop repeated until the value of v is greater than f_2. If STEP f_3 is omitted, $+1$ is assumed.

NEXT v: see FOR.

REM: remarks or comments which are not to form part of the executable program.

END: final statement of a program.

OPERATIONS

+	addition
−	substraction
*	multiplication
/	division
^	raise to a power

RELATIONSHIPS

=	equal to
<	less than
≤	less than or equal to

>	greater than
≧	greater than or equal to
≠	not equal to

FUNCTIONS

SQR	(f)	returns the square root of expression f.
ABS	(f)	returns the absolute value of f.
INT	(f)	returns the greatest integer less than f.
SIN	(f)	returns the sine of angle f rad.
COS	(f)	returns the cosine of angle f rad.
ATN	(f)	returns the angle in radians whose tangent is f.
LOG	(f)	returns the natural logarithm of f.
EXP	(f)	returns the value of e raised to the power f.
RND	(0)	returns a random number between 0 and 1.

Variables in BASIC may be given names up to two characters, but must always start with a letter. If a second character is used it must be a number. Lists or arrays may be specified by putting a subscript in parentheses after the variable name, as in X(5). If a subscript greater than ten is to be used, the program must include a dimension statement such as

```
100 DIM X(35),Y(100)
```

Clearly this elementary form of BASIC does not have the facilities needed to control experiments, or to collect laboratory data. For such purposes, we need to add functions which relate to strict time and allow communication with laboratory peripherals. A simple laboratory system with a real-time clock and 12 bit input and output registers might have the following additional functions:

DEL	(f)	delay program execution for f ms.
CLK	(f)	operate the real-time clock
		$f = 0$ read and stop
		$f = 1$ read and restart
		$f = 2$ zero and stop
		$f = 3$ zero and restart
BIN	(f)	return the status of bit f in the input register.
BON	(f)	set bit f of the output register.
BOF	(f)	reset bit f of the output register.

Because these functions must be included in a legal BASIC statement, the user is often forced to construct an artificial statement of the form

```
150 LET Z=BON(3)
```

just to operate a user function. Z is a dummy variable, and is present only

because a variable is required by the BASIC syntax. A more elegant solution
is to introduce a new statement to BASIC purely for the purpose of exercising
user functions. We could call it OPERATE, and then write statements of the
form:

```
150 OPERATE BON(3)
```

In the examples which follow, we will assume that an OPERATE statement has
been added to our hypothetical version of BASIC.

The fixed ratio schedule used as an example in the preceding sections could be
programmed in BASIC as follows:

```
  1 REM FR10 SCHEDULE
  2 REM RESPONSE:      INPUT REGISTER BIT 2
  3 REM REINFORCEMENT: OUTPUT REGISTER BIT 1
 10 LET R=0
 20 OPERATE BOF(1)
 30 FOR I=1 TO 10
 40    IF BIN(2)=1 THEN 40
 50    IF BIN(2)=0 THEN 50
 60 NEXT I
 70 OPERATE BON(1)
 80 OPERATE DEL(3000)
 90 OPERATE BOF(1)
100 LET R=R+1
110 GOTO 30
120 END
```

When the program is first started, the statement in line 20 ensures that the bit in
the output register which is used for reinforcement is cleared. Lines 40 and 50
control the progress of the program, ensuring that there is a transition from
logic 0 to logic 1 on input register bit 2 before control is allowed to pass beyond
these statements. The FOR loop between lines 30 and 60 counts 10 such
transitions before the program reaches line 70, at which point reinforcement is
dispensed by a 3000 ms output. In practice, the starting and stopping of an
experiment is usually controlled by detecting the state of additional logic
inputs, which can be set by the experimenter. This program counts the number
of reinforcements at line 100, and it could be extended to print out the total
number of reinforcements when the experimenter signals the end of a session.
The program as written here would, of course, continue indefinitely, and would
need to be stopped by intervention from the computer console.

When running experiments from a computer, it is useful to be able to set
experimental parameters at the time the program is run. The probability
reinforcement procedure described in Section 4.3.3 and implemented in
Figure 4.19 by modular programming equipment could be programmed in
BASIC as follows:

```
  1 REM PROBABILITY REINFORCEMENT SCHEDULE
  2 REM RESPONSE:      INPUT REGISTER BIT 2
  3 REM REINFORCEMENT: OUTPUT REGISTER BIT 1
 10 LET R=0
 20 OPERATE BOF(1)
```

```
 30 PRINT "PROBABILITY"
 40 INPUT P
 50 IF BIN(2)=1 THEN 50
 60 IF BIN(2)=0 THEN 60
 70 IF RND(0)>P THEN 50
 80 OPERATE BON(1)
 90 OPERATE DEL(3000)
100 OPERATE BOF(1)
110 LET R=R+1
120 GOTO 50
130 END
```

This program allows the experimenter to select the probability of reinforcement every time the program is run. At line 30, the program asks for a probability in the range 0 to 1, and the typed value is assigned to variable P at line 40. At line 70, the value of P is compared with an equiprobable random number in the range 0 to 1 every time a response is detected. Reinforcement follows if the random number is less than or equal to P.

At the end of a computer-controlled experiment, it is usual to print out a summary of the data. To start with a simple example, we give a program for a fixed interval schedule of reinforcement. This program operates in the same manner as the modular programming example in Figure 4.20, with the addition of a control bit on the input register which is used to start and stop the experiment.

```
  1 REM FIXED INTERVAL SCHEDULE
  2 REM RESPONSE:        INPUT REGISTER BIT 1
  3 REM REINFORCEMENT:   OUTPUT REGISTER BIT 1
  4 REM START EXPERIMENT: SET INPUT REGISTER BIT 11
  5 REM STOP EXPERIMENT:  CLEAR IT
 10 FIXED INTERVAL SCHEDULE
 15 LET R=0
 20 OPERATE BOF(1)
 30 PRINT "INTERVAL IN SECONDS"
 40 INPUT T
 50 IF DIN(11)=0 THEN 50
 60 FOR I=1 TO T
 70    OPERATE DEL(1000)
 80 NEXT I
 90 IF BIN(11)=0 THEN 180
100 IF BIN(1)=1 THEN 90
110 IF BIN(11)=0 THEN 180
120 IF BIN(1)=0 THEN 110
130 OPERATE BON(1)
140 OPERATE DEL(3000)
150 OPERATE BOF(1)
160 LET R=R+1
170 GOTO 60
180 PRINT "NUMBER OF REINFORCEMENTS =";R
190 END
```

In the following program for simple reaction time, data is stored during the course of the experimental session for subsequent statistical processing. The intertrial intervals are randomized, and, at the start of the program, a dialogue at the teletypewriter allows the experimenter to specify the number of trials and the minimum and maximum durations of the intertrial intervals.

```
1 REM RT EXPERIMENT
2 REM RESPONSE:          INPUT REGISTER BIT 5
3 REM STIMULUS:          OUTPUT REGISTER BIT 1
4 REM START EXPERIMENT: SET INPUT REGISTER BIT 0
10 DIM T(100)
20 OPERATE BOF(1)
30 PRINT "NO. OF TRIALS (MAX. 100)"
40 INPUT N
50 PRINT "MIN. INTERVAL (<4095 MS)"
60 INPUT L
70 PRINT "MAX. INTERVAL (<4095 MS)"
80 INPUT U
90 IF BIN(0)=0 THEN 90
100 FOR I=1 TO N
110   LET T1=L+(U-L)*RND(0)
120   IF BIN(5)=1 THEN 110
125   OPERATE DEL(T1)
130   OPERATE BON(1)
140   OPERATE CLK(3)
150   IF BIN(5)=0 THEN 150
160   LET T(I)=CLK(0)
170   OPERATE BOF(1)
180   IF BIN(5)=1 THEN 180
190 NEXT I
200 REM SESSION OVER. CALCULATE MEAN AND STANDARD DEVIATION
210 LET S=0
220 FOR I=1 TO N
230   S=S+T(I)
240 NEXT I
250 LET M=S/N
260 PRINT "MEAN RT =";M;"MILLISECONDS"
270 LET S=0
280 FOR I=1 TO N
290   LET S=S+(T(I)-M)↑2
300 NEXT I
310 LET V=S/(N-1)
320 PRINT "STANDARD DEVIATION =";SQR(V)
330 END
```

The program includes some tests which ensure that the subject makes responses at the appropriate times. At line 120, a check is made that the subject has not anticipated the stimulus, and, at line 180, progress to the next randomized intertrial interval is held up until the subject releases the response key. The stimulus is presented continuously from line 130 until a response is detected at line 150. The response latencies are stored in the array T which is dimensioned in line 10. If the raw data is needed for more sophisticated analyses, possibly with data from other subjects, then the response latencies could be output on punched paper tape. It would be more convenient, however, to write the data into a file on disc or magnetic tape, so that the data could be accessed by an analysis program when all the experimental sessions have been completed.

12.2.3 *Experimental-control languages*

BASIC and the other commonly used high-level languages FORTRAN and ALGOL were, of course, not designed for controlling experiments, but for mathematical and scientific computation. High-level languages are often described as problem-oriented, in contrast to assemblers, which are machine-oriented languages. The intention in providing a problem-oriented language is to allow the user to program at the level of the concepts he would normally use when thinking about the problem which is to be solved. Because so many man hours are involved in writing high-level languages, computer manufacturers usually provide only the standard scientific- and business-oriented languages. Some researchers and scientific instrument manufacturers, however, have written various languages oriented to the problem of experimental control. The most successful in the field of psychology have been those designed for the time-shared control of a number of operant conditioning experiments, such as ACT (Millenson, 1973) and SCAT (Stadler, 1969). The fairly low data rates and standardized procedures in such experiments make it possible for an inexpensive minicomputer to control many experimental chambers. In other areas of psychological experimentation, the critical time demands of refreshing CRT displays or sampling ADC channels do not usually permit time sharing, and the wide variety of procedures has meant that there has been little general acceptance of a language oriented to experimental control. Accordingly, most programming for experimental control in areas other than operant conditioning has used assembly language or modified BASIC or FORTRAN. Wood, Sette and Weiss (1975) have prepared a useful review of computer languages and operating systems for experimental control in psychology.

As an example of an experimental-control language, we will describe the SKED system (Snapper and Kadden, 1973) which was designed for the control of operant conditioning experiments. The system allows a single minicomputer to control up to ten experimental chambers or boxes, each having up to 12 stimulus and response lines. The SKED language is based on a state-notation system for describing reinforcement schedules in terms of sequences of states which change according to the ocurrence of responses or time pulses. Snapper, Knapp and Kushner (1970) have advocated the general use of state diagrams for the precise description of schedules of reinforcement, and the SKED language is merely a process for transcribing state diagrams into a form suitable for input to a computer.

Any state in an experiment has two critical parameters:

(1) the prevailing stimuli which are to be presented,
(2) the events which govern transition to the next state.

Figure 12.11a shows how a state and transition may be represented in graphical form. The circle representing the state is divided into two parts. The upper part identifies the state by number, and the lower part shows the stimulus conditions which are associated with the state. Transitions from one state to another are represented by arrows labelled with the event which governs the transition from one state to the other. The state diagram for a simple reinforcement schedule is shown in Figure 12.11c. Note that the identifying codes S1 and S2 in the lower parts of the circles refer to stimulus 1 and stimulus 2, not to state 1 and state 2.

260

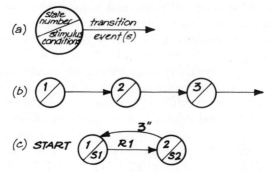

Figure 12.11. *(a) SKED state notation. Each state in an experimental procedure is represented by a circle with a vector labelled by the event governing transistion to the next state; (b) a sequence of three states, each being identified by a number; (c) A simple continuous reinforcement schedule.*

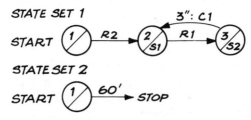

Figure 12.12. *State diagram for continuous reinforcement schedule. The number of reinforcements is counted by C1, and the parallel state set 2 is used to terminate the session after 1h. S1 is the keylight, and S2 provides reinforcement. R1 is the response key, and R2 is used to start the session. The units of time are denoted by ' (minutes) and " (seconds).*

Many procedures need two or more parallel state sets. At any given time, only one state from each set is operative. A basic use for a second state set is to provide a session timer. Figure 12.12 shows a second state set added to the continuous reinforcement schedule so that the session will terminate after 1 #. A counter C1 has also been added to count the reinforcements and make the state diagram consistent with the modular programming example in Figure 4.17. R2 is a switch which is closed to start the session.

When using the SKED system, the continuous reinforcement schedule would be programmed as follows:

```
/CONTINUOUS REINFORCEMENT SCHEDULE

S.S.1,
S1,
        R2:ON1------------>S2    /START SESSION
S2,
        R1:OFF1;ON2------->S3    /GIVE REINFORCEMENT
S3,
        3":OFF2;ON1;C1---->S2

S.S.2,
S1,
        60'-------------->STOP /SESSION TIMER
        $
```

S.S.1. and S.S.2. refer to state sets 1 and 2, respectively. Within a state set, each state is identified as S1, S2, S3 etc., and is followed by the event which governs a transition. For example, the occurrence of R2 during state 1 of state set 1 causes a transition to state 2, accompanied by the switching on of stimulus 2.

The SKED runtime system allows further compiled programs to be loaded from paper tape while existing control programs are running. Control programs can be started and stopped from the console teletypewriter, and the values of counters associated with any program can be printed out as required, or punched on paper tape for subsequent computer analysis. Because the timesharing for the runtime system does not normally permit compilation to take place simultaneously, it is desirable to have one machine for the runtime system and a second machine for compiling programs and analysing data. As well as a compiler and a runtime system, the SKED software includes a debugging program which simulates the SKED interface, allowing a compiled program to be run on the computer used to compile the control programs. This allows the experimenter to test and modify his program from the console teletypewriter before transferring the compiled output to the machine which is controlling the experiments.

Versions of the SKED language have been developed for various PDP-8 configurations, and there is no reason why the system could not be implemented on other minicomputers. Full details of the various current SKED systems are available from the SKED Users' Group, Department of Psychology, Western Michigan University.

To conclude our brief review of the SKED system, we will give state diagrams and programs for the remainder of the examples of schedules of reinforcement in Chapter 4. The continuous reinforcement schedule of Figure 12.12 is easily converted to a fixed ratio schedule which corresponds to Figure 4.18 by changing the label on the state-2-to-state-3 transition from R1 to 10R1 (Figure 12.13). The program then becomes:

```
/FR10 SCHEDULE

S.S.1,
S1,
```

262

```
                R2:ON1------------>S2    /START SESSION
    S2,
                10R1:OFF1;ON2----->S3    /GIVE REINFORCEMENT
    S3,
                3":OFF2;ON1;C1---->S2    /GIVE REINFORCEMENT

    S.S.2,
    S1,
                60'-------------->STOP /SESSION TIMER

         $
```

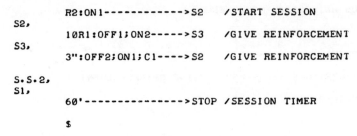

Figure 12.13. *State diagram for a fixed ratio schedule of reinforcement (FR10).*

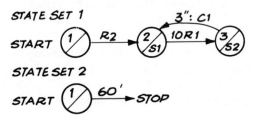

Figure 12.14. *State diagram for reinforcement with a probability of 0·1. The probability is generated by the gating function R1&A(2) and state set 2.*

Probabilities can be included in the transitions. Figure 12.14 shows a state diagram for a probability reinforcement schedule. The transition labelled R1 & A(2) between state 2 and state 3 of state set 2 is contingent upon R1 occurring while state set 2 (equated to A) is in state 2. The time transitions in state set 2 are such that this set is in state 2 for only 10% of the time. This method of generating probabilities is similar to that used in the modular programming example of Figure 4.19. The SKED program would be written as follows:

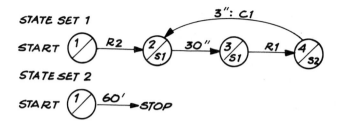

Figure 12.15. *State diagram for a fixed interval 30 s schedule of reinforcement.*

```
/PROBABILITY SCHEDULE P=0.1

S.S.1,
S1,
        R2:ON1------------>S2    /START SESSION
S2,
        R1&A(2):OFF1;ON2-->S3    /GIVE REINFORCEMENT
S3,
        3":OFF2;ON1;C1---->S2

S.S.2=A,
S1,
        .09"------------->S2
S2,
        .01"------------->S1     /P=.1

S.S.3,
S1,
        60'--------------->STOP /SESSION TIMER

        $
```

Figure 12.15 shows a fixed interval schedule corresponding to Figure 4.20. The SKED program is

```
/FIXED INTERVAL 30 SECONDS

S.S.1,
S1,
        R2:ON1------------>S2    /START SESSION
S2,
        30"--------------->S3
S3,
        R1:OFF1;ON2------->S4    /GIVE REINFORCEMENT
S4,
        3":OFF2;ON1;C1---->S2

S.S.2,
S1,
        60'--------------->STOP /SESSION TIMER

        $
```

The DRL schedule of Figure 4.21 is shown in state-diagram form in Figure 12.16. The SKED program is

264

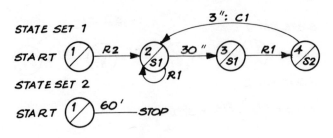

Figure 12.16. *State diagram for a DRL schedule.*

```
/DRL 30 SECONDS

S.S.1,
S1,
        R2:ON1------------>S2      /START SESSION
S2,
        30"--------------->S3
        R1---------------->S2      /ONLY CHANGE FROM FI 30
S3,
        R1:OFF1;ON2------->S4      /GIVE REINFORCEMENT
S4,
        3":OFF2:ON1:C1---->S2

S.S.2,
S1,
        60'-------------->STOP /SESSION TIMER

        $
```

The last schedule is the Sidman avoidance procedure of Figure 4.22. The state diagram is illustrated in Figure 12.17, and the SKED program is

```
/SIDMAN AVOIDANCE CONDITIONING

S.S.1,
S1,
        R2:ON1------------>S2      /START SESSION
S2,
        R1---------------->S2
        10":ON2----------->S3      /GIVE SHOCK
```

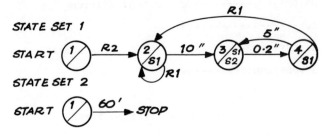

Figure 12.17. *State diagram for the Sidman avoidance procedure. S1 is the keylight and S2 the shock. The response–shock time is 10 s, the shock duration is 200 ms and the shock–shock interval is 5 s.*

```
S3,
        .2":OFF2----------->S3    /SHOCK-SHOCK INTERVAL
        R1:OFF2------------>S2    /TERMINATE SHOCK

S.S.2,
S1,
        60'-------------->STOP /SESSION TIMER

        $
```

12.3 Summary

A laboratory computer is a flexible tool which allows a wide range of experiments to be controlled. It can also provide means for recording and analysing experimental data.

To be generally useful, a laboratory computer system needs a backing store, an operating system and a laboratory interface. Unless specially written programs are available for the intended application, it is also necessary to have a specialist available in at least a supporting capacity.

Depending on the timing requirements of an experiment, programs for experimental control can be written in a variety of languages. Special languages have been designed for controlling psychology experiments, and some of them allow time-shared control of a small number of low data rate experiments. Descriptions have been given of languages exemplifying the various classes of programming languages, together with specimen programs for some of the more commonly used operant conditioning procedures.

References

Adrian, E. D., and Matthews, B. H. C. (1934a). 'The interpretation of potential waves in the cortex', *Journal of Physiology*, **81**, 440–471.

Adrian, E. D., and Matthews, B. H. C. (1934b). 'Berger rhythm: potential changes from occipital lobes in man', *Brain*, **57**, 355–385.

Alpern, M. (1962). 'Types of movement', in H. Davson (Ed.), *The Eye. Vol. 3—Muscular Mechanisms*, New York, Academic Press.

Apter, M. J., and Westby, G. (Eds.) (1973). *The Computer in Psychology*, London, John Wiley & Sons.

Ax, A. F., Singer, S. J., Zachery, G., Gudobba, R. D., and Gottlieb, J. S. (1964). 'Psychophysiological data retrieval and utilization', *Annals of the New York Academy of Sciences*, **115**, 890–904.

Azrin, N. H., and Powell, J. (1968). 'Behavioral engineering: the reduction of smoking behaviour by a conditioning apparatus and procedure', *Journal of Applied Behavior Analysis*, **1**, 193–200.

Baer, D. M. (1962). 'A technique for the study of social reinforcement in young children: behavior avoiding reinforcement withdrawal', *Child Development*, **33**, 847–858.

Baker, L. E. (1971). 'Biomedical applications of electrical-impedance measurements', in B. Watson (Ed.), *IEE Medical Electronics Monographs 1–6*, Peter Peregrinus.

Barker, A., and Brown, B. H. (1973). 'Simple impedance pneumograph and volume integrator', *Medical and Biological Engineering*, **11**, 352–353.

Bauer, J. A., Woods, G. D., and Held, R. (1969). 'A device for rapid recording of positioning responses in two dimensions', *Behavior Research Methods and Instrumentation*, **1**, 157–159.

Berger, H. (1929). 'Über des Elektrenkephalogramm des Menschen', *Archiv für Psychiatrie und Nervenkrankheit*, **87**, 527–570, translated by P. Gloor, *Electroencephalography and Clinical Neurophysiology*, supplement, **28**, 37–73.

Bijou, S. W., and Baer, D. M. (1966). 'Operant methods in child behavior and development', in W. K. Honig (Ed.), *Operant Behavior: Areas of Research and Application*, New York, Appleton–Century–Crofts.

Bitterman, M. E. (1966). 'Animal learning', in J. B. Sidowski (Ed.), *Experimental Methods and Instrumentation in Psychology*, New York, McGraw–Hill.

Bitzer, D., and Skaperdas, D. (1973). 'The design of an economically viable large-scale computer-based education system', *CERL Report X-5*, Computer-based Education Research Laboratory, University of Illinois, Urbana, Illinois.

Boole, G. (1854). *The Laws of Thought* (reprinted 1958), New York, Dover.

Bornstein, M. H., and Cox, N. (1974). 'A continuous interference-filter monochromator', *Behavior Research Methods and Instrumentation*, **6**, 31–32.

Boynton, R. M. (1966). 'Vision', in J. B. Sidowski (Ed.), *Experimental Methods and Instrumentation in Psychology*, New York, McGraw–Hill.

Bradley, P. B. (Ed.) (1975). *Methods in Brain Research*, London, John Wiley & Sons.

Brenner, J. (1967). 'Heart rate', in P. H. Venables and I. Martin (Eds.), *Manual of Psychophysiological Methods*, Amsterdam, North-Holland Publishing Co.

Brophy, J. J. (1972). *Basic Electronics for Scientists*, 2nd edition, New York, McGraw–Hill.

Brown, C. C. (Ed.) (1967). *Methods in Psychophysiology*, Baltimore, Md., Williams & Wilkins Co.

Bureš, J., Petráň, M., and Zacher, J. (1967), *Electrophysiological Methods in Biological Research*, New York, Academic Press.

Caton, R. (1875). 'The electric currents of the brain', *British Medical Journal*, 2, 278.

Caton, R. (1877). 'Interim report of investigations on the electric currents of the brain', *British Medical Journal*, 5 May supplement.

Cavonius, C. R. (1974). 'A method of mixing lights to produce homogeneous illumination', *Behavior Research Methods and Instrumentation*, 6, 29–30.

Cherry, C. (1964). *On Human Communication*, London, Chapman & Hall.

Cleary, A., Mayes, T., and Packham, D. (1976). *Educational Technology: Implications for Early and Special Education*, London, John Wiley & Sons.

Cohen, A., and Denenberg, V. H. (1973). 'A small-animal activity-analysing system for behavioural studies', *Medical and Biological Engineering*, 11, 490–499.

Cohen, M. M., and Massaro, D. W. (1976). 'Real-time speech synthesis', *Behavior Research Methods and Instrumentation*, 8, 189–196.

Coombs, C. F., Jr. (Ed.) (1972). *Basic Electronic Instrument Handbook*, New York, McGraw–Hill.

Cooper, R. (1971). 'Recording changes in electrical properties of the brain', in R. D. Myers (Ed.), *Methods in Psychobiology—Vol. 1*, London, Academic Press.

Coren, S., and Miller, J. (1973). 'The use of photographic exposure meters as photometers', *Behavior Research Methods and Instrumentation*, 5, 357–360.

Craske, B., and Smith, D. G. (1974). 'A two-dimensional eye position and movement transducer of high sensitivity and stability', *Quarterly Journal of Experimental Psychology*, 27, 137–140.

Davenport, J. W., Chamove, A. S., and Harlow, H. F. (1970). 'The semiautomatic Wisconsin general test apparatus', *Behavior Research Methods and Instrumentation*, 2, 135–138.

DEC (1974). *OS/8 Handbook DEC-S8-OSHBA-A-D*, Maynard, Mass., Digital Equipment Corporation.

Delgado, J. M. R. (1967). 'Aggression and defence under cerebral radio control', in C. D. Clemente and D. B. Lindsley (Eds.), *Aggression and Defence*, Los Angeles, University of California Press.

Dodge, R., and Cline, T. S. (1901). 'The angular velocity of eye movements', *Psychological Review*, 8, 145–157.

Donchin, E., and Heffley, E. (1975). 'Minicomputers in the signal-averaging laboratory', *American Psychologist*, 30, 299–312.

Downing, A. C. (1972). 'The teletracker', *paper presented at the International Symposium on Simple Nervous Systems, Glasgow*, Royal Society of Edinburgh and the Scottish Electrophysiology Society.

Downing, A. C. (1976), *Personal communication*, Department of Psychology, University of Newcastle upon Tyne.

Edelberg, R. (1967). 'Electrical properties of the skin', in C. C. Brown (Ed.), *Methods in Psychophysiology*. Baltimore, Md., Williams & Wilkins Co.

Edelberg, R., Greiner, T., and Burch, N. R. (1960). 'Some membrane properties of the effector in the galvanic skin response', *Journal of Applied Physiology*, 15, 691–696.

Edwards, E. (1964). *Information Transmission*, London, Chapman & Hall.

Eisman, E. (1969). 'Monitoring drinking: a method compatible with the recording of electrophysiological phenomena', *Behavior Research Methods and Instrumentation*, 1, 300–301.

Estrin, T., and Uzgalis, R. (1969). 'Computerized display of spatio-temporal EEG patterns', *IEEE Transactions on Biomedical Engineering*, **16**, 192–196.

Féré, C. (1888). 'Note sur des modifications de la résistance électrique sous l'influence des excitations sensorielles et des émotions', *Comptes Rendus de la Société de Biologie (Paris)*, **8**, 217–219.

Fine, S., and Weinman, J. (1973). 'The use of photoconductive cells in plethysmography', *Medical and Biological Engineering*, **11**, 455–463.

Finger, F. W. (1972), 'Measuring behavioral activity', in R. D. Myers (Ed.), *Methods in Psychobiology*, Vol. 2, London, Academic Press.

Flegg, H. G. (1971). *Boolean Algebra*, London, Macdonald.

Galvani, P. F. (1970). 'Air puff-elicited startle: habituation over trials and measurement of a hypothetical emotional response', *Behavior Research Methods and Instrumentation*, **2**, 232–233.

Geddes, L. A., and Baker, L. E. (1975). *Principles of Applied Biomedical Instrumentation*, 2nd edition, New York, John Wiley & Sons.

Geddes, L. A., Baker, L. E., Moore, A. G., and Coulter, T. W. (1969). 'Hazards in the use of low frequencies for the measurement of physiological events by impedance', *Medical and Biological Engineering*, **7**, 289–296.

Gellermann, L. W. (1933). 'Chance orders of alternating stimuli in discrimination experiments', *Journal of Genetic Psychology*, **42**, 206–208.

GenRad (1976). *A Handbook of Behavioral Research Equipment*, revised edition, Bolton, Mass. Enviromedics Division, GenRad, Inc.

Gildermeister, M., and Ellinghaus, J. (1923). 'Über die Abhängigkeit des galvanischen Hautreflexes von der Temperatur der Haut', *Pflüger's Archiv für die Gesamte Physiologie*, **200**, 262–277.

Greatorex. C. A. (1971). 'Indirect methods of blood-pressure measurement', in B. Watson (Ed.), *IEE Medical Electronics Monographs 1–6*, London, Peter Peregrinus.

Greenfield, N. S., and Sternbach, R. A. (Eds.) (1972). *Handbook of Psychophysiology*, New York, Holt, Rhinehart & Winston.

Gregory, R. L. (1969). 'Apparatus for investigating visual perception', *American Psychologist*, **24**, 219–225.

Harlow, H. F., and Bromer, J. (1938), 'A test-apparatus for monkeys', *Psychological Record*, **2**, 434–436.

Hart, B. L. (1969). *Experimental Neuropsychology: A Laboratory Manual*, San Francisco, W. H. Freeman & Co.

Hart, B. L. (Ed.) (1976), *Experimental Psychobiology: A Laboratory Manual*, San Francisco, W. H. Freeman & Co.

Hill, J. H., and Stellar, E. (1951). 'An electronic drinkometer', *Science*, **114**, 43–44.

Horner, J. L., Longo, N., and Bitterman, M. E. (1961). A shuttle box for the fish and a control circuit of general applicability. *American Journal of Psychology*, **74**, 114–120.

Horowitz, H. (1969). 'Observation room windows', *American Psychologist*, **24**, 304–308.

Horsley, V., and Clarke, R. H. (1908). 'The structure and function of the cerebellum examined by a new method', *Brain*, **31**, 45–124.

IES (1959). *IES Lighting Handbook*, 3rd edition, New York, Illuminating Engineering Society.

Ingling, C. R., Jr. (1970) 'The calibration of neutral density wedges', *Behavior Research Methods and Instrumentation*, **2**, 45–48.

Jackman, K. L., and Cowgill, R. C. (1970). 'Design and laboratory tests of a long-life FM transmitter for tagging small animals', *Behavior Research Methods and Instrumentation*, **2**, 230–231.

Jasper, H. H. (1958). 'International Federation of Societies for Electroencephalography and Clinical Neurophysiology. Appendix IX: The ten-twenty electrode system of the International Federation', *Electroencephalography and Clinical Neurophysiology*, **10**, 371–375.

Julesz, B. (1971). *Foundations of Cyclopean Perception*, Chicago, University of Chicago Press.

Kemeny, J. G., and Kurtz, T. E. (1971). BASIC Programming, 2nd edition, New York, John Wiley & Sons.

Korn, G. A. (1973). *Minicomputers for Engineers and Scientists*, New York, McGraw-Hill.

Leong, C. K. (1975). 'An efficient method for dichotic tape preparation', *Behavior Research Methods and Instrumentation*, **7**, 447–451.

Lippold, O. C. J. (1952). 'The relation between integrated action potentials in a human muscle and its isometric tension', *Journal of Physiology*, **117**, 492–499.

Lippold, O. C. J. (1967). 'Electromyography', in P. H. Venables and I. Martin (Eds.), *Manual of Psychophysiological Methods*, Amsterdam, North-Holland Publishing Co.

Lott, D. F. and Woll, R. J. (1966). 'A device permitting one-way vision without a mirror image', *Perceptual and Motor Skills*, **23**, 533–534.

Lykken, D. T. (1959). 'Properties of electrodes used in electrodermal measurement', *Journal of Comparative and Physiological Psychology*, **52**, 629–634.

Mackay, R. S. (1970). *Bio-Medical Telemetry*, 2nd edition, New York, John Wiley & Sons.

Mackworth, J. F., and Mackworth, N. H. (1958). 'Eye fixation recorded on changing visual scenes by the television eye marker', *Journal of the Optical Society of America*, **48**, 429–435.

Mackworth, N. H., and Thomas, E. L. (1962). 'Head-mounted eye marker camera', *Journal of the Optical Society of America*, **52**, 713–716.

Margerison, J. H., St. John-Loe, P., and Binnie, C. D. (1967). 'Electroencephalography', in P. H. Venables and I. Martin (Eds.), *Manual of Psychophysiological Methods*, Amsterdam, North-Holland Publishing Co.

Marshall, C. (1967). 'Research electroencephalography', in C. C. Brown (Ed.) *Methods in Psychophysiology*, Baltimore, Md., Williams & Wilkins Co.

Masterson, F. A., and Campbell, B. A. (1972). 'Techniques of electric shock motivation', in R. D. Myers (Ed.), *Methods in Psychobiology*, Vol. 2, London, Academic Press.

Mathews, M. V. (1969). *The Technology of Computer Music*, Cambridge, Mass. MIT Press.

Mayes, T. (1976). *Personal communication*, Department of Psychology, University of Strathclyde, Glasgow.

Millenson, J. R. (1973). 'On-line sequential control of experiments by an automated contingency translator', in B. Weiss (Ed.), *Digital Computers in the Behavioral Laboratory*, New York, Appleton–Century–Crofts.

Monty, R. A., and Senders, J. W. (Eds.) (1976). *Eye Movements and Psychological Processes*, Hillsdale, N. J., Lawrence Erlbaum Associates.

Murch, G. M. (1972). 'CIE *x*, *y* coordinates from an inexpensive projection colorimeter', *Behavior Research Methods and Instrumentation*, **4**, 3–5.

Myers, R. D. (Ed.) (1971). *Methods in Psychobiology—Volume 1*, London, Academic Press.

Myers, R. D. (Ed.) (1972). *Methods in Psychobiology—Volume 2*, London, Academic Press.

Mylrea, K. C. (1966). 'A sixteen-unit projector with microsecond turn-on time', *American Journal of Psychology*, **76**, 314–317.

Nealis, P. M., Engelke, R. M., and Massaro, D. W. (1973). 'A description and evaluation of light-emitting diode displays for generation of visual stimuli', *Behavior Research Methods and Instrumentation*, **5**, 37–40.

Newhall, S. M., Nickerson, D., and Judd, D. B. (1943). 'Final report of the OSA subcommittee on the spacing of the Munsell colors', *Journal of the Optical Society of America*, **33**, 385–418.

Olsen, G. H. (1968). *Electronics: A General Introduction for the Non-specialist*, London, Butterworths.

Paskewitz, A. (1975). 'Biofeedback instrumentation: soldering closed the loop', *American Psychologist*, **30**, 371–378.

Passman, R. H. (1974). 'The smoked plastic screen: an alternative to the one-way mirror',

Journal of Experimental Child Psychology, **17**, 374–376.

Pert, A., and Bitterman, M. E. (1969). 'A technique for the study of consummatory behavior and instrumental learning in the turtle', *American Psychologist,* **24**, 258–261.

Phister, M. (1958). *Logical Design of Digital Computers,* New York, John Wiley & Sons.

Plutchik, R. (1974). *Foundations of Experimental Research,* 2nd edition, New York, Harper & Row.

Poincaré, H. (1905). *Science and Hypothesis* (English translation), London, Walter Scott Publishing Co.

Poulton, E. C. (1962). 'On simple methods of scoring tracking error'. *Psychological Bulletin,* **59**, 320–328.

Poulton, E. C. (1964). 'Postview and preview in tracking with complex and simple inputs', *Ergonomics,* **7**, 257–266.

Riggs, L. A. (1964). 'A projection color mixer', *American Journal of Psychology,* **77**, 129–134.

Riggs, L. A. (1965). 'Light as a stimulus for vision', in C. H. Graham (Ed.), *Vision and Visual Perception,* New York, John Wiley & Sons.

Robinson, D. W., and Dadson, R. S. (1956). 'A re-determination of the equal-loudness relations for pure tones', *British Journal of Applied Physics,* **7**, 166–181.

Rosenthal, R. (1976). *Experimenter Effects in Behavioral Research,* enlarged edn. New York, Irvington Publishers, Inc.

Shackel, B. (1967). in P. H. Venables and I. Martin (Eds.), *Manual of Psychophysiological Methods,* Amsterdam, North-Holland Publishing Co.

Shagass, C. (1972). *Evoked Brain Potentials in Psychiatry,* New York, Plenum.

Shannon, C. E. (1948). 'A mathematical theory of communication', *Bell System Technical Journal,* **27**, 379–423 and 623–656.

Skinner, B. F., and Campbell, S. L. (1947). 'An automatic shocking grid apparatus for continuous use', *Journal of Comparative and Physiological Psychology,* **40**, 305–307.

Skinner, J. E. (1971). *Neuroscience: A Laboratory Manual,* Philadelphia, W. B. Saunders & Co.

Snapper, A. G., and Kadden, R. M. (1973). 'Time-sharing in a small computer based on a behavioral notation system', in B. Weiss (Ed.), *Digital Computers in the Behavioral Laboratory,* New York, Appleton–Century–Crofts.

Snapper, A. G., Knapp, J. Z., and Kushner, H. K. (1970). 'Mathematical description of schedules of reinforcement', in W. N. Schoenfeld (Ed.), *The Theory of Reinforcement Schedules,* New York, Appleton–Century–Crofts.

Sobel, A. (1973). 'Electronic numbers', *Scientific American,* **228**, June, 65–73.

Spelman, F. A., and Pagano, R. R. (1969). 'Beating the *L* out of inductive transients', *American Psychologist,* **24**, 225–229.

Sperling, G. (1971). 'Flicker in computer-generated visual displays: selecting a CRO phosphor and other problems', *Behavior Research Methods and Instrumentation,* **3**, 151–153.

Stadler, S. J. (1969). 'On the varieties of computer experience', *Behavior Research Methods and Instrumentation,* **1**, 267–269.

Stiles, W. S., and Crawford, B. H. (1933). 'The luminous efficiency of rays entering the eye pupil at different points', *Proceedings of the Royal Society,* **112B**, 428–450.

Tarchanoff, J. (1890). 'Über die galvanischen Erscheinungen in der Haut des Menschen bei Reizungen der Sinnersorgane und bei verschiedenen Formen der psychischen Tätiskeit', *Pflüger's Archiv für die Gesamte Physiologie,* **46**, 46–55.

Taylor, M., and Creelman, C. D. (1967). 'PEST: efficient estimates on probability functions', *Journal of the Acoustical Society of America,* **41**, 782–787.

Thorsheim, H. I., Anderson, D. E., and Schultz, L. C. (1974). 'An inexpensive circuit for beta, alpha, theta or delta EEG biofeedback', *Behavior Research Methods and Instrumentation,* **6**, 33–36.

Tursky, B., Shapiro, D., and Schwartz, G. E. (1972). 'Automated constant cuff-pressure system to measure average systolic and diastolic blood pressure in man', *IEEE Transactions on Biomedical Engineering*, **19**, 271–276.

Tyler, J. E. (1973). 'Applied radiometry', *Oceanography and Marine Biology Review*, **11**, 11–25.

Uttal, W. R. (1968), *Real-Time Computers: Techniques and Applications in the Psychological Sciences*, New York, Harper & Row.

Valentinuzzi, M. E., Geddes, L. A., and Baker, L. E. (1971). 'The law of impedance pneumography', *Medical and Biological Engineering*, **9**, 137–163.

Venables, P. H., and Christie, M. J. (1973). 'Mechanisms, instrumentation and recording techniques', in W. F. Prokasy and D. C. Raskin (Eds.), *Electrodermal Activity in Psychological Research*, New York, Academic Press.

Venables, P. H., and Martin, I. (1967a). 'Skin resistance and skin potential', in P. H. Venables and I. Martin (Eds.), *Manual of Psychophysiological Methods*, Amsterdam, North-Holland Publishing Co.

Venables, P. H., and Martin, I. (Eds.) (1967b). *Manual of Psychophysiological Methods*, Amsterdam, North-Holland Publishing Co.

Veraguth, O. (1909). *Das Psycho-Galvanische Reflexphänomen*, Berlin, Karger.

Vo-Ngoc, B., Poussart, D., and Langlois, J. M. (1971). 'Automatic recognition of sleep spindles using short-term spectral analysis', *Behavior Research Methods and Instrumentation*, **3**, 217–219.

Walsh, J. W. T. (1958). *Photometry*, 3rd edition, London, Constable & Co.

Warner, L. H. (1932). 'The association span of the white rat', *Journal of General Psychology*, **41**, 57–89.

Weinman, J. (1967). 'Plethysmography', in P. H. Venables and I. Martin (Eds.), *Manual of Psychophysiological Methods*, Amsterdam, North-Holland Publishing Co.

Weiss, B. (Ed.) (1973). *Digital Computers in the Behavioral Laboratory*, New York, Appleton–Century–Crofts.

Weiss, M. S. (1973). 'Safe, constant current, electric-shock stimulator', *Medical and Biological Engineering*, **11**, 506–508.

Wood, R. W., Sette, W. F., and Weiss, B. (1975). Interfacing the experimenter to the computer: languages for psychologists', *American Psychologist*, **30**, 230–238.

Young, L. R., and Sheena, D. (1975). 'Survey of eye movement recording methods', *Behavior Research Methods and Instrumentation*, **7**, 397–429.

Zucker, M. H. (1969). *Electronic Circuits for the Behavioral and Biomedical Sciences*, San Francisco, W. H. Freeman & Co.

APPENDIX 1

Electronic Circuit Symbols

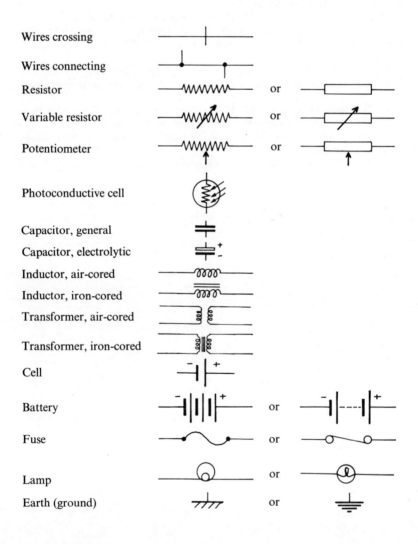

Wires crossing	
Wires connecting	
Resistor	or
Variable resistor	or
Potentiometer	or
Photoconductive cell	
Capacitor, general	
Capacitor, electrolytic	
Inductor, air-cored	
Inductor, iron-cored	
Transformer, air-cored	
Transformer, iron-cored	
Cell	
Battery	or
Fuse	or
Lamp	or
Earth (ground)	or

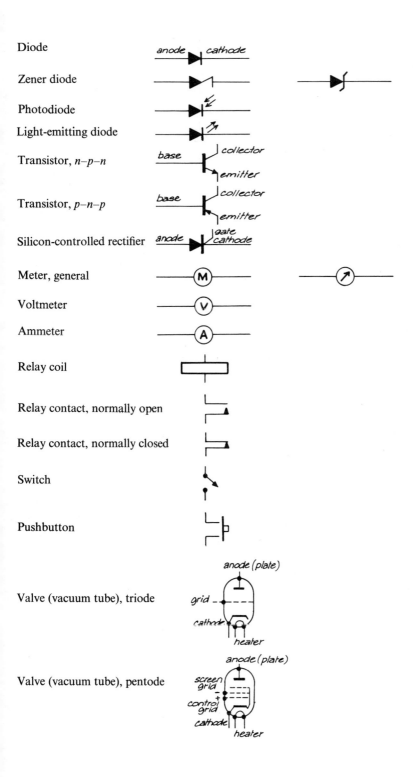

Diode	
Zener diode	
Photodiode	
Light-emitting diode	
Transistor, *n–p–n*	
Transistor, *p–n–p*	
Silicon-controlled rectifier	
Meter, general	
Voltmeter	
Ammeter	
Relay coil	
Relay contact, normally open	
Relay contact, normally closed	
Switch	
Pushbutton	
Valve (vacuum tube), triode	
Valve (vacuum tube), pentode	

274

Microphone

Loudspeaker

APPENDIX 2

Selected SI Units

The International System of Units represents an attempt to standardize and simplify scientific language. It is increasingly being adopted by scientific bodies throughout the world, and is likely to become universally accepted in a few years.

BASE UNITS

Physical quantity	SI unit	Abbreviation
length	metre	m
mass	kilogram	kg
time	second	s
current	ampere	A
absolute temperature	kelvin	K
luminous intensity	candela	cd
amount of substance	mole	mol

NOTE: (1) The degree Celsius (°C) scale is the kelvin scale minus 273·15.

(2) Although the base unit for mass is the kilogram, masses are still expressed as multiples of the gram. Thus, 10^{-5} kg should be written as 10 mg.

DERIVED UNITS

Physical quantity	SI unit	Abbreviation
area	square metre	m^2
volume	cubic metre	m^3
velocity	metre per second	$m\,s^{-1}$
force	newton	$N\,(m\,kg\,s^{-2})$
pressure	pascal	$Pa\,(N\,m^{-2})$
work, energy	joule	J
power	watts	$W\,(J\,s^{-1})$
electrical charge	coulomb	C
voltage, p.d., e.m.f.	volt	V
resistance	ohm	Ω

conductance	siemens	S
capacitance	farad	F
inductance	henry	H
luminous flux	lumen	lm
illuminance	lux	lx
luminance	candela per square metre	$cd\,m^{-2}$
frequency	hertz	Hz

SUPPLEMENTARY UNITS

The units for plane and solid angles are radian (rad) and steradian (sr), respectively. The degree ($1°$) is equal to ($\pi/180$) rad.

SI PREFIXES

Multiplication factor	Prefix	Symbol
$1\,000\,000 = 10^6$	mega	M
$1\,000 = 10^3$	kilo	k
$100 = 10^2$	hecto	h
$10 = 10^1$	deca	da
$0{\cdot}1 = 10^{-1}$	deci	d
$0{\cdot}01 = 10^{-2}$	centi	c
$0{\cdot}001 = 10^{-3}$	milli	m
$0{\cdot}000\,001 = 10^{-6}$	micro	μ
$0{\cdot}000\,000\,001 = 10^{-9}$	nano	n
$0{\cdot}000\,000\,000\,001 = 10^{-12}$	pico	p

APPENDIX 3

Glossary

Å

See *Ångstrom unit*.

a.c.

See *alternating current*.

a.c. amplifier

An *amplifier* which will not handle d.c. or low-frequency signals. Audio amplifiers are a.c. amplifiers. To be distinguished from *d.c. amplifier*.

a.c. coupled

Not *directly coupled*, and therefore the frequency response will not extend down to d.c.

ACT

Automated Contigency Translator. An experimental control language devised by Millenson (1973).

active electrode

In electrophysiology, an electrode so placed that its potential is maximally affected by the bioelectric phenomenon under investigation. To be distinguished from an *inactive electrode*.

ADC

See *analogue–digital converter*.

admittance

The reciprocal of *impedance*.

aesthesiometer

An instrument for measuring the tactual 2-point threshold.

AF

Audio frequency. Usually taken to mean from about 20 Hz to 20 kHz.

aliasing

Problem caused by failing to filter out high frequencies before sampling a signal, usually by means of an *analogue–digital converter*. If frequencies higher than half the sampling rate are present, they produce spurious data at frequencies below half the sampling rate. See *sampling*.

alternating current (a.c.)

A flow of current in which the direction reverses periodically. The average value over a complete period is zero. The number of cycles per second is termed the *frequency*.

alternating voltage

A voltage which periodically reverses in direction and has a mean value of zero over each period, as in the public electricity supply. The amplitude of an alternating voltage can be changed by a *transformer*.

AM

Amplitude modulation. See *modulation*.

ampere (A)

The SI unit of *current*. It is defined in terms of the force of the magnetic field between a pair of current-carrying conductors.

amplifier

A device whose output is a magnified function of its input, and which draws power from a supply rather than from the input.

anaglyph

Stereoscopic pairs printed in superimposed different colours, usually red and blue, for viewing through coloured glasses.

analogue computer

A machine designed to perform arithmetical functions upon numbers represented in the machine by continuously variable quantities, such as electrical current or voltage. Analogue computers are often used to simulate complex physical systems. To be distinguished from *digital computer*.

analogue–digital converter

A unit which converts an analogue signal into a digital representation. Allows a digital computer to sample voltage levels.

AND

In logic, giving an output deemed to be logic 1 only when all the inputs are at logic 1.

Ångstrom unit

A non-SI unit often used for wavelengths of light. Ten Ångstrom units are equal to one nanometre.

anomaloscope

In colour vision, an instrument for measuring colour anomaly. The subject is required to match spectral yellow to a red-green mixture.

anode

The electrode at which electric current enters a device, and therefore the electrode at which electrons flow out of it. Generally the positive electrode.

asserted

In digital logic, at logic 1, enabled.

attenuator

A device designed to reduce the amplitude of a signal without introducing distortion. It may be fixed or variable, and is usually calibrated in decibels. Variable attenuators are often used to control the stimulus intensity in psychoacoustic research.

Avometer

A popular moving-coil multimeter. A trade name.

bandwidth

The range of frequencies over which an instrument will operate. It is usually measured to the *half-power points*.

bar

A unit of atmospheric *pressure* equal to 10^5 Pa, or approximately 1 atm.

base

Normally the control electrode of a junction *transistor*.

battery

In electronics, a number of *cells* connected in series to produce a greater potential. Often used loosely also to mean a single cell.

baud

A unit of rate of transmission of data. It is usually employed in serial data communication, and refers to the actual *bits* per second which can be transmitted over the line.

b.c.d.

Binary-coded decimal.

bias

In a transistor or valve, a fixed voltage which sets the operating point of the device. In a tape recorder, it is a high-frequency signal which allows the audio signal to be recorded on the tape with minimum distortion.

biofeedback

An extension of psychophysiology in which a subject is given knowledge of results in an attempt to improve his control of some physiological variable.

biopolar recording

In electrophysiology, using two *active electrodes*. To be distinguished from *unipolar recording*.

bistable

A circuit with two stable states. It can store 1 *bit* of information. Alternative names are flip–flop or latch.

bit

A contraction of binary digit. A unit of information content corresponding to the decision between one of two possible states. The information capacity of a storage device is the logarithm to base 2 of the number of possible states of the device.

bridge

In a *rectifier*, it is a full-wave rectifier circuit in which there are four arms, each containing a *diode*. Other kinds of bridge circuits are used for precision measurement of electrical quantities, such as resistance.

busbar

A heavy conductor used to make a common connection between several circuits.

C

On switch contacts means common. See *switch*.

capacitor

An electronic component comprising a pair of sheet conductors which are separated by a thin insulating layer known as a dielectric. Capacitors store electric charge when a potential difference exists between the two conductors. In a.c. circuits, the *reactance* of a capacitor decreases as the frequency increases, and therefore high-frequency signals will pass through a capacitor more easily than low-frequency signals.

carrier

In data communications, a steady signal which is modulated to carry information. In semi-conductors, mobile electrons or holes which carry current. Majority carriers are the type which carry more than half the current, and minority carriers are the type which carry less than half the current.

cathode

The electrode at which electric current flows out of a device, and therefore the electrode at which electrons enter it. Generally the negative electrode.

cathode-ray tube (CRT)

An electron tube in which a beam of electrons can be controlled to produce a spot of light on the tube face. The spot can be deflected in the X and Y directions to produce a visual display, as in a television set or oscilloscope.

CCTV

See *closed-circuit television*.

cell

In electricity, a single source of electrochemical potential. See *battery*.

ceramics

Oxides of one or more metals. Originally pottery materials, but modern ceramics have a wide range of useful properties.

channel capacity

The maximum number of *bits* per second which can be transmitted over a communication channel.

chip

In electronics, a circuit fabricated as a single piece of *semiconductor* material and designed to perform a specific function or group of functions. Usually an *integrated circuit*.

choke

An obsolete term for *inductor*.

chopper

An electronic or electromechanical switch which is used to interrupt a low-frequency or d.c. signal at a higher frequency. It allows the signal to be amplified by an *a.c. amplifier*.

chronoscope

An early form of time-interval meter used in reaction-time studies.

clear

See *reset*.

clock

A device for measuring and indicating time. In digital electronics, a source of pulses, not necessarily at a regular frequency, which are used to synchronize logic operations.

closed-circuit television (CCTV)

A television system in which the camera, receiver and controls are directly connected by cables. Therefore no aerials are used for transmission or reception.

CO

Changeover contacts. See *switch*.

coil

Conductors wound in a series of loops to form an *inductor*.

collector

One of the three electrodes in a *transistor*. The electrode to which the *majority carriers* flow inside the device. In an *n–p–n* transistor, it is the anode; in a *p–n–p transistor*, it is the cathode.

colour wheel

An apparatus for spinning colour discs to achieve colour mixing.

common-mode rejection

A figure of merit for a *differential amplifier*. It indicates the performance of the amplifier in suppressing unwanted signals common to the two inputs. It is a ratio of the wanted to the unwanted gain, and is usually expressed in *decibels*.

complement

In logic, *negation*.

computer

See *analogue computer*, *digital computer*. By itself, the term computer usually implies a digital computer.

condenser

An obsolete name for *capacitor*.

conductance (G)

The reciprocal of *resistance*. The *SI* unit of conductance is the siemens (S). The mho is an obsolete name for the unit.

conductor

A substance which offers little resistance to the flow of electricity. In electronics, often copper wire. To be distinguished from *semiconductor* and *insulator*.

core

In *transformers* and *inductors*, the metal or *ferrite* which acts as a path for the magnetic flux, giving increased *inductance*. In computers, the immediate-access memory based on miniature ferrite beads. In some modern computers, it is replaced by semiconductor RAM.

c.p.s.

Cycles per second. See *hertz*.

CPU

Central processing unit (of a computer).

CRO

Cathode-ray oscilloscope. See *oscilloscope*.

crosstalk

Unwanted transfer of information from one channel of communication to another.

CRT

See *cathode-ray tube*.

crystal

In electronics, usually a quartz crystal, which employs piezoelectric resonance to achieve precise control of an *oscillator* frequency. Also the active element in one kind of microphone or gramophone pickup. See *piezoelectric effect*.

c/s

Cycles per second. See *hertz*.

current

The rate of flow of electricity. Electric current always involves the movement of charged particles, usually electrons. Because electrons are negatively charged, they flow in the opposite direction to conventional current. See *ampere*.

DAC

See *digital–analogue converter*.

data logger

Device for recording data in a form suitable for automatic analysis. Generally implies a system which *samples* at a low rate and over a long time period. Usually records the data in chronological order.

dB

See *decibel*.

d.c.

See *direct current*. Sometimes means *directly coupled*.

d.c. amplifier

The d.c. can be taken to mean either *direct current* or *directly coupled;* in either case it means an *amplifier* with a frequency response which goes down to d.c. or zero frequency. The amplifier will, therefore, amplify very low frequencies. It is sometimes called a directly coupled amplifier, because *capacitors* are not used to couple the stages of the amplifier as in an *a.c. amplifier*. However, see *chopper*.

d.c. coupled

See *d.c. amplifier*.

d.c. voltage

Illogical jargon for *direct voltage*.

debug

To test and correct errors in a computer program.

decibel (dB)

A measure of the ratio of two values of power. It is expressed as ten times the logarithm to base 10 of the power ratio. When voltage and current ratios are expressed in decibel form, 20 times the log ratio is used, because power varies as the square of the voltage or current.

degauss

To demagnetize, usually by applying an a.c. magnetic field and slowly removing it.

dielectric

A nonconducting material. See *capacitor*.

differential amplifier

An *amplifier* which responds to the difference in voltage between two similar input circuits, ideally rejecting voltages which are alike on the two inputs. Used in physiological amplifiers. See *common-mode rejection*.

digital computer

A machine capable of performing operations on data represented in digital form, that is in the form of discrete elements coded to represent numbers. In most digital computers, the binary system is used, and each element can adopt either of the values 0 or 1. Although the basic processes performed by an electronic digital computer are simple, they can be performed at extremely high speeds, enabling the computer to carry out quite complex tasks. A computer system usually consists of input devices, a central processing unit, backing stores and output devices. To be distinguished from *analogue computer*.

digital–analogue converter (DAC)

A unit which converts a digital signal into a continuous voltage or current. Often used to drive an oscilloscope or plotter in a computer system.

diode

A device which permits current to flow in one direction only.

direct current (d.c.)

Current which is unidirectional, and does not change in value.

direct voltage

A unidirectional voltage which does not change in value.

directly coupled

See *d.c. amplifier*.

disc

In computers, a circular plate with a magnetic surface. It rotates at high speed, and is used as a backing store. Discs can have capacities of many million computer words. Small plastic discs known as floppy discs have a smaller capacity, but are cheap and often used on small systems.

drain

The electrode to which the *majority carriers* flow in a *field-effect transistor*. The anode in an *n*-channel FET, and the cathode in a *p*-channel FET.

DTL

Diode–transistor logic. A system of semiconductor logic in which the decisions are made by a group of diodes and the output is fed through a transistor.

dynamic

Sometimes an abbreviation for *electrodynamic*.

earth

In electronics, the conducting mass of the earth or any conductor electrically connected to it. At zero potential with respect to earth. Ground is an alternative term.

ECG

See *electrocardiogram*.

ECL

Emitter-coupled logic. A family of digital *integrated circuits*.

EDR

Electrodermal response. See *skin conductance, skin potential, skin resistance*.

EEG

See *electroencephalogram*.

EHT

Extra-high tension, usually referring to the high-voltage supply for a CRT.

EKG

See *electrocardiogram*.

electrocardiogram (ECG or EKG)

A record of the electrical activity associated with the heart.

electrodynamic

Refers to electricity in motion. Usually moving electromagnets, as in electric motors and moving-coil loudspeakers.

electroencephalogram (EEG)

A record of the electrical activity of the brain.

electron

An elementary particle with a negative charge. The vehicle of current flow in a good conductor.

electroluminescence

The glowing of a phosphor under the influence of an electric field.

electrolyte

A substance which produces a conducting medium when dissolved in water or some other liquid. The resulting solution is also often termed an electrolyte.

electromyogram (EMG)

A record of the action potentials of muscle fibres.

electrooculogram (EOG)

A record of eye movements using the bioelectric potentials around the eyes.

electroretinogram (ERG)

A record of changes in potential of the retina.

electrostatic

Refers to electric charges at rest. A potential difference but no current flow, as when paper is attracted to a charged plastic comb.

e.m.f.

Electromotive force or source of voltage. The *SI unit* is the *volt*.

EMG

See *electromyogram*.

emitter

One of the three electrodes in a *transistor*. The electrode from which the majority carriers flow through the device. In an *n–p–n* transistor, it is the cathode; in a *p–n–p* transistor, it is the anode.

enable

In digital logic, to present an input which will cause a device to operate. Normally a logic 1.

EOG

See *electrooculogram*.

ERG

See *electroretinogram*.

ergograph

An apparatus for recording the regularly repeated contractions of a single muscle system, for example the hand. Used in the study of fatigue.

event recorder

A chart recorder which records the occurrence of single events on each channel. Usually has a low-speed chart drive.

false

In logic, at logic 0.

farad (F)

The *SI unit* of capacitance. A *capacitor* has a capacitance of one farad when a charge of one coulomb produces a potential difference of one volt across its terminals. It is a very large unit, and the microfarad and picofarad are used in practice.

feedback

A technique whereby, for any system which has an input and output, part of the output is redirected to the input. In an amplifier, feedback will increase or decrease the gain depending on the relative phase of the input and the returned signals. If the returned signal reduces the effective input signal, the gain is reduced, and the process is termed negative feedback. It gives reduced distortion, and extends the frequency response of an amplifier. If the returned signal increases the effective input signal, it is termed positive feedback. This increases gain and can cause the amplifier to become unstable. Positive feedback is used in oscillator circuits. In psychology, the term feedback is often applied to knowledge of results in training procedures.

ferrite

Synthetic *ceramic* materials with good magnetic properties.

FET
See *field-effect transistor*.

FFT

Fast Fourier transform. See *Fourier transform*.

field-effect transistor (FET)

A transistor in which the effect of an electric field applied at the gate controls the resistance between the drain and source electrodes. The gate has a very high input impedance.

filter

In electronics, a device for controlling the *bandwidth* of a signal by attenuating unwanted frequencies. In optics, an element which selectively transmits specified wavelengths of light. A neutral-density filter provides uniform attenuation of light over a wide range of wavelengths.

flip-flop

See *bistable*.

flux

A term used to describe the flow of particles, such as photons, or of lines of force, as in magnetism.

FM

Frequency modulation. See *modulation*.

force

In mechanics, that which changes or tends to change a body's motion in a straight line. Loosely, a measure of push or pull derived from ideas of muscular effort. The *SI unit* is the *newton*.

form A, B or C

Configurations of switches on relays. See *switch*.

Fourier transform

A mathematical operation which decomposes a time-varying signal into its frequency components. The fast Fourier transform (FFT) is an efficient method for use on digital computers. The inverse Fourier transform will reconstruct a time-domain signal from the complex-frequency components.

frequency

The number of cycles of a periodic quantity which occur in unit time. The *SI unit* of frequency is the *hertz*.

fundamental frequency

The lowest sine-wave component of a periodic quantity.

fuse

A device for protecting electrical circuits. It contains a fusible link which melts and therefore breaks the circuit when the rated current is exceeded.

gain

An increase in the level of a signal, usually as a result of amplification. The gain of interest may be in voltage, current or power, depending on the application. It is expressed as a ratio, often in *decibels*.

galvanometer

An instrument for measuring small electric currents.

gate

In a *field-effect transistor*, the control electrode. In digital logic, a logic element with more than one input channel, the output state being determined by the input state.

graphics terminal

A computer terminal which allows graphs and other figures to be drawn on a CRT screen.

ground

See *earth*

GSR

Galvanic skin reflex. See *skin conductance, skin potential, skin resistance*.

half-power point

The point in a frequency-response curve which represents half the power intensity of the point corresponding to maximum power. Also called the 3 dB point.

harmonic

In a periodic signal, a frequency component with a frequency which is an integral multiple of the *fundamental frequency*.

henry (H)

The *SI unit* of *inductance*. The value of inductance which produces an e.m.f. of one volt when the current changes at a rate of one ampere per second.

hertz (Hz)

The *SI unit* of *frequency*. One cycle per second.

hole

In semiconductors, a mobile electron vacancy in the atomic structure of the semiconductor.

hum

In electronics, unwanted signals at mains frequency or a harmonic of mains frequency.

Hz

See *hertz*.

IC

See *integrated circuit*.

IGFET

Insulated gate *field-effect transistor*.

impedance

A measure of the opposition to the flow of alternating current in a circuit. The ratio of the r.m.s. electromotive force to the r.m.s. current.

impedance matching

Ensuring that the *input* and *output impedances* of interconnected electronic equipment are appropriate. Loosely, the impedances should be equal for maximum power transfer. For maximum voltage at the input of the driven equipment, the output impedance should be low and the input impedance high. For maximum current flow, both impedances should be low. It all depends on the requirement: power, voltage or current transfer.

inactive electrode

In electrophysiology, an electrode which is used to make contact with the body fluids in such a way that its potential is not greatly affected by bioelectric phenomena, including that which is under investigation. To be distinguished from *active electrode*.

inductor

An electronic component which stores electricity in a magnetic field. A coil of wire, usually with a metal or ferrite *core* to facilitate the magnetic circuit.

input impedance

The *impedance* presented to an external source of current by the input circuit of an instrument.

inhibit

In digital logic, an input which, when enabled, prevents the normal operation of the device.

insulator

A substance through which electric current does not flow readily. In electronics, plastics are often used as insulators. To be distinguished from *semiconductor* and *conductor*.

integrated circuit (IC)

An electronic circuit which has been fabricated as an inseparable assembly of *semiconductor* elements on a single silicon chip. Complete electronic circuits such as logic gates and amplifiers packaged as small components.

inverter

In logic, an element with a single input which performs the operation of *negation*. In power supplies, a device which converts a *d.c.* to an *a.c.* supply.

I/O

Input and output of an instrument or computer.

ion

An atom with more (negative ion) or less (positive ion) electrons than its normal number.

i.p.s.

Inches per second.

junction

In semiconductors, a transition between layers having different electrical characteristics. In a thermocouple, the contact between two different metals.

kilo- (k)

The *SI* prefix for multiplication by 10^3.

kymograph

An instrument for making graphic records on a revolving drum. Largely superseded by the *polygraph*.

latch

See *bistable*.

LED

See *light-emitting diode*.

light-emitting diode (LED)

A solid-state lamp.

LSI

Large-scale integration. The technology of fabricating *integrated circuits* with a complexity equal to many logic gates on a single chip.

litre (l)

A unit of volume equal to 1 dm^3 or 1·760 pints.

majority carrier

See *carrier*.

manometer

An instrument for measuring fluid pressure.

manipulandum

In operant conditioning, a response key. Also operandum.

mega- (M)

The *SI* prefix for multiplication by 10^6.

memory drum

An apparatus which allows a series of visual items to be presented to a subject in regular succession.

metre (m)

The *SI unit* of length. Equal to 39·37 inches.

micro- (μ)

The *SI* prefix for multiplication by 10^{-6}.

microcircuit

An *integrated circuit*.

microcomputer

A *digital computer* based on a *microprocessor*. It does not usually support a wide variety of peripherals, being mainly used to give sophisticated control of a small number of devices.

micron (μ)

A non-SI unit of length equal to 1 μm.

microprocessor

The central processing unit of a *microcomputer*. Does not include storage, and is often on a single chip.

milli- (m)

The *SI* prefix for multiplication by 10^{-3}.

minicomputer

A low-cost *digital computer* which is still able to support a wide range of peripherals. Generally has a 12 or 16 bit word, and is suitable for use in a laboratory computer system

minority carrier

See *carrier*.

modem

A modulator–demodulator. A device which allows digital data to be transmitted over telephone lines.

modulation

The process, or the result of the process, in which some characteristic of a carrier frequency is varied in sympathy with another signal. The main types are frequency and amplitude modulation.

module

A device which is designed as one of a series of compatible standard units.

monostable

A device with only one stable state, but capable of being triggered for a brief period into a second state by an external pulse. It therefore provides pulses of fixed duration. An alternative name is one-shot. In relay programming systems, often called a pulse former.

MOSFET or MOST

Metal–oxide–silicon *(field-effect) transistor*. Has a high *input impedance*, and is often used in *integrated circuits*.

multivibrator

An *oscillator* with a pulsed or non-sinusoidal output.

multiplex

To transmit a number of messages concurrently over a single physical channel.

NAND

In logic, giving an output deemed to be logic 0 only when all the inputs are at logic 1. NOT AND.

nano- (n)

The *SI* prefix for multiplication by 10^{-9}.

NC

Normally closed. See *switch*.

NO

Normally open. See *switch*.

negation

In logic, giving an output deemed to be logic 1 only when the input is at logic 0.

newton (N)

The *SI unit* of *force*. Equal to the weight of 1 kg.

noise

In electronics, an undesired electrical disturbance within the frequency band of interest. White noise contains frequencies over the whole of the band of interest.

NOR

In logic, giving an output deemed to be at logic 0 whenever any one or more inputs are at logic 1. NOT OR.

NOT

In logic, *negation*.

n–p–n transistor

A *transistor* with an *n-type emitter* and *collector* and a *p-type base*.

n-type semiconductor

A *semiconductor* in which the free-electron density exceeds the *hole* density.

octave

An interval between two frequencies such that one frequency is twice the other.

offline

A part of a computer system which is not directly under the control of the central processor. Not *online*.

ohm (Ω)

The *SI unit* of electrical *resistance*. A potential difference of one volt across a resistance of one ohm will cause a current of one ampere to flow.

olfactometer

An apparatus for measuring the threshold of smell.

one-shot

See *monostable*.

online

Able to communicate directly with, or be controlled by, a computer system.

operandum

See *manipulandum*.

ophthalmoscope

An instrument for viewing the retina and the interior of the eye.

OR

In logic, giving an output deemed to be at logic 1 whenever any one or more inputs are at logic 1.

oscillator

A circuit or instrument which produces a periodic signal, such as a sine or square wave.

oscillograph

An instrument which records the waveform of an electrical signal on paper. A pen recorder.

oscilloscope

A laboratory instrument which gives a visual representation of a changing electrical quantity on a *cathode-ray tube*.

output impedance

In a source of an electrical signal, the *impedance* which appears to be in series with the source.

pascal (Pa)

The *SI unit* of *pressure*. Equal to one newton per square metre.

p.c.b.

Printed-circuit board. See *printed circuit*.

p.d.

Potential difference or voltage.

perimeter

An apparatus for mapping the visual field, for example in studying colour zones.

peripheral

In computers, an abbreviation for peripheral equipment. Usually input–output equipment connected to a computer system.

PGR

Psychogalvanic reflex. See *skin conductance, skin potential, skin resistance*.

phase

In a.c. circuits, the fraction of a period which has elapsed from some fixed origin.

photocell

A contraction for photoelectric cell. A light-sensitive device which converts light changes to changes of some electrical property, often resistance.

photoconductor

A semiconductor which changes in electrical resistance when stimulated by light.

photometer

An instrument for measuring the intensity of light.

photomultiplier

A very sensitive *photocell*.

photon

In physics, a fundamental particle or quantum of electromagnetic energy, particularly in the region of the visible spectrum. In visual research, an obsolete name for the *troland*.

pico- (p)

The *SI* prefix for multiplication 10^{-12}.

piezoelectric effect

The development of a potential difference across the faces of some natural *crystal* and synthetic *ceramics* when they are subjected to mechanical strain. These materials also produce a mechanical force when a voltage is applied.

plethysmograph

An apparatus for measuring changes in the volume of parts of the body.

***p–n–p* transistor**

A *transistor* with a *p-type emitter* and *collector* and an *n-type base*.

polarization

In an *electrolyte*, the movement of negative *ions* to a positive electrode and positive ions to a negative electrode. Reduces the performance of a cell and causes changes in base potential in electrophysiology. In optics, the treatment of light so that the waves oscillate parallel to a single axis. Polarizing filters are available in sheet form under the trade name Polaroid.

polygraph

A multichannel pen recorder.

power

The rate of doing work. The *SI unit* is the *watt*.

power amplifier

An *amplifier* which is designed to convert a voltage signal to power which can drive a device such as a loudspeaker.

preamplifier

An *amplifier* which is designed to increase the voltage level of a signal, often so that it can drive a *power amplifier*.

pressure

In mechanics, the *force* per unit area. The *SI unit* is the *pascal*.

printed circuit

An insulated board (often glass fibre) containing a pattern of copper tracks, usually formed by acid etching a complete sheet of copper-laminated board. The electronic components are soldered to the tracks, which are thus analogous to the connecting wires in a conventional circuit.

pseudoscope

An instrument for transposing the left and right eye fields of view, so that a binocular disparity is reversed.

p-type semiconductor

A *semiconductor* in which the *hole* density exceeds the free-electron density.

pulse former

See *monostable*.

pursuit rotor

An apparatus for measuring visual–motor coordination.

push–pull amplifier

An *amplifier* in which the input signal is processed to produce two signals of equal but opposite phase. The signals are amplified and then recombined to form the output signal. The technique reduces some kinds of distortion.

RAM

See *random-access memory*.

random-access memory (RAM)

Storage designed to give a constant access time for any location addressed, regardless of the location previously addressed. Usually implies *semiconductor* memory, rather than *core* memory.

raster

In television, the pattern of lines scanning the cathode-ray tube or camera tube.

reactance

The non–resistive element of *impedance;* the part due to *capacitance* and *inductance*. Its value varies with frequency.

rectifier

A *diode* used to convert an a.c. supply to d.c.

redundancy

In information theory, the proportion of the maximum uncertainty which is not utilized in a message. In computer systems, redundancy is often used for error checking and error correction.

reed switch

A switch comprising two gold-plated tongues of a soft magnetic material sealed into a glass tube filled with an inert gas. When a magnetic field is applied, the tongues make contact, completing the circuit. If a solenoid is wound around the switch, the complete assembly is known as a reed relay. Some reed switches have an additional contact, giving a changeover action.

relay

A solenoid-operated switch.

reset

In digital electronics, to make a *bistable* or a memory *bit* take the value deemed to be logic 0. Alternative term is to clear.

resistance

The tendency of materials to oppose the steady flow of electric current. The *SI unit* is the *ohm*.

RF

Radio frequency. A frequency which could be used for radio transmission. From about 20 kHz to a few thousand megahertz.

ripple

The small alternating voltage which remains in the output of a d.c. power supply.

RTL

Resistor–transistor logic. A system of semiconductor logic.

sampling

Recording the value of a variable at intervals of time. The sampling theorem states that a signal is completely described if it is sampled at a rate which is at least twice as great as the highest frequency contained by the original.

SCAT

State Change Algorithm Translator An experimental control language and interface system marketed by GenRad, Inc.

SCL

See *skin conductance*.

SCR

In electronics, see *silicon-controlled rectifier*. In psychophysiology, see *skin conductance*.

semiconductor

A material which has an electrical resistance between that of *conductors* and that of *insulators*. Its resistance can be reduced by adding small amounts of impurities. Semiconductors are the basic materials from which *transistors* and *integrated circuits* are manufactured. The term is often used to mean such a device.

servosystem

An automatic control which is designed to control the output so that it closely follows the input. Uses negative feedback.

set

In digital electronics, to make a *bistable* or memory *bit* take the value deemed to be logic 1.

shift register

A series of *bistables* arranged to allow a pattern of bits to be shifted to the left or right.

SI units

The international standard metric system of units. See Appendix 1.

silicon-controlled rectifier (SCR)

Device for controlling the power available when rectifying an a.c. supply.

SKED

An experimental control language (Snapper and Kadden, 1973).

skin conductance (SC)

The electrical *conductance* of skin, usually palmar. Measured either as skin conductance level (SCL) or skin conductance response (SCR). Obsolete terms are EDR, GSR and PGR.

skin potential (SP)

The electrical potential of skin, usually palmar. Measured either as skin potential level (SPL) or skin potential response (SPR). Obsolete terms are EDR, GSR and PGR.

skin resistance (SR)

The electrical *resistance* of skin, usually palmar. Measured either as skin resistance level (SRL) or skin resistance response (SRR). Obsolete terms are EDR, GSR and PGR.

solenoid

A coil, usually tubular in shape, for producing a magnetic field. Often includes a soft iron armature which is attracted by the coil, thus providing an electromechanical actuator.

solid-state

Generally, using *semiconductor* devices rather than *thermionic valves*.

source

In electronics generally, the origin of a signal. In semiconductors, the electrode from which the majority carriers flow in a *field-effect transistor*. The cathode in a *p*-channel FET, and the anode in an *n*-channel FET. In computing, an abbreviation for the source program. A program in the form prior to assembly or compilation.

spectrum analysis

The process of determining the magnitudes of the frequency components of a signal.

sphygmomanometer

An instrument for measuring blood pressure.

spirometer

An instrument for measuring respiratory volume.

stepper motor

A motor which rotates a fixed fraction of a turn for each input pulse.

strain gauge

A *transducer* which converts small mechanical movements into electrical signals.

stroboscope

An instrument which produces brief flashes of light at a controllable rate. Used to study rotating or oscillatory movements.

switch

A mechanically operated device which is capable of making or breaking an electrical circuit. The main types of switch arrangement are:

Single-Pole Single-Throw (SPST). Two types:
  normally open (NO) or relay form A
  normally closed (NC) or relay form B
Single-Pole Double-Throw (SPDT). Also called:
  changeover (CO) or relay form C

tachistoscope

An apparatus for controlling the duration of presentation of visual stimuli. Most tachistoscopes have more than one field, and a means for switching between fields. Sometimes abbreviated to T-scope.

tachometer

An instrument for measuring the speed of rotation.

Teletype

A popular *teletypewriter*. A trade name.

teletypewriter

An input/output device used as a terminal for a *digital computer*. When it is switched *online*, the keyboard sends data to the computer, which echoes back the characters to the printer. The computer output is also printed on the paper roll. The teletypewriter is sometimes replaced by a *visual-display unit*.

thermionic valve

A vacuum tube in which the cathode is heated to provide a source of electrons. Can be used to *amplify* and *rectify*.

thyristor

An alternative name for a *silicon-controlled rectifier*.

time constant

The time taken for a circuit to rise to 63.2% of its final value, or to fall to 36·8% of its value. The time constant of a resistor–capacitor circuit is CR, and the time constant of a resistor–

inductor circuit is L/R. The low-frequency controls on a physiological amplifier are often labelled in time constants. With a short time constant, the low-frequency response will be reduced.

tolerance

The permissible deviation of a quantity from some desired value.

transducer

Converts changes in one modality (heat, light, movement etc.) into another modality. Usually to or from an electrical signal.

transformer

A device based on electromagnetic induction which transforms an alternating electrical signal in one circuit to another circuit, usually with a change of current or voltage.

transistor

A *semiconductor* device with three electrodes which is capable of amplification.

triac

A semiconductor device similar to a *silicon-controlled rectifier*, but able to control a.c. power.

troland

In visual research, a measure of the illumination on the retina. The product of the luminance of the surface of the stimulus, in candelas per square metre, and the pupil size, in millimetres.

true

In logic, in the state deemed to be logic 1.

truth table

In logic, a table which defines the input and output relations of a logic system.

T-scope

An abbreviation for *tachistoscope*.

TTL

Transistor–transistor logic. A family of *integrated-circuit* logic elements.

tube

In electronics, a *cathode-ray tube* or *thermionic valve*.

unipolar recording

In electrophysiology, using one *active* and one *inactive electrode*. To be distinguished from *bipolar recording*.

valence electrons

The outer ring of *electrons* in an atom which form the bond between atoms.

vacuum tube

See *thermionic valve*.

valve

See *thermionic valve*.

VDU

See *visual-display unit*.

video tape recorder (VTR)

A tape recorder on which television sound and vision signals can be recorded and replayed.

vidicon

A television-camera tube with a photoconductive target. It is the type most frequently used in *closed-circuit television*.

visual-display unit (VDU)

A replacement for a *teletypewriter* which uses a *cathode-ray tube* instead of a printed paper output.

voice key

An instrument used to detect verbal responses.

volt (V)

The *SI unit* of electromotive force and potential difference.

VOM

Volt–Ohm–Milliammeter. A moving-coil multimeter.

watt (W)

The *SI unit* of *power*. It is the amount of energy expended per second by a current of one ampere under a voltage of one volt. A single bar of an electric fire dissipates about one kilowatt.

wavelength

The distance between two successive similar phases of a periodic function.

Zener diode

A voltage-stabilizing device.

Author Index

Numbers printed in italic refer to the references.

303

Subject Index

A page number in bold type refers to an entry in the glossary (Appendix 3) under a similar heading.

Memory drum, 3, 149, 172, **291**
Mercury,
  sliprings, 194
  strain gauge, 204, 206, 209, 299
  vapour lamp, 134
Meter,
  circuit symbol, 273
  digital, 87
  high impedance, 90–92
  moving-coil, 88
  multimeter, 87–90, 279, 301
Metre, 275, **291**
Mho, 282
Micro-, μ, 276, **291**
Microcircuit, 291 *see also* Integrated circuit
Microcomputer, 228, **291**
Microelectrode, 194
Micron, μ, **291**
Microphone, 102–110, 192, 207, 272, 282
Microprocessor, **291**
Microswitch, 32, 36, 44, 182–183, 191–192
Milli-, m, 276, **291**
Millisecond stopclock, 98–99 *see also* Timer/counter
Minicomputer, 10, 231–232, 235, 237–265, **291**
Minority carrier, 69–70, **280**
Mirror, semireflecting, 146–147, 186
Mirror scale, 90
Modem, **292**
Modular,
  electronic instruments, 3, 97, 98
  programming equipment, 32–50, 237
Modulation, 71, 92, 280, **292**
  amplitude, 292
  frequency, 82, 227, 292
  Z, brightness, 168, 169
Module, 33–49, **292**
mol, mole, 275
Monochromator, 145
Monostable, 45, 85, 95, **292**
MOSFET, **292**
MOST, 77, 79, **292**
Motor responses, 182–192
Movie,
  camera, 162–163
  cartoon as reinforcer, 179
  projector, 163–164
Moving-coil meter, 88
Moving-coil microphone, 106–107
Multimeter, 87–90, 279, 301
Multiplex, 247, **292**

Multivibrator, 85, 93, 95, **292**
Munsell Color System, 145
Muscle action potential *see* EMG
MUSIC V, 239
Mutual inductance, 57

n, nano-, 276, **292**
N, newton, 275, 287, **292**
NAND, logic, 24, 31, **292**
Nano-, n, 276, **292**
Needle electrode, 210, 211, 214
Negation, **292** *see also* Inverter
Negative feedback, 125, 127, 129, 180, **287,** 297
Neutral-density filter, 143–144, **287**
Neutral-density wedge, 144
Newton, N, 275, 287, **292**
Nit, 139
Nixie tube, 164–165
Noise, 6–7, 103, 106, 107, 115–116, 240–241, **293**
  flicker, 122
  Johnson, 122
  rating scale, 117–118
  white, 3, 121, 184, 293
Non-material reinforcement, 179
NOR, logic, 24, 31, **293**
NOT, logic, **293** *see also* Inverter
n-p-n transistor, 71–73, 75, **293**
n-type semiconductor, 66–67, **293**
Number systems, 8–11
Numeric indicators *see* Alphanumeric displays

Observation screen, 177, 186
Octal notation, 10, 248, 251
Octave, 128, **293**
Octave-band filter, 128
Offline, **293**
Ohm, Ω, 54, 275, **293**
Ohm's law, 54–56, 61, 199
Ohmmeter, 89 *see also* Meter
Olfactometer, **293**
One-shot, monostable, 45, 85, 95, **292**
One-way screen, 177, 186
Online control, 240, 242, **293**
Open-field test, 190–191
Operandum, **293** *see also* Manipulandum
Operating system, computer, 242, 251
Operators, Boolean, 22–24
Ophthalmograph, 218
Ophthalmoscope, **293**
Optical,
  bench, 153

316

318